STARTING FROM QUIRPINI

Starting from
QUIRPINI

THE TRAVELS AND PLACES OF A BOLIVIAN PEOPLE

Stuart Alexander Rockefeller

Indiana University Press · *Bloomington and Indianapolis*

This book is a publication of

Indiana University Press
601 North Morton Street
Bloomington, Indiana 47404-3797 USA

www.iupress.indiana.edu

Telephone orders   800-842-6796
Fax orders   812-855-7931
Orders by e-mail   iuporder@indiana.edu

Manufactured in the United States of
America

Library of Congress Cataloging-in-
Publication Data

Rockefeller, Stuart Alexander, [date]–
  Starting from Quirpini : the travels and
places of a Bolivian people / Stuart Alexander
Rockefeller.
      p. cm.
  Includes bibliographical references and
index.
  ISBN 978-0-253-35497-6 (cloth : alk.
paper) — ISBN 978-0-253-22210-7 (pbk. :
alk. paper) 1. Indians of South America—
Bolivia—Estancia Quirpini—Ethnic iden-
tity. 2. Indians of South America—Bolivia—
Estancia Quirpini—Economic conditions.
3. Estancia Quirpini (Bolivia)—Economic
conditions. 4. Estancia Quirpini (Bolivia)—
Social life and customs. 5. Migrant labor—
Argentina—Buenos Aires. I. Title.
  F3319.1.E85R63 2010
  305.800984′14—dc22
                              2009052671

1 2 3 4 5 15 14 13 12 11 10

*In memory of
my mother Barbara
my father Rodman
and
Zyllia, who almost*

CONTENTS

ACKNOWLEDGMENTS

One of the first things you learn in anthropology is that no one does anything 'on their own.' Like any kind of production, research and writing are social activities. Over the years I have been aided by the favors and input of so many people that I could not possibly remember all, or even most of them.

The book has benefited immensely from the insightful feedback and moral support of innumerable colleagues and mentors, notably Tom Abercrombie, Claudio Lomnitz, Laurie Kain Hart, Setha Low, Hylton White, Susan Paulson, Judith Friedlander, Roger Rouse, Andy Orta, Rob Albro, Barnie Bate, Carmen Medeiros, Jesse Shipley, Mateo Taussig-Rubbo, Ray Fogelson, Alejandro Giusti, and Jean Comaroff. In writing the book, I have received valuable help at different times from two assistants: the promising young anthropologist Diego Cagüeñas, and my cousin Joanna Howard. Terence Turner, Nancy Munn, Paul Friedrich, and Alan Kolata of the Anthropology Department at the University of Chicago were great sources of inspiration and intellectual guidance. My fellow graduate students in anthropology at Chicago formed a challenging and supportive community that was ideal for stimulating creative work. The students in my spring 2009 "Introduction to Cultural Anthropology" courses at Fordham University read the book manuscript; their impressions and advice were most helpful.

In Bolivia I incurred countless debts to countless people. From the stranger who kindly shared his blanket as we waited out a *campesino* roadblock in the freezing highlands near Potosí, to the insightful, supportive audience members at the first public presentation of my Argentina material in Sucre, I have repeatedly relied on the generosity of spirit that is so evident among Bolivians, and often shared by expatriate scholars. First of all I thank Pilar Giménez, whose friendship and intelligence made her a great support during my sojourns in Sucre, and who played a key role in helping me find the relationships that would enable me to enter San Lucas. Antonio Sánchez de Lozada and his wife Lulé shared with me their home, wisdom, and love of Bolivia; without them this project never would have come to be. When my search for a field site was stalled, Erick Langer suggested that I look at San Lucas, for which I am ever grateful. Primo Nina Llanos, language teacher extraordinaire, and the equally gifted Mamerto Torres, did more than just teach me Quechua; they shared their knowledge and guided my growing understanding of the culture of the Quechua-speaking people of the area. In Sucre I was lucky to find myself in the midst of a lively group of scholars, given focus by the energies of Gabriel Martínez and Veronica Cereceda. I spent many happy hours comparing notes, ideas, and complaints with Gary Urton and Julia Meyerson, Antero Klemola, Colin Gomez, and Elka Weinstein. Luis Oporto at the Museo Nacional de Etnografía y Folklore in La Paz gave me crucial help, and Denise Arnold and Juan de Dios Yapita, as well as Wilbert Tejerina, Alison Spedding, and Rossana Barragán were good company, always ready to share their profound insights into Bolivia.

All of my research would have been impossible without the active support of many people in Quirpini, San Lucas, and Buenos Aires. Miguel Paco and Emiliana Puma housed me, fed me, vouched for me, and spent hours answering my naïve questions; their children, especially Javier, were my good friends. The friendship and support of Anisa Ibarra and Felix Villcasana, Genaro Mamani and Carminsa Santos, Filomón Villcasana, and Justinano Cruz made my work in Quirpini much more enjoyable and productive. Nicanor Huarachi guided me to Buenos Aires and looked after me while I was there. Mamerto Barrios, a San Luqueño living in Sucre, gave me a valuable entrée to the town. Adolfo Otondo and his family, as well as Macedonio Valverde, were of inestimable help.

It would make perfect sense to mention all of my friends, and all those who have helped me over the years, but I will limit myself to a few people to whom I owe special thanks: John Hyslop, Craig Morris, Antoinette Molinié, Adele Greene, Althea Viafora-Kress, Jessica Bejamin, and Stephen Keogh. The financial support from my grandmother, Mary Clark Rockefeller, helped with fieldwork. I hardly know how to thank my oldest intellectual companion and one of my closest friends, David Graeber. Many of the ideas in the book might well have originated with him (as did this line; see Graeber 2001:vii); nearly all were refined in the course of our many conversations, which have been an endless source of ideas and inspiration since we were in high school.

And, finally, I give all my love and plenty of thanks to Julia D'Amico, for sharing a new world with me, and for her love and support, and to our children Jack and Sage, for endless distractions and delight.

All photographs are by the author with the exception of that facing title page, taken by Miguel Paco.

PART 1 ～ INSCRIPTIONS

Introduction: Disorientations

Where Was I?

It is customary for ethnographers to begin by giving their readers some information that will "orient" them as to the place, time, and subject matter of the book they are about to read. In a book about places, however, it is crucial that we accept some measure of disorientation. Like the stars at night, which disappear when you look at them directly, places are never where we expect them to be. They do not contain themselves but sprawl across the terrain. They are never the same as themselves but constantly unfold in time, becoming what they might be only through their dynamic interconnections with other places, and the movement of people, things, and ideas within and through them. They are never the same to everyone who inhabits or encounters them; instead they are the objects of interpretive struggles played out through ideas, objects, and bodies.

The first time I really had to confront the sprawling nature of places was when I returned from my main bout of fieldwork in 1994, and repeatedly had to respond to the question, "Where did you go?" The question was harder to answer than I had anticipated, and not only because my research was multisited. The answer that this question called for was: I went to Quirpini, a village of Quechua-speaking *campesinos* in highland Bolivia. But that response would accept the implication that my research location and the whereabouts of the people I studied was bounded and unique, that there was a "place" that could be said to contain them. In addition, it would elide a good part of my travels. I could say that I went to Bolivia and Argentina, or that I traveled about the "Southern Cone," but these replies would be much too broad, and invoke places that were often irrelevant to what I and the people around me were doing, and where we were going. I could answer that I spent a year and a half working in and around Quirpini, spending a good deal of time in the nearby town of San Lucas, home to the Spanish-speaking regional elite, and then traveled with a campesino from Quirpini to Buenos Aires, where I lived for a little while in a multiethnic immigrant neighborhood on the outskirts of that city, traveling around the urban area to visit the places where Quirpini migrants worked. This answer would be rather longer and more detailed than what most people were looking for.

Giving an honest and adequate answer to the question of where I did my fieldwork, or where Quirpinis live, would be even more involved. In fact, it would require significantly "missing the point" of the question. This is where the disorientation comes in. Attempting to answer questions of this sort started me in the direction that has culminated in the writing of this book. This book is about movement, and it is about places. It is about the ways in which the Quechua-speaking people of Quirpini make the places they live in and live in the places they make. Much of this making (we could call it "creation" or, following Lefebvre [1991], "production") takes place through movement and efforts to influence and control movement. As a starting point, then, I will take the reader on a visit of my own initial disorientation, and give some hint of how I began the lengthy process of figuring out where I was.

WANDERING QUIRPINI

The first time I walked about Quirpini I scarcely encountered any people. I had been there briefly once before and had met some Quirpinis, but on this occasion I was not visiting anyone and just wanted to look around. As I walked among the spiny trees and between the ravines of Quirpini's dry terrain, try-ing not to impose myself but filled with curiosity, I saw many of the places that made up the world I would inhabit for the next two years. I walked to the community from the town of San Lucas, the place I was most familiar with at this early point in my fieldwork. The road took me south from the town, through the tiny community of Tambo Mokho and a couple of kilometers across a dry plain cut by a few seasonal streambeds. It was July, and the day was sunny and cool, as most winter days in the area are. Nearing Quirpini, the road, only recently built to replace an older route connecting San Lucas to the main highway, ascended the western side of the valley, skirting the edge of the irrigated land. Presently I found the access road that descended from this new route to an old road that ran near the river and defined the central area of Quirpini, insofar as such a dispersed community can be said to have a center. To the east and west, high ridges rose several hundred meters, brush lightly covering the tan earth. To the north, downriver, the view opened up toward San Lucas and I could see distant hills far outside the valley, although the town was hidden from view. Upriver, to the south, I saw a peculiar mountain looming above the top of the valley, with broad diagonal stripes near its top as if from some tilted sedimentary rock formation; far beyond this formation rose a high, conical, snow-covered peak, the only dramatic vista in a decidedly low-key scene. The land had a spare beauty, reminding me at times of arid parts of the southwestern United States.

Going down the access road I saw the school, surrounded by adobe walls, between the old road and the river. Outside the school's wooden gates was a small dusty semicircle some twenty meters across, lined with adobe benches and featuring a flagpole. As I wandered further I saw adobe houses, many enclosed by low walls, strung loosely along the old and new roads, or set among bare fields of earth the same color as the houses and the ridges. Wherever I went there seemed to be some kind of path; the community was laced by a tracery of ways to get from one place to another. Between the river and the new road was a broad uncultivated area cut by gullies, with sparse brush and low trees; I saw a few birds but no animals. Here and there immense eucalyptus trees, green even in winter, towered over everything. A rustling grove of the giant trees behind the main buildings of the school was particularly striking. I think that on this visit I saw the San Lucas River as it passes through Quirpini, a trickle of water deep in its own ravine some ten meters below the valley floor. Across it I could see more fields and houses, beyond which the brush-covered slopes rose to the cliffs that marked the eastern rim of the valley. On my next visit I had to cross the river, clambering down a narrow trail cut in the steep bank, stepping over the stream in its sandy bed, and finding a path up the other side.

Although I was fascinated by the place and thrilled with its beauty, I was aware that none of what I saw made much sense to me. I did not even know what it was that I did not know. Everything I saw was static—was, in Raymond Williams's sense, just part of a landscape,[1] a collection of views with no evident order except as objects of my observation. Over the next twenty-four months, as I took part in many aspects of the life of Quirpini and the San Lucas valley, I gradually came to understand something about the scenes and places I had wandered through. What changed in my understanding of the terrain of Quirpini and the whole area was that I came to grasp, by talking to people and taking part in their activities, what moved across the land and how. In this way I came to have some understanding of the places that I had walked through on my early visit. The school, for instance, was not only where the children of Quirpini gathered every day for lessons; it was also an important ritual center, particularly during Carnival, as well as the site of the community's general meetings, and where communal authorities gathered. It was especially significant, then, that most public activity at the school was under the control of the teachers, all Spanish-speaking members of the regional elite based in San Lucas. In fact, the school was not only a symbolic center of Quirpini, as evinced to me by the many ways in which people converged on the place throughout the year, it was also the main place where Quirpini interacted with the dominant strata of Bolivian society: visiting dignitaries always addressed the community in the school; when I sought permission to stay in the community I had to go to the school.

Similarly, the houses I saw looked to me simply like houses. I intuited some things about them based on my own store of cultural knowledge and ethnographies I had read. I felt, for instance, that I should not approach them too closely without calling out a greeting. What I knew little about was the dense network of relationships that connected them and the ways in which people moved between and within them.

Even at this early point, of course, I knew something about the community and the area. This was my second visit to San Lucas, the eponymous regional capital, where I had been asking about rural villages in the hope of locating a place to conduct the main part of my fieldwork. The area was inhabited entirely by people who were bilingual in Quechua and Spanish or who spoke only Quechua. Most of the Quechua-speakers were rural agriculturalists, or campesinos, often thought of as indigenous. They lived in several dozen villages of a few hundred people each, spread across the cold, dry highlands of the area or in the one large valley that cut through the highlands and contained the region's best land and most plentiful water. Both San

Lucas and Quirpini were located in this valley, at an altitude of about three thousand meters. San Lucas, situated some five kilometers north of the Quirpini school, was home to most of the people in the region who spoke Spanish as their first language; these people, I already knew, formed a regional elite that dominated not only the valley but the surrounding highlands as well. I knew that people in the valley farmed irrigated fields and that the campesinos communities had once been organized into extensive social/geographical institutions called *ayllus*.[2] I was aware, too, that many men living in the area traveled frequently to Argentina for wage labor. Yet my knowledge was abstract, partial, and outdated. I did not yet know that the extensive ayllus of the area were largely defunct, devolved into individual communities, or that the most effective intercommunal institution was the campesino labor union, or that rainfall had decreased so much in the last decade that most people of the valley had abandoned their non-irrigated fields. In fact, until a few days before this trip I had thought that the name of this community was not "Quirpini" but "Jatun Kellaja," a name now rarely used that I had seen on a map in the Agrarian Reform office.

Although I could learn something about Quirpini just by walking around, articulating the parts of the terrain through my own movement, as long as what I saw appeared static, like the elements of a landscape, as long as I was not engaged with the life of the place so as to appreciate the movement that interconnected everything there, then what I was seeing was not the place itself. It would not be inaccurate to say that I did not actually encounter much of anything on that first walk; I was merely wandering through a shadow—a snapshot—that would only become real for me when I saw how it moved.

With time I learned that the direction from San Lucas to Quirpini is not actually "south" but "up": the cardinal directions in the San Lucas River valley are "up" and "down," in relation to the river's flow. The mountains I had seen were important *mallkus,* or powerful spirits that are identified both with mountains and condors. The distant snowy peak was called Liki; it was a mountain feared and respected throughout southern Chuquisaca and Potosí, said to be full of condors and valuable minerals. The mountain is actually in the territory of ayllu Calcha, and few people I knew had ever been near it. The closer mountain was Antahawa, the most important and powerful mallku in the valley. Most Quirpinis draw their irrigation water from a spring that rises in the mountain; Antahawa is thus the "owner" of the water, and Quirpinis go there every year to offer sacrifices for the continued supply of water.

I was later to learn that because I had arrived after the end of the harvest, which is the ideal time for people to travel for wage labor, many people were working in the cities. With no work to do in the fields at this time, most of the other people were working in their houses or pasturing animals on the mountainsides. It took me even longer to recognize the relationship between migration and the organization of land in Quirpini. As I detail later in this book, the local market for land largely exists because of labor migration; some Quirpinis leave the area permanently and sell their land to others (usually close kin) who can afford to buy the land because of their own migration for work.

It also took me some time to understand that the road I had taken to reach Quirpini was a divisive political issue. When I arrived Quirpini was in a state of transition due to the recent opening of the new road. The old road had passed through two of the three subdivisions of the community, called *zonas*, crossing the river in the process. The new one went along the edge of just the largest zona and did not cross the river. During the time I lived in the area, the bypassed zona, called Sakapampa, made vigorous but futile efforts to maintain the old road in order to stay accessible to truck traffic. Back on the other side of the river, several families had already moved their homes near the new road; some had opened stores to sell candy and soda; those who lived by the old road had closed their shops.

As for the river, although even I could tell that it became a raging torrent in the rainy season, it took me months to appreciate that it was just one part of a valley-wide system for distributing the water that flowed from Antahawa and other sources. In the semi-desert climate of Quirpini, the main factor limiting the extent of cultivated fields is not lack of land but lack of water. As a result, people of the valley manage and share the water with great care. One of the most important political institutions within each community is the *larqha* (literally, canal), the group of landholders who share rights to water from a specific source, via a specific irrigation canal. At numerous points water is drawn from the river into irrigation canals and then returned to the river at many other points, according to a schedule agreed on among the larqhas. At any point along the length of the valley there is usually far more water flowing through the irrigation canals than there is in the main channel of the river.

Even the eucalyptus trees reflected a complex and malleable spatial reality. Eucalyptus is native to Australia; the trees were introduced in South America in the nineteenth century. All the eucalyptus trees in Quirpini were planted; they are valued for their straight timber, their ability to grow fast in poor, dry soil, and their medicinal leaves. Yet they must not be planted near fields, as they are notorious for "sucking up" all the available nutrients and water in the soil, leaving nothing for crops; as a result, they are usually found in the most marginal areas, unsuitable for planting. The trees in the schoolyard had been planted a couple of decades earlier, in hopes that they would eventually provide cash for the school. While I was in Quirpini, the school contracted with an itinerant woodsman to cut them down and sell the lumber. This provided a tidy sum that helped the school build a new classroom, and also dramatically changed the feel of the school's land.

Finally, on my early visit, I was convinced that I was walking around in "Quirpini"; strictly speaking this was not incorrect, but it wasn't very correct, either. The people I lived with orient their actions in many ways, and a recurring theme of this book is sensitivity to the invoked contexts of people's actions and travels. As we will see most clearly in chapter 4, Quirpini often presents itself as the context for people's actions, but just as often it does not, and there are many occasions when people act not "in" Quirpini but with an orientation to their houses or their networks of kin and friends. There were times when placing people's activities in Quirpini inhibited my ability to understand them.

In other words, I learned with time that Quirpini is not a place on a map, nor is it a territory that contains a culture or a people. It is, rather, a pattern of movements, a conjunction of forces, a set of spatial strategies and struggles, a situational context for people's actions. My challenge during fieldwork was to move beyond the landscape, to recognize that the land that people inhabit, that they work, is never a static object for contemplation. My challenge in this book is to show how the people of Quirpini inhabit places of their own constant making, and that a part of the way they make it is by their movement.

FINDING LA SALADA

Well over a year after this first walk through Quirpini, I arrived in Buenos Aires. Again I was alone and coming to a strange place, but the circumstances of my arrival could hardly have been more different. I was on a long-distance bus from the Bolivian border, nearing the end of my overland trip from Quirpini to La Salada, an immigrant neighborhood on the outskirts of the Argentine city, where a number of Quirpini families had settled; this was a route well traveled by Quirpinis. I was alone because my traveling companion, a Quirpini named Nicanor Huarachi, had a ticket for an earlier bus, which I missed because of my difficulty getting through customs at the Argentine border (Nicanor had no trouble with customs, having Argentine citizenship papers). The city loomed impenetrably in my mind as I anticipated trying to find the house of Nicanor's cousin in La Salada. Nicanor had given me sketchy directions about which city buses I should take to get there, but I had little confidence in my ability to execute his instructions well enough to find him in the urban maze. That I had been robbed in a particularly humiliating fashion in the border town of Yacuiba did nothing to improve my outlook.

By now I was relatively adept at navigating Quirpini spatially and socially. I had left behind the community's comfortably familiar confines to visit migrants in the unknown metropolis, accompanied only by one of my Quirpini acquaintances, my only link to Quirpinis in Buenos Aires. Were Nicanor not waiting for me at the bus station, I feared I would be lost, as would the whole second part of my fieldwork project.

To my relief, he was there when I got off the bus; in fact, he seemed to have been even more anxious over our separation than I was, terrified lest I not be on the next bus. He bundled me onto a series of local buses that took us all the way across the city into the southern suburb of Lomas de Zamora. A few kilometers outside the city, we descended from our final bus into a marginal-looking commercial district, and walked to the residential neighborhood where some Quirpinis could be found. Nicanor led me a few blocks until we arrived at a fenced lot with two houses, one of cinderblock, one of tar paper. We went to the cinderblock house and knocked on the door. This, Nicanor told me, was the home of Santiago Gómez, his cousin, who would surely put us up for the night. Santiago appeared to be nervous at the unexpected appearance of a strange *gringo*; he told Nicanor that he already had guests for the night and directed us to his cousin's house across the street. We knocked there, only to discover that the cousin had recently moved out, abandoning her husband and children. The husband, Paulino Flores, was not from San Lucas, did not know Nicanor, and had only one bed in his truly decrepit shack, but nevertheless he put us up for the night.

The next morning La Salada was very quiet. But the stillness was different than that of Quirpini. This was the quiet of the workday and of domestic space; every adult I met in the neighborhood was from elsewhere and had come to Buenos Aires for work or to accompany someone who was working. By mid-morning on a weekday at least half the population of the area had departed and would not return until the evening. There were no fields to be worked and few public spaces; people entertained visitors and celebrated minor fiestas in their houses.

Over the next few weeks I set about putting together a somewhat coherent idea of the space of La Salada and Buenos Aires, with the help of the Quirpinis I got to know in the area. This process was very different from the one I conducted in Quirpini, not only because La Salada is so different a place but also because the Bolivians I knew in Buenos Aires were sojourners in someone else's space, and they knew it. As a result, getting a deeper grasp of the way they lived in space did not necessarily bring me to a full understanding of Buenos Aires or even of La Salada. Instead, I learned to navigate the bus routes along the city's outer edge that took them to the construction sites where most of them worked. I quickly mastered a space that was made up of the names of bus routes and streets but was markedly spare in other geographical features. This thin quality of my interlocutors' knowledge of the urban terrain differed strikingly from their rich and detailed knowledge of the land in and around Quirpini. On walks, even well into the mountains above the village, people were perfectly familiar with the names of each place we passed, knew where each alternate path led. Much of the geographical and historical information that I eventually learned about the city and the place of immigrants in it was of no relevance at all to the people I was spending time with; in learning about urban development policies or the history of migrant housing in Buenos Aires, I was learning a spatial depth that was relevant to them only in its consequences.

I suspect that this is true of cities in general. They are made up of spaces so complex and so dependent on the interconnection of people with dramatically different histories, prospects, values, and habits that no one version of "lived" space can be taken to be "the" space of the city. In learning something of the lived space of Quirpinis and other people from the San Lucas area in Buenos Aires, I was learning only one distinctive and marginal aspect of the urban space, largely populated by people who straddled the two spatial realities.

Although the space of Quirpini was what it was in part (and increasingly) due to the travels of migrants, understanding what the space of Buenos Aires was for Quirpinis was a markedly different matter than understanding the space of Quirpini. There was no place that Quirpinis could fill with their spatial orientations, nor any that they wished to. Although the space that Quirpini migrants were helping to create was undoubtedly transnational, their aspirations were not—the Quirpinis I knew wanted either to settle in Argentina or return to Bolivia.

Construction of a Chapel

I finally did meet someone on that early visit to Quirpini, and in the course of our conversation he introduced me to what would become one of the themes of my field experience. He wanted to build a chapel. This was a project that would transform the space of Quirpini and that exemplifies the malleability and created nature of the community's terrain. Following the politics and the work of constructing this chapel was one of the ways in which I came to understand Quirpini as a terrain as well as the community's insertion into regional and super-regional relations of power. The chapel was a key part of my introduction to spatial politics, and following its progress was an important aspect of my coming to understand Quirpini as a place.

I met Hilarión Condori as he was constructing a new field on the edge of his property. He was a short, quick man in his forties, who showed none of the reserve I had come to expect from campesinos. In time I would come to know him as an ambitious and intelligent person with a rather obsessive personality. To my pleasant surprise, after briefly asking me what I was up to, he launched into a long, rambling monologue, mostly taken up with complaints about the lack of rain. He also told me that he was a catechist, one of a few people in the community specially trained by the Church to teach their fellows Catholic doctrine.

His greatest ambition as a catechist was to realize the construction of a chapel in Quirpini. He told me that "we" were soon going to build the chapel with the support of the priest, whose church was in the nearby town of San Lucas. This was a good thing, because currently, when the priest visited Quirpini, he had to hold services in the school, which was not fitting. If there were a chapel, the priest would visit more often. I was later to learn that weekly religious celebrations were conducted by the catechists and held in the school, but hardly anyone came unless they were approaching some major sacrament and were required to attend services.

With his use of the term "we," Hilarión clearly meant that the people of Quirpini would build the chapel, I soon came to think that he was the only Quirpini with much interest in the project. Over the succeeding months I periodically mentioned the plan, but for the most part people just blandly agreed that the community needed a chapel; there was never any suggestion that "we" were going to do anything about it. A few argued that it was not worth the trouble and expense. For over a year nothing happened. I came to assume that the chapel would never be built. Even the other two catechists in Quirpini showed little enthusiasm for it.

Then, in the latter part of 1993, all this changed. Whereas the priest (for the initiative was indeed his) at first had offered to collaborate in some un-specified way on building the chapel, he now announced that the Church would buy all the necessary materials, and pay for the services of an engineer to design and supervise the project. Quirpini would provide only the work and adobe bricks. Once the priest had committed himself to this support, results came quickly.

For the last few years the Catholic Church in the area had been encourag-ing communities to build their own chapels. This was part of a broad politics aimed to help free the Quechua peasant communities of the San Lucas region from the control of the town's Spanish-speaking elite. One of the expressions of the town's dominance over the villages was the centrality of the Church to the region's ritual life. One could not baptize a child or have a religious wed-ding or properly celebrate a number of important annual fiestas without going to the Church. In this role the Church was part of a system that concentrated transformative social powers in the town. Other parts of this system included the notary, who recorded births, marriages, and (theoretically) deaths, as well as the judge and the mayor, who could adjudicate certain disputes, and the shopkeepers and traders, who could transform goods into money and vice versa. The Quechua-speaking residents of the rural areas were obliged to travel to town in order to realize these transformations.

The two priests who had served successively in San Lucas since the mid-1980s, Juan Miranda and Vicmar Miranda,[3] were of progressive sym-pathies and tried to loosen the power of the town's elite. In this spirit they helped many small rural communities, including Quirpini, obtain authori-zation to build their own cemeteries so they would not have to carry their dead to San Lucas to bury them; they also made efforts to advocate for the campesinos in regional politics, as well as encourage various campesino organizations independent of the town, such as Mothers' Clubs. They tried to undermine the ritual cycle whereby campesinos were frequently obliged to celebrate major religious fiestas by going into town and visiting notables or the Church. People in Quirpini used to celebrate Easter in town but had recently stopped doing so, with the priest's encouragement. They still went into town on Carnival and visited the town's notables, but Vicmar Miranda, who was the priest during most of my time in the area, was openly ambivalent about this custom and sometimes made a point of not being present to receive the visits. Encouraging communities to build their own chapels was a part of this de-centering of the town in relationship to the region; by doing this, and visiting these chapels regularly to conduct masses, Miranda was able to move some of the focus of campesino Catholic ritual life into the communities. A corollary of this effort was trying to strengthen the organization of the region's communities. He was concerned that because of labor migration, the growth of evangelical Christianity, and increased contact with the rest of the world, the region's campesinos were abandoning their traditional culture and political structures without adopting anything to replace them. He felt that the Church could act to strengthen communal culture and society.

Apart from anything the priests were doing, San Lucas had been losing its dominant position over the communities of the region for several decades. The highland communities outside the San Lucas River valley had, to a considerable extent, thrown off the political influence of the town, and the dominant class of relatively white Spanish-speakers in the town no longer enjoyed the privileged position it once did. In this situation, with power in the region moving out of the town, it made sense for the local Church to change with the times and not tie its own position too closely with that of the town elite.

In addition, the regional Church was sensitive about the growing number of people converting to evangelical (non-Catholic) Christian sects. Evangelical churches led by campesinos were popping up not only in San Lucas but in private houses throughout the region, including in Quirpini. As the ability of San Lucas to command ritual submission declined, the Catholic Church was finding that it had no presence in most of the region, while its main rivals had a beachhead in every population center. Although Juan Miranda never connected the issues of evangelical Christians and the chapel, it seemed unlikely that the convenience of having an institutionally sanctioned Catholic center in every village escaped him.

It is telling, then, that the only obstacle to the plan to build the chapel was the objection of the relatively small number of evangelical Christian families in Quirpini (fewer than ten out of a hundred households). They felt it was wrong that a Catholic building should be constructed as a communal project. As in much of Bolivia, the evangelical population of the San Lucas area was small but growing, and clearly constituted a threat to the hegemony of the Catholic Church. This dispute made it clear that the Church's concern was partly to defend its own "turf" by means of the chapel. Father Miranda argued that the chapel was crucial to any effort to strengthen Quirpini as a community; by implication, he was arguing that the Church's centrality to the rural communities of the area was a fact that outweighed any considerations of religious favoritism. The issue was resolved in a series of town meetings (*reuniones generales*) with the agreement that evangelical households would contribute the same amount of work as Catholics but would work on the school (the only other communally held building in Quirpini) rather than on the chapel.

With this issue out of the way, the *reunión* quickly decided how to proceed. Under the guidance of the school director, who usually ran the meeting, it was agreed that everyone would contribute a certain number of adobe bricks for the walls and several hours of work on construction. The chapel was to be situated near the geographical middle of the community, on some un-irrigated land across a ravine from the school and above the cemetery. The owner of this unproductive land donated it to the community, and it became part of what could be a nascent center of Quirpini. Not far from the chapel was Quirpini's new cemetery. Finally, a three-member committee was elected to supervise the work. Theirs would be the heaviest responsibility, as one of them would have to be present whenever work was going ahead, and they were expected to keep records of everyone's contribution and make sure no one came up short.

This arrangement was not uncommon for group labor projects. Each household was responsible for making bricks out of the soil of their own land, in their own time, with water from their own allotment for irrigation, and each was responsible for bringing it to the building site. Each household also had to provide a set number of man hours, building the chapel walls out of these adobes. Every adult male in Quirpini knows how to make adobes and build walls, so this was labor that fell equally on each household.

Work proceeded apace, and as far as I knew everyone fulfilled their obligations. The Church provided windows, doors, tiles, and other architectural items that were not available in Quirpini, and hired an architect who turned up periodically to direct the work. The priest also visited from time to time.

The chapel was finished not long before I was to leave, and was inaugurated with a Mass and a short fiesta. The central event of the fiesta was a folkloric performance for the new priest, who had recently replaced Vicmar Miranda. He was asked to sit at a small table, and a crowd of Quirpinis watched him closely as members of the community performed a succession of traditional songs and dances.

By this time most Catholic Quirpinis had come to support the chapel enthusiastically, and plans had been made that would radically revise the spatial order of the community around it. Most significant, it was decided that all the saints held in the community would be moved to the new chapel. There were three, each owned by a different family: Santa Rosa de Lima, sometimes called the patron of Quirpini; San Antonio; and Santiago. Until this time these saints had each resided in one of the three zonas of Quirpini, and their celebrations usually drew people from their respective zonas.

My encounter with the building of Quirpini's chapel exposed me to many of the themes that would become central to my understanding of how Quirpinis live in space. First of all, around the chapel people were working out aspects of the relationship between Quirpini and the regional capital San Lucas, home to nearly all the Spanish-speaking elite of the area. A key struggle between these groups involves the elite's constant demands that campesinos come to San Lucas to effect most of the transformations that are realized through the Church, the state, or the market. The relations of the local Catholic Church to both these factions was also played out in the construction of the chapel. In light of the way I explicate spatial politics throughout the book, it is worth noting that although advocating for chapels throughout the region was partly a power move by the priest, he exercised and augmented his power not through commands but through inducements to get people to transform the space of their community in a way that would affect both their future patterns of movement and, it was implied, the priest's. I argue that a key means of exercising power is to respond to people's movement so as to try to influence or control it.

But the chapel was not just negotiated—it had to be built. This meant work: carrying out repetitive tasks like making adobe bricks and mortaring them in place, planning the location of the chapel, designing it, and deciding who would do the work and how it would be done. Creating the chapel as a place, then, depended on people's repeated attendance at reuniones generales, on Father Miranda's involvement with the community, on his bringing window and roofing materials, on the periodic visits of an engineer to plan the structure, and on the Catholics making and delivering adobe bricks and coming to the chapel site to put together the bricks, windows, and roof. Finally, the chapel would never succeed as a place if Quirpinis (and the priest) did not go there regularly, make it part of their spatial practice. It finally looked as if it would succeed as a place because it was being incorporated into Quirpinis' ritual ways of making their social space. Thus the building of the chapel not only provided temporal bookends for my field experience in Quirpini but exemplifies some of the key themes of this book.

About the Title

The reader may have noticed that the book's title references Walt Whitman's sweeping poem "Starting from Paumanok" (Whitman 2002 [1855]). Whitman's poem is a paean to (North) American mobility—to the wild dynamism of nineteenth-century America in its rude variety, which Whitman both observes and identifies himself with. Paumanok is an Algonquian name for Long Island, where Whitman was born. At the simplest level I found his title useful to underline an important insight: the people I worked with were not "in" Quirpini—for them it was a starting point from which they roamed across a vast terrain, just as Whitman saw Long Island as his own starting point. I wanted to claim for Quirpinis the restless, embracing mobility that Whitman claims for Americans.

At the same time this book can be seen as a counter-poem to "Starting from Paumanok." For Whitman, Americans are a people of ceaseless movement; the nation's dynamism is identified with their mobility, and it is that dynamism that contrasts America to much of the rest of the world, as future to past. One of the clearest lessons of globalization is that America has no monopoly on such people; migrants, tourists, and business travelers alike (not to mention anthropologists) restlessly crisscross the world, and their travel is a central part of the global integration and transformation that some anthropologists celebrate in an almost Whitmanian fashion (see, for instance, Appadurai 1996a, 1996c). Although Whitman does casually include South America in his celebration of the American future, people such as the Quirpinis I worked with would not have fit into his vision of a restless, forward-looking people. He makes this clear in his dismissive reference to Native Americans:

> And for the past I pronounce what the air holds of the red aborigines.
>   The red aborigines,
>   Leaving natural breaths, sounds of rain and winds, calls as of birds
>   and animals in the woods, syllabled to us for names,
>   Okonee, Koosa, Ottowa, Monongahela, Sauk, Natchez,
>   Chattahoochee, Kaqueta, Oronoco,
>   Wabash, Miami, Saginaw, Chippewa, Oshkosh, Walla-Walla,
>   Leaving such to the States they melt, they depart, charging the
>   water and the land with names. (2002:stanza 17)

He leaves Paumanok off the list, but it is easy to work out that Whitman, one of the "new race" of Americans, takes as his starting point a place with an "aborigine" name. It is a kind of homage to the "red aborigines" but one that is based on their identification with a disappearing wild nature and their utter separation from the future, which Whitman's Americans embody. The "aborigines," like the "Dead poets, philosophs, priests / Martyrs, artists, inventors, governments long since" of the Old World, serve to ground Whitman's New Man in the past which he is in the act of surpassing. "Quirpini" would have fit comfortably in Whitman's list of "aborigine" place-names, as would "Potosí," "Cuzco," "Lima," "Bogotá" or "Mexico," but the situation is quite different for Quirpinis than for Long Islanders. Quirpinis share in an indigenous heritage with the people who named the place from which they are starting, and are most likely in large part descended from them. They find themselves on the same side of the indigenous versus Eurocentric divide as the name of their community, and on the opposite side from Whitman, as well as Bolivian literary society.

In borrowing Whitman's title, I am refuting his relegation of Native peoples to the past. In fact, one aim of the book is to show that Quirpinis are very much agents in their own present and that their actions are molding the future. Far from departing and leaving their names, they and their fellows are building and feeding cities, transforming international borders, re-forming the national identities of Argentina and Bolivia.

Theorizing Lived Spaces, Big and Small

When Whitman has the "aborigines" leave behind place-names, then disappear, he is not only erasing Native Americans from history. The same device draws a temporal dividing line between his forward-looking, dynamic Americans and the places in which and through which they move and act; the places are already there, a support for action, but not a result of it. Here, too, my book stands opposed to Whitman's poem in that I refuse to separate action and the places in which it happens. Why must we suppose that the transformative mobility that Whitman celebrates is something new? How were the places his Americans were reinventing created in the first place if not through the movement, work, and struggles of precisely the "red aborigines" who Whitman sees as static?

Heightened sensitivity to the problem of talking about place, and particularly the refusal to treat locality as a matter that can be dispensed with before taking in more weighty cultural matters, is not new to anthropology. Eric Mueggler (2001:10) eloquently exemplifies this refusal when he critiques ethnographic writing that "finds place to be a container for social being or a surface on which social life is played out," and instead stakes out a position that both place and time are not "given in nature or power; both are made." Mueggler invokes what is by now a well-known dichotomy in philosophical and social scientific debates about spatiality: place as a container for action (or for identity, or for something else) versus place as something constantly produced by action, inextricably bound up with the actions that take place within it. In a similar vein Munn rejects the "commonplace assumptions" that "space is static and to be contrasted with the dynamism of time," and "that spatial boundaries are . . . fixed" (1986:464–465). Pandya criticizes the common anthropological approach that treats space as "a prefabricated stagelike structure," arguing that our subjects live it as something "created by the ongoing practice of movement" (1990:774, 776). The people of Quirpini constantly enact and reenact the space they live in—the arena in which movement takes place is not immune to the effects of that movement. In other words, social space is always lived space, and it is always embodied.

As Low and Lawrence-Zúñiga (2003a) show in the introduction to their collection, *The Anthropology of Space and Place*, there has long been a tradition of thought in anthropology that focuses on embodied space, with the implicitly phenomenological assumptions accompanying that approach. In effect, the problem anthropology encounters today is that there is a disjuncture between the approaches represented in part 1 of their book ("Embodied Spaces") and part 5 ("Transnational Spaces"). There is still a disjuncture between the anthropology of lived space and that of large-scale space. My central theoretical goal in this book is to show a way that this disjuncture might be overcome. My chief methodological assertion is that this can best be achieved by scaling "up" from the space of bodies and experience to the large-scale spaces of nations' population movements and other large-scale phenomena, and by maintaining an unwavering awareness that space, considered as a social phenomenon, is the product of action and movement.

EMBODIED TRANSNATIONAL SPACES

"Locating culture" (in Low and Lawrence-Zúñiga's phrase) and locating social relations has become a complex and urgent problem, as people, images, goods, and values move more rapidly and routinely between ever more distant places. It is becoming increasingly clear that culture and society happen at multiple scales. The collection of articles edited by Gupta and Ferguson (1997b) includes valuable insights into how to understand large-scale cultural phenomena, particularly identity in the context of the nation-state. One inspiration for my approach to locality is their observations that anthropologists have too often "taken the local as given, without asking how perceptions of locality and community are . . . constructed" (1997a:6), and treated 'the local' as "the original, the centered, the natural, the authentic, and opposed to 'the global,' understood as new, external, artificially imposed and inauthentic" (1997a:7). Rouse's (1991, 1992, 1995) work on Mexican immigrants in the United States was also very helpful; he engages many of the issues raised by the experience of transnational migration with a nuance and attention to details of practice that take him beyond simple generalizations. His notion of "transnational migrant circuits," the intensive and enduring movement of people, goods, and information between distant localities to the point that the localities can be lived as a single social space (Rouse 1991), has been a particularly useful tool for understanding the articulation of places, and I have adapted and employed it throughout this volume.

A number of anthropological works have been written during the last fifteen or so years that endeavored to take account of the challenges posed by globalization and transnationalism, while taking seriously the reality and dynamism of places. A few notable examples are Tsing's ethnographic and theoretical work (2002, 2005); Bestor's research on the global fish trade (2002, 2004); Ong's wide-ranging ethnographic work (e.g., 1999) with women workers and migrants; Rouse's work (1991) with Mexican migrants; Favero's writing (2003) on Indian markets; and Escobar's magnum opus (2008) on Afro-Columbian social movements. In my own view, all this work offers the hope of realizing the implications of LeFebvre's dictum that "no space disappears in the course of growth and development: *The worldwide does not abolish the local*" (1991:86; italics in original). Not all these authors may choose to align themselves with Lefebvre and his approach to space, or indeed with one another, but they share a commitment to recognizing the multi-scalar nature of social reality, and the way that any understanding of people's situations today must be capable of non-reductively relating different scales of activity and organization. In this book I am proposing another way to grasp the importance of lived places in relation to much larger-scaled realities.

These authors implicitly write in distinction to an earlier approach to globalization, which constituted the first concerted effort by anthropologists and other social scientists to come to grips with the new realities of global integration. This work, faced with the manifest (but theretofore widely neglected) entanglement of the spaces of people's experiences with an array of vast institutions producing public order, economic value, information, entertainment, and more, and the no longer deniable reality of global mobility, tended to argue for a radical disjuncture between scales. They saw the global and the mobile eroding the ontological status of places. The work of Arjun Appadurai (1996) stands out here, with his argument that social and cultural life happens in a variety of "scapes," and that cultural life is becoming "deterritorialized." Another notable example of this approach is Kearney's work (1991, 1994; Nagengast and Kearney 1990) on transnational Mixtec identity.

An important early strain of thought about globalization starts by attributing most agency and dynamism to large-scale entities—to global markets or corporations or regional economies. Authors such as Castells (1989, 1996a, 1996b) and Sassen (1998, 2001), as well as Appadurai (1996, 2002), argue that individual agency and locality are increasingly subordinated to, or effaced by, large-scale global forces, often called "flows." But rather than taking the ethnographic approach of "studying up" (see Nader 1974), these authors choose to study aggregates, looking not at bureaucratic practices or the way bankers act in the world but at marketing trends, policy changes, and demographic data. They do not look at people with the power to act on a large scale but rather at what those people themselves look at.

In seeking to embrace a dynamic and interconnected model of large-scale structures of action, these writers end up draining "place" of all dynamism. This downgrading of "place" starts with a refusal to move beyond the traditional idea of locality as a "container" or "stage" for action. The kind of place that is "deterritorialized" is the most rigid imaginable, one that resists entry and exit, and tends toward stasis. This model of place suffers from the dualism that Munn (1996) critiques, lending itself to an extreme dichotomization between static place and dynamic transnational movements, one that also has powerful implications for the relationship of different scales.

It is worth recalling here that, in Whitman's poem, the only things the "red aborigines" leave behind as they vanish in the face of the restless, ultramobile American future were place-names. In some respects, these authors are, as I am, embarking on a Whitmanian project, shorn of its racist and triumphalist assumptions. But Appadurai, Castells, and Sassen, in particular, by focusing on historical rupture and large-scale dynamism, maintain Whitman's underlying dualism between that which is taking part in the future, and that which is left behind. In their writings, places and actors take the place of red aborigines.

If these approaches to the global and the large-scale tend to efface locality, many phenomenological approaches to space that emphasize action and experience have great difficulty accounting for the interaction of disparate scales in the constitution of places, treating places as necessarily small-scale. For the philosopher Edward Casey (1998), "space" is an abstraction, defined from no particular point and prior to its own occupation by any body; it is defined by coordinates. In contrast, "place" is defined by the presence of a body; it is bodily but thus small-scale. Casey argues forcefully that the Enlightenment privileging of space over place represented a philosophical dead end and a turning away from the experienced world. Similarly, Tuan (e.g., 1977, 1996) contrasts "cosmos," the vast, unlived space of policymakers and the like, to "hearth," the small, embodied space of experience and attachment.

In *The Production of Space* Henri Lefebvre (1991) distinguishes two ways of thinking about space that resemble Casey's "space" versus "place," but ultimately his distinction is considerably more subtle and useful. Lefebvre contrasts "abstract space" and "social space," where abstract space is the map-like universalistic conception of space entirely divorced from action or the perspective of any actor. Like Casey's "space," it is space that just "is," prior to anything that happens in it. "Social space" is the space people live in, the product of human labor and action. Instead of calling the two terms mutually exclusive, as Casey does, Lefebvre's approach accounts for them both. Abstract space, he argues, is simply a special form of social space that is lived as if it were prior to the action that produces it. This step allows him to talk about space that, though produced, is not as closely tied to immediate bodily presence as is Casey's "place"; he can thus take seriously large-scale political spaces such as cities and nations. Lefebvre developed this approach partly in reaction to Henri Bergson's philosophy of "duration," which posits an ontological distinction between space and time, and separates time from human activity (see Bergson 1946; Lefebvre 1959, 1991; and Shields 1999). Instead, Lefebvre treats space and time together, and approaches them both as social products.

For Lefebvre, not only dynamic "social space" but also the supposedly abstract and pre-human "abstract space" is the result of action; it is produced. Here his Marxism, particularly his dialectical analysis of space, gives him the tools to understand large-scale economic and political structures that constrain and structure our experiences and actions while passing themselves off as "natural." Lefebvre's resultant historicization of the sort of uniform space that Casey dismisses has been an invaluable tool for a generation of geographers and social scientists who are committed to treating spatial practice as well as the large-scale structures that condition it.

In chapter 3 I talk about the "production" of a cornfield, and throughout the book I claim that places are produced. In using the word "production" I am following Lefebvre's (1991) adaptation of Marx's term. For Lefebvre, production is an inherently human activity and implies action oriented to an end (see Marx 1977:284). Production is also an inherently material process that involves the movement of the body, the limbs, and a variety of materials, as well as the movement of information. Note, however, that the product and the action's end, or purpose, need not be congruent. Crucial to Lefebvre's model of production is that people's intentional, productive activity can give rise to, or contribute to the production of, products that they did not anticipate—such as space or a city.

Here I should make it clear that in talking about "production" and "creation" I am in no way talking about origins or the creation of something ex nihilo. Rather, I am concerned to understand a world that is always-already there, a world in which people live and act. This approach is premised on the idea that social reality undergoes a constant process of creation. This ongoing and recurrent creation is always able to lead to change and periodically gives rise to something entirely new. In this view, the words "create" and "recreate" are virtually synonymous; I emphasize the ways in which creativity underlies any social world, and that the persistence of social forms, far from being natural or static and opposed to creation, is the result of constant creative action.

SCHEMAS, REPETITION, AND SCALING UP

A key term in much work concerned with embodied space is "schema," drawn from Merleau-Ponty's (1962) foundational work on the phenomenology of space. He uses the idea to address the structure and possibilities of the spatial field of one's body. It is our bodily schema that connects the parts of our bodies into a single phenomenal whole that allows me, for instance, to always know where my ear is and how far I must reach to touch my nose. Schemas—shared, ever present, and ever shifting—orient us in the world.

When people engage with a space repeatedly, they develop a schema of the possibilities and difficulties of the place. This is not the same thing as a mental map, nor is it just a series of habits; it cannot even be fully attributed to individuals. Rather, it is the complex of memories, rules, customs, and practices that are attached to a place. As Hanks (1990:81–84), drawing on Johnson (1987) and Merleau-Ponty (1962), points out, a schema incorporates mind and body and is super-individual. It cannot be called to mind in its entirety and is fully available only when a person or people are in the place to which the schema applies. Hanks emphasizes the implicit, bodily aspects of schemas, but it is useful to include in the idea some overt and collective elements (such as stories explaining why certain places are to be avoided) and other elements that are material (such as the shape and position of a doorway or the marks left by hundreds of feet on a path). A person or institution may enforce a pattern of movement, altering spatial schemas.

The development of phenomenology into an ethnographic tool for grasping space through schemas rather than structures that precede action, and focusing on lived, bodily space, owes a great deal to the work of Nancy Munn. In her writings on Papua New Guinea (1977, 1986) and on Australian Aboriginal spatiality (1996), Munn treats space (or, more precisely, spatial relations) as the product of actions guided by "generative schemas." For Munn, who draws liberally on Merleau-Ponty as well as on LeFebvre, it is nonsensical to think of space or time in the absence of each other or as abstractions that exist in their own right. I am following Munn, then, when I treat the places that Quirpinis inhabit and transit as the products of movement, and thus always temporal.

In this book I use the idea of schema to denote a pattern that appears in various media and is generative of action. By "media" I mean the concrete stuff that manifests patterns; such a pattern might appear in a dance, in a ritual, in a written or spoken text, in someone's memory, or in an oral tradition. It might be inscribed in a pattern of buildings, or it might appear only in the interactions of certain people, as in a family. Hanks (1990) details the schema of a Maya house; he shows what sorts of actions are implied, or disallowed, in certain spaces, the ways in which action in different parts of the house relate to one another, and generally what formal principles constrain the construction and inhabiting of the house. A schema is neither an action nor the idea of an action; it is the form of an action.

If schemas are patterns that guide action and make it comprehensible, any action can best be seen, not only as unique (although they always are unique in some way) but also as the playing out of a pattern that was already implicit in a social situation, a space, a memory. It is a playing out that instantiates and reproduces the pattern. If schemas underlie social action, then action always contains an element of repetition.

In contrast to those, like de Certeau (1984), who identify repetition with the deadening routines of modern life, I argue for a direct connection between repetition and creativity. In developing this approach, I draw on a heterogeneous collection of literary and linguistic work, notably Roman Jakobson's poetics, particularly as read by Turner (Jakobson 1960, 1970; Jakobson and Jones 1970; Jakobson and Lévi-Strauss 1973; Turner 1977), Jacques Derrida's concepts of iterability and citationality (Derrida 1971), and Judith

Butler's theory of perfomativity and gender identity (Butler 1988, 1993, 2006; see also Bell 1999; Loxley 2007; and Jagger 2008). What these approaches have in common is that they each treat repetition (of linguistic features or of actions) as the condition of the value, or significance, of those features or actions in relation to an encompassing context (whether a poem, a text, or a prevailing ideology about gender and identity). Although Jakobson makes the clearest case for the power of repetition to organize the text within which it appears, his approach suffers from his complete silence on the issue of agency—neither poet nor reader plays any discernable role in producing what in the end is a free-floating structure, untethered to practice. Turner's innovation on Jakobson is to treat poems as products of action but ones that play a role in governing the conditions of their own creation. Derrida does not leave out acting subjects, so much as he negates them: in his approach iterability is not just a source of sense; it also reveals that it is not subjects who speak but the systems of signification that speak through them. I find the more nuanced approach to subjects and agency in Butler's discussions of performativity (see, especially, Butler 2006) very apt for understanding Quirpinis' decidedly ambiguous possibilities for agency. Through their actions they partially make their own worlds, and influence other worlds, but they do so under conditions, and as subjects, that often render those actions questionably their own. Like gender identity as ordinarily performed, nearly all the effects of Quirpinis' (and others') actions that I focus on, nearly all the spaces and relationships produced, were not intended by anyone; in many cases they go entirely unnoticed.

If repetition (and by extension schemas) render action intelligible, they do so by relating it to larger scales of action and significance. This point brings us back to the disjuncture I mentioned earlier: How can we relate lived space to the very large-scale processes, places, and phenomena—transnational migration, global distribution of consumer goods, states' cultural ambitions, financial markets, mass media, and the like—that constitute much of the conditions under which people act, and that, increasingly, rural people like Quirpinis actively engage? To put the question differently, can we scale place and action "up" from small- to large-scale? As a starting point, I contend that we have no choice, as large-scale structures don't scale "down" very well; starting out by looking at bureaucrats, corporations, or media, though important in itself, does not easily lead one to any sort of ethnographic grasp of the people and communities operated on by these systems. By starting with small-scale places, with the interaction of bodies and the schemas governing those interactions, I am taking an approach that necessarily opens our understanding of those places and actions to the multiple contexts that constrain and guide them. The approach I have outlined, then, implies a dynamic model of the spatial practices of Quirpinis that can be scaled up, to include progressively larger phenomena in a way that it can help us understand places of different scale and character, such as the Bolivia-Argentina border, and the city of Buenos Aires.

The places inhabited by Quirpinis are articulated through the movement of, among other things, water, mountain-spirits, kin, government documents, money, corn, manufactured clothing, and people. Even a small community like Quirpini is constituted by a complex tangle of movements operating to different ends and at different scales. When the constraint on, or impetus for, motion come from the regional elite, the Bolivian nation, the Argentine government, or other sources of authority, the result is a dialectical unfolding of a place as an interpretive and material struggle. One effect of these struggles is that people enact places that are "oriented to" (to use the phrase that Weber [1999:2] puts at the heart of social action) certain other places or institutions; they are acting within a specific context.

Scaling up, then, is a particularly apt way to relate a lived space to the contexts that affect it, and is also a natural complement to the other elements of the method I have sketched so far: attention to movement; approaching action through the schemas that guide them, and the repetitive patterns of which they are a part; and a dialectical approach to movement and efforts to control or constrain that movement. By approaching spaces and places at the scales of experience, and investigating the ways in which larger-scale institutions and forces manifest themselves in experience, a work like this one is more likely to remain true to the many scales at which reality happens.

MOVEMENT AND EMBODIMENT AMONG THE ANDEANISTS

It is perhaps fortunate for this project that it starts from a place in the Andes—researchers working with indigenous people of the region have long recognized that Andean social life is best grasped in its dynamism and through the idiom of movement. Since Zuidema's (1964) crucial analysis of Inca ritual and statecraft in terms of travels through a representation of social space, and Murra's (1972, 1978, 1985) development of a dynamic model of Andean subsistence and circulation, movement and the interconnection of localities with distant realms have been central to many understandings of Andean culture and society (see, for instance, Saignes 1995). In addition, anthropologists have pieced together an understanding of the "hydraulic" Andean cosmology, in which the world is animated by the ceaseless and repetitive movement of fluids through the earth, the sky, and all living bodies (see, for example, Bastien 1978, 1985; Urton 1981; and Arnold 1987).

Expanding on Zuidema's ethnohistorical insights, Sallnow's (1987) classic study of pilgrimage shows the extent to which the Andean terrains are encountered as a space of travel, and as indigenous social worlds that depend on the dynamic interaction of distant places and contrasting realms. Orta (2004) deftly combines the themes of travel and the movement of fluid to illuminate the shifting valence of travel in an Aymara community. More recently work on Andean migration has begun to pay attention to the importance of migrants' transnational movement and the circuits they sustain (see, for instance, Cortes 2002; Hinojosa Gordonava 2007; Nobrega 2007; Paerregaard 2002, 2008; and Meisch 2002).

Most important for this book, however, has been Abercrombie's (1998) magisterial treatment of the history and present of a Bolivian Aymara community, *Pathways of Memory and Power*. By paying attention to the bodily and metaphorical travels and pathways of the people of K'ulta, Abercrombie manages to grasp the space of an Andean community in its multi-scalar and dynamic complexity. His close attention to the poetic organization of movement and spatial "rhymes" and homologies to describe social structure has been a significant inspiration for my work.

Structure of the Book

In keeping with the theme of scaling up, the main spatial movement of this book is from small to large, from the intimate spaces of houses and community to the region, the Bolivian nation, the border with Argentina, and the distant metropolis of Buenos Aires. The body of the book is divided into three parts. Part 1, "Inscriptions," contains, in addition to this introduction, the first chapter, "Places and History in and about Quirpini," which offers provisional concreteness that will help readers begin to trace the movements that make up my subjects' places. In addition to basic ethnographic background, I provide a history of the region and of factors in the area's current articulation with national and international spaces and dynamics, always emphasizing and developing a descriptive idiom centered on movement.

Part 2, "Facets of a Place," includes three chapters about aspects of Quirpini and social formations that exist within it. As I do throughout the book, in these chapters I describe both places and social relations in dynamic terms, as the products of action and movement.

Chapter 2, "Bicycles and Houses," concerns the creativity of movement, the ways that places in Quirpini are created and re-created through action and circulation, and the relationship of movement, place and power.

Chapter 3, "The Geography of Planting Corn" is mostly taken up with a spatial poetics of what Quirpinis do when they plant corn. Planting corn is the most labor-intensive and ritualized agricultural activity in Quirpini, carried out through a system of labor reciprocity called *mink'a*. In planting corn Quirpinis not only insure their family's subsistence, but they also reproduce the fields which grow the corn as well as the social networks through which they do all sorts household production and that are the foundation of their social lives.

In chapter 4, "Carnival and the Spatial Practice of Community," I turn to a discussion of the space of Quirpini as a whole, particularly as it is enacted in the fiesta of Carnival. I expand on the themes of chapter 2, presenting some schemata that structure the ways in which Quirpinis move around their community and region, and by which the places they inhabit are structured. Here I problematize the centrality of borders in much current literature on places. Quirpini as a community and space is enacted in multitude ways, and only some involve reference to borders.

Although commercial, migrant, and large-scale political engagements are a theme throughout the book, in part 3, "From Quirpini," I focus directly on the many external entanglements that affect the world of Quirpinis. In the three chapters that comprise this part of the book, I look at the regional political system, which concentrates power in the hands of the elite class of San Lucas, on the invocation of the Bolivian state in Quirpini, and on migration to Buenos Aires.

In chapter 5, "Ethnic Politics and the Control of Movement," I explore ethnic politics in the San Lucas region, and address a question that challenged me in the field: If space in Quirpini is so fluid, and, in effect, constantly being re-created, how did the San Lucas–based elite maintain their position of regional power? In other words, what was the nature of the power relation between Quirpini and San Lucas? The chapter analyzes how the region's Spanish-speaking "white" elite maintained its political dominance by controlling the terms on which movement and collective action take place in and around Quirpini.

Chapter 6 is devoted to a problem of significantly larger scale: the presence of the Bolivian nation in Quirpini. Through a reading of an annual school pageant celebrated in Quirpini and the messages it encodes about what it is to be a Bolivian, I show how Bolivia manages to impress itself in myriad ways on Quirpini. I argue, further, that it is possible to work upward from local actions and movement to larger-scale structures and patterns of action such as the Bolivian nation. By attention to the creative role of movement and the importance of context in constraining what can be created by an action, we can approach issues of scale in a way that does not elide the local.

In chapter 7, "Where Do You Go When You Go to Buenos Aires?" I address the general prevalence and impact of migration on Quirpini, tracing the role of long-distance travel in several people's life-courses. The bulk of the chapter is taken up with a geographically thick description of my trip to Buenos Aires with Nicanor, focusing, in particular, on the way that spaces like the Bolivia-Argentina border and the structure of the Argentine capital have been and are being transformed by large-scale international travel. A key issue here is what happens as Quirpinis confront the challenge of adapting the techniques of movement and power that are generally adequate to create a world "at home" to a new environment.

In the concluding chapter, I first return to Quirpini, as most migrants repeatedly do, and consider the changing ways in which the community is being produced as a locality, and discuss the continuously transformed long-distance entanglements in which they are involved. Here I look at the numerous sites and scales of movement that engage and influence Quirpini. I do so to demonstrate that understanding Quirpini as a locality requires us to situate the community's multiple heterogeneous spatial realms, large and small.

Writing this book presented a double challenge. The first was to represent the places that Quirpinis inhabit and move through. The second challenge was to do so in a way that would inform anthropological thinking about places, specifically how they are implicated in the small- and large-scale movement of people, things, and ideas. Displacement, I contend, is the permanent condition of places, and the many places that Quirpinis occupy and traverse can only be grasped by looking beyond them.

Fundamentally this book is an ethnographic study, but it is driven by theoretical concerns. One of these is to show that we cannot understand people's spatial worlds without detailed attention to their spatial practice; in other words, spatial theory needs ethnography. I ask for the reader's trust and patience, then, if at times I indulge in detailed spatial descriptions whose import is not immediately clear, and at other times use a broad brush to evoke the places I portray. Although I am describing the spatial practices of a specific group of people, it is not my concern to emphasize, or to underplay, their uniqueness. Some of the patterns of action I describe can be found in many other conjunctures; others are particular to the Andes or to Quirpinis. Similarly, the question of how culturally "Andean" their lives and practices are is of little interest, except insofar as it interests them or interests someone (such as the local priest) whose actions affect them. Quirpinis cannot be understood outside the framework of Andean history and culture, but that framework does not fully contain them.

Having extolled disorientation and indulged in a pastiche of events, locations, and antecedents, I must relent and give the reader a sense of what I am getting at and the people I am talking about. Before we start—before we really even get to Quirpini—I must provide context—social, geographical, historical, and theoretical—for the main part of the book. In the following historical and ethnographic account of the places Quirpinis frequent, I emphasize the dynamism, mobility, and struggles over mobility that have given rise to the lived space of Quirpinis.

1 · *Places and History in and about Quirpini*

Quirpini is a community of about five hundred people in the San Lucas River valley. The valley is the historical heart of the loosely defined San Lucas region, in the southern highlands of Chuquisaca, one of nine "departments" into which Bolivia is divided. Bounded to the east by the Pilcomayo River, to the north and west by the Department of Potosí, the San Lucas region is geographically and agriculturally varied, ranging from the low, hot valleys to highlands that soar beyond four thousand meters above sea level (see Figures 1.1, 1.2, and 1.3, which locate San Lucas and Quirpini in relation to Bolivia). The south of Chuquisaca is one of the poorest areas in Bolivia, characterized by low rainfall, difficult terrain, and poor communication with the rest of the country. San Lucas lies near the southern extreme of the vast zone stretching across much of highland Bolivia, Peru, and Ecuador, where rural people mainly speak the Quechua or Aymara languages, and occupy the bottom rungs of a racialized social hierarchy.[1]

The Crossroads

A traveler enters the San Lucas River valley from Padcoyo, a village on the main road between Potosí and Tarija. Padcoyo is the *cruce,* or crossroads, for the town of San Lucas as well as the highland areas around it. Before the road was improved in the 1970s, Padcoyo was by all accounts an insignificant hamlet, but by the 1990s it had a population of several hundred people, as well

Figure 1.1. Map of the Southern Cone, showing San Lucas and
Buenos Aires underlined and the route I followed from Quirpini
to Buenos Aires. Based on *Oxford Atlas of the World* 2001:167.

as a few restaurants for travelers, a high school, some government offices, and a weekly market. The town consisted mainly of a kilometer-long string of low adobe houses stretched along a bend in the graded dirt truck road, and surrounded by fields. Trucks rumbled through Padcoyo every hour or so, carrying various combinations of agricultural products, furniture, ores, livestock, and people. This is the main road to southern Bolivia and the most important connection between the Bolivian highlands and Argentina; nearly all the traffic was trucks, although jeeps carrying development officials passed through from time to time, as did the occasional bus.

Figure 1.2. Map of Department of Chuquisaca, showing the provinces of Sur Cinti and Nor Cinti, as well as the locations of San Lucas, Quirpini, and Padcoyo. Based on Instituto Nacional de Estadística 1999:8.

While I was in the area, it was not uncommon to see a battered jeep or other vehicle waiting near the middle of Padcoyo, at the start of a smaller dirt road heading north, and nearby a few men and women waiting with large bundles wrapped up in brightly colored cloth. These cars were taxis, waiting for a carload of people and cargo to carry to San Lucas. The road they followed passes through Quirpini, and this was the road I usually took. Two hundred or so meters south of this road, another, even smaller road heads east, crossing a dry plain and heading toward distant mountains. There were rarely any cars waiting to carry people in this direction, and only a few vehicles a day traveled on it.

These two roads mark the major geographical and ecological divide of the area, a divide which has also become political. The second road goes to the highland communities of the San Lucas region, then over the distant mountains, and down to the tropical valley of the Pilcomayo River. The highland area is mostly made up of *puna*, or high arid hills and plains. Much of the area is more than four thousand meters above sea level. Villages here (there are no major towns) are located alongside seasonal river beds, by springs, or near flat areas with arable land. To the east are a number of small mines. In the western part of the highlands, however, there is little source of livelihood except for agriculture and herding.[2] People primarily grow wheat, barley, potatoes, and some quinoa. This area has experienced extremely high levels of out-migration.[3]

The communities of this highland area, as well as the highlands of Qhocha, to the west of the San Lucas valley,[4] were, until the Agrarian Reform that began in 1953, entirely under the control of haciendas, large landholdings in which the owner controlled not only the land but the indigenous campesinos living there, who worked the land for the benefit of the owner. This situation was utterly transformed by the Agrarian Reform as, over some years, the residents of the various communities reclaimed nearly all the land in the highlands. Politically, the highland areas (Qhocha as well as the eastern highlands) were dominated by the campesino union, called the Confederación Sindical Única de Trabajadores Campesinas Bolivianas, or CSUTCB.

This was the latest in a series of unions to represent campesinos nationwide (Hahn 1992:73–74). The regional union headquarters is in the highland town of Pututaca, and the union power base is in the eastern highlands. Although the regional Spanish-speaking elite were dominant in the San Lucas valley, in the highlands their power was often matched by that of the union.

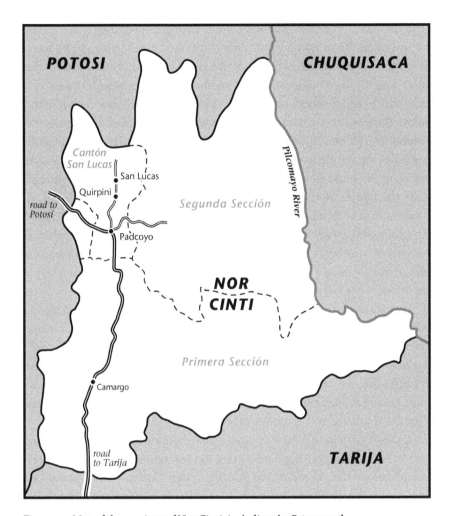

Figure 1.3. Map of the province of Nor Cinti, including the *Primera* and *Segunda Secciones* and Cantón San Lucas. The map also shows the main Potosí-Tarija road, Padcoyo, and the two roads that enter the San Lucas region from Padcoyo. The northern one passes through Quirpini, and then San Lucas. Based on Instituto Nacional de Estadística 1999:45.

The other road, the one with the taxis, leads to the political and economic heart of the region. The trip to San Lucas took about an hour in good weather, although in the rainy season the trip could take longer, and after a heavy rain the road became impassable until the waters subsided. This road crosses the same dry plain as the highland road, then goes through the hamlet of

Mishkhamayu. After Mishkhamayu the road begins a winding descent into the San Lucas River valley, which flows from the Qhocha plain to the west. Here the landscape changes dramatically: water is plentiful at the head of the valley, and the desert-like conditions on the plain are replaced by numerous green shrubs and trees among the many small fields tucked into the side of the valley. There is also a scattering of houses, usually near the fields. This is the community of Cumuni, which during my time in the field was completing the process of separating itself from Quirpini and merging with Mishkhamayu (see chapters 4 and 5). In contrast to the cold and dry puna of the highland areas, the upper valley, in an ecological zone called *valle alto* (high valley) or *cabazera de valle* (headwater valley),[5] whose main settlements lie at about three thousand meters altitude, has relatively plentiful water[6] and is sheltered from severe weather by the steep mountains surrounding it. Agriculturalists here primarily grow corn (for food and sale) and peaches (for sale); other important crops include fava beans and wheat.

Immediately below Cumuni the valley narrows and arable land disappears. In the next widening of the valley, a couple of kilometers below, lies the community of Quirpini. Here the river is no longer visible from the road, as it runs in its own canyon some ten meters below the valley floor. Quirpini straddles the river, with houses and fields to the east and west; unlike Cumuni, it has a defined center, marked visually by the school's eucalyptus trees when I arrived, and by the whitewashed chapel when I departed.

Below Quirpini is Tambo Mokho, a small community on the edge of the town of San Lucas. The land here is drier, the vegetation thinner. Few houses or fields are visible where the road passes through Tambo Mokho, as most of them are clustered around the few arable fields on a seasonal river a few hundred yards to the west; all that is visible is a small school and scattered *mulli* trees. Below Tambo Mokho the road enters San Lucas, a stronghold of the region's Spanish-speaking elite in a terrain mainly inhabited by campesinos. But before we arrive in San Lucas, some historical and social background is in order.

"Campesino" is the term by which Quirpinis designate their social position and which members of the Spanish-speaking San Lucas elite use to refer to the Quechua-speaking residents of the many small villages of the region. The best treatment of this subtle, untranslatable word for rural agriculturalists, especially those considered to be of indigenous background, is provided by

Hahn (1992:3–4). In *The Divided World of the Bolivian Andes,* Hahn argues that the term, as used in Bolivia, does not simply denote a "peasant" but "signals the existence of the two worlds that make up that country." It refers to "an inhabitant of the countryside . . . whether . . . that inhabitant be a peasant, a craftsperson, a rural merchant or . . . a farmer," but it also suggests someone who is "of" the countryside, particularly an indigenous person: "the word *campesino* came to replace the word *indio.* This use became official speech after the 1952 revolution with the intention of dignifying the ethnic category of Indian." So the word also signifies "those people who were of and remained a part of the 'indigenous way of life'; those people who . . . were indigenous to the land of which the Europeans and their descendants were alien."

A third term, *mestizo,* or person of mixed indigenous and European race, came into use early in the colonial period; today other such "intermediate" terms as *cholo/chola* further complicate the picture. Nevertheless, in the San Lucas area, social hierarchies are fundamentally dual in nature, based on a distinction between the mainly rural, Quechua-speaking agriculturalists, variously called "campesinos," "indigenas," or, rarely, "indios," and the Spanish-speaking elite of San Lucas, often called *caballeros* or *gente decente.* Indeed, the intermediate terms commonly used elsewhere barely play a role in San Lucas; the terminology and dress associated with cholos is evident mostly among campesinos, and the structural position that mestizos occupy in many rural areas has devolved to the high-status group whose members publicly claim European origins. In talking about the identity and values of this elite and the larger caste of which they claim membership, I will often employ the term *criollo.* By this term I refer to the values of the social classes that have dominated Bolivia, and most other Spanish American nations, since the times of independence. Prominent elements of criollo value systems are the Spanish language, and allegiance, often expressed in racial terms, to a culture that sees itself as an "American" variant on an Iberian, and thus "European," model. Bearers of these views see themselves as emphatically "civilized" (not "indigenous" or "traditional"), ambivalently modern, and distinctively national.[7]

The designation "campesino" is telling. As Hahn's gloss makes clear, it relegates indigenous peasants (like Whitman's "red aborigines") to the past. It also implies that the people so designated are 'rooted,' both connected to the soil and immobile. The word contrasts with the elite designation *caballero,* or "horseman." Rhetorically, a caballero is above the ground and mobile.

Contrary to the image of immobile campesinos, for millennia, people throughout the rural Andes have maintained links of kinship and prestation across hundreds of kilometers, linking areas across multiple ecological zones. For example, until the Land Reform, Quirpini held land far afield, particularly in the hot Pilcomayo River valley, in a version of what Murra calls a "vertical archipelago" (1972, 1978, 1985). Several communities in the highlands around the valley had themselves been satellites of other ethnic groups, although their connections with their home regions were broken long ago, as the highlands were incorporated into haciendas under the Spanish colony (Presta 1990). In other words, people of the Southern Andes have a centuries-old tradition of routinely traveling great distances in order to subsist. As Saignes (1995:170) puts it: "The practice of migration is deeply rooted in Andean history."

The ethnic makeup of the San Lucas region itself is partly the product of a different kind of movement—the forced relocation of peoples for reasons of state. Before and during the Inca period, the upper San Lucas River valley and surrounding highlands were the site of repeated fighting between Aymara-speaking agriculturalists, apparently part of the Chichas people (Bouysse-Cassagne 1978, esp. 1059 [map]), and the warlike Chiriguanos, who frequently raided from the lowlands (Abercrombie 1998). Abercrombie (1998) argues that the Incas, during their brief control of the southern Andes, moved people into the area from three of the component polities, or diarchies, of the Quillacas federation near Lake Poopó, in what is now Oruro.[8] Under Spanish colonial rule, the lords of the reduced Quillacas federation maintained ties with the area (then called Payacoyo). Over the centuries several other ethnic groups established satellites in the highlands outside the central valley, including the Visijsa (Yura) and people from Chaquí (Presta 1990; Zulawski 1995). In the late sixteenth century[9] the town of San Lucas de Payacoyo was founded as part of the colonial system of *reducciones*, whereby indigenous people were obliged to live in these towns conceived on an idealized Spanish model, abandoning the dispersed residences they had occupied before the Spaniards arrived. The reducciones were intended to facilitate the "civilizing" of the Indians, as well as rendering them subject to greater observation and control by colonial and Church authorities (see Larson 1998:64–74).

In the course of the next few centuries the San Lucas region became effectively independent of Quillacas. The three groups sent as colonists from Lake Poopó developed into the component ayllus (Kellaja, Asanaque, and

Yucasa) of the new polity, all ruled by a Kellaja lord. According to Presta (1990), the area as a whole came to be known as "Kellaja." At some point late in the colonial period, or possibly even in the nineteenth century, people of the area shifted from speaking Aymara to Quechua, a linguistic change that took place across southern Bolivia and continues to this day in parts of the country. No one I met in the area had any memory of their ancestors speaking Aymara, or indeed having a historical connection to people from Oruro.

Today Quirpini is also known as *Jatun Kellaja* ("Great" or "Big" Kellaja), as it was formerly the major part of the area's dominant ayllu. Two prevalent surnames in the area reinforce the idea that Quirpini once played a politically central role in the region. In Sakapampa, the richest of the three current zonas of Quirpini, the most common surname is Huarachi, and in the nearby community of Avichuca (once a part of Quirpini and still seen as belonging to Jatun Kellaja) most families are named Colque; the names "Colque" and "Guarache" were both generally used by the rulers of Quillacas prior to the Spanish conquest (Abercrombie 1998:160–161).

From early colonial times the cash-based economy introduced by the Europeans has coexisted with various non-cash and non-market forms of circulation.[10] A key non-cash market has been conducted through the travels of long-distance traders, called *llameros* for the llamas that they used to transport goods. Trading salt from Uyuni, or potatoes and ritual materials from the altiplano for corn and other valley products, the llameros for centuries have helped connect the highlands of Potosí and Oruro culturally and materially with the temperate valleys of Chuquisaca and Cochabamba. They still pass through the San Lucas area, mainly on the way to the lowland pepper-producing zones; many have foregone their llamas for trucks. Llameros compete with a growing number of regional fairs that bring people and products from different ecological and economic spheres. Whereas the llameros engage in barter, fair vendors prefer selling their goods for money, and thus not only do they articulate various regions but they also provide an important connection between the cash economy of Bolivia and the rural hinterland.

Apart from transplanted populations and travels along archipelagos, the terrain of the Southern Andes has long been molded by travels related to work. After the devastating epidemics of European diseases at the time of the early colonies (see Larson 1998:52; and, esp., Cook 1981), probably the most dramatic demographic phenomenon in the colonial period was the *mita*, the system of obligatory service adapted by the Spaniards from an Inca model to recruit a mass labor force for the silver mines of Potosí from eighteen provinces of the southern Andes. As instituted under the Viceroy Toledo in the late sixteenth century, the mita obliged all male *originarios*, or residents of their ancestral communities, between the ages of eighteen and fifty to spend several months of every seven years working in the mines (see Cole 1985). Tens of thousands of Indians were sent to Potosí every year; many died, and many remained in the city. The mita's most dramatic demographic effect was indirect. Along with the system of native tribute, it gave indigenous people, particularly the men on whom the burden of forced labor and tribute fell most heavily, reason to leave their home communities and go either to the cities, where they entered the labor market, or to other rural areas, where they had no rights to land but also no obligations to pay tribute or work in the mita.[11] Those who went to new rural areas were called *forasteros*, or "foreigners," by Spanish administrators; keeping this massive internal migration under control became a central, and largely unrealized, goal of colonial policy (Larson 1998:97–98, 102–115).

The San Lucas area played an atypical role in the resultant movement of people. In the sixteenth to the mid-seventeenth century, the region now called Camargo, south of San Lucas, became a major wine-producing area, and it still is today; however, wine production was hobbled by the area's sparse population. To attract a force of free laborers to work in viniculture and wine production, the colonial government excepted any native people living in the province from mita obligations (Zulawski 1995). As anticipated, this rule produced a flood of forasteros from other provinces. Though few of these immigrants found their way to the San Lucas region, evidence suggests that people from the area themselves frequented the southern part of the province for work (Zulawski 1995:185). One might speculate that the popularity of the area as a site for satellite communities had to do not only with the area's excellent climate and relatively good agricultural conditions but also with the hope of escaping from the dreaded silver mines of Potosí.

With independence from Spanish control in 1825, city and countryside in the southern part of the new nation of Bolivia became far more disarticulated than previously. Southern Bolivia suffered tremendously in the wars of independence, but by the 1840s the wine and sugarcane industries in the southern parts of Cinti Province were rebounding (Langer 1989:92), providing a magnet for laborers from the San Lucas area and beyond. The scant evidence that exists suggests that the mid-century was a time of relative prosperity and autonomy for the indigenous people of San Lucas. This began to change under the presidency of Melgarejo in the 1860s and even more so under that of Frías, whose 1874 *Ley de Exvinculación,* or Law of Expropriation, initiated a major assault on communal land rights in the name of liberal economics (Larson 1985:310). From the late nineteenth century into the early decades of the twentieth the haciendas in the highlands above the central valley of San Lucas grew, and the communities surrounding the town periodically had to defend themselves from encroachments by white landowners (Zulawski 1995; Langer 1989:93). As the century progressed, the Southern Bolivian economy became increasingly moribund as a result of the collapse of the silver mining industry and increased foreign competition for local products (Langer 1989:28–35).

The haciendas stopped expropriating communal lands, instead trying to extract as much value as possible by imposing increasingly harsh conditions on their peons (see Platt 1982, for an analysis of a similar situation in Potosí). Langer (1989:108) argues that this intensified exploitation triggered a general uprising of hacienda workers in the late 1920s. In San Lucas the event was remembered as a llamero uprising; no one in Quirpini or the town recalled any local involvement in the conflict. This was also a period of relatively low mobility for the Quechua campesinos, broken only by the disastrous Chaco War against Paraguay in the 1930s, for which they were taken to fight in the remote and inhospitable southeastern regions of the country. An elderly member of the San Lucas town elite told me that the main road into town had been built for the war.

San Lucas was too far from the mines of Potosí and Oruro for many people to be tempted by work there, and the cities were not attracting much labor. People in Quirpini told me that they traveled to northwest Argentina as early as the 1940s, but this was not a popular trip; the sugarcane plantations of Salta and Jujuy were more accessible to those in Potosí who lived near the north-south train line (Whiteford 1981). At the same time, wage employment came to the area in the twentieth century with the opening of a number of small mines, and I was told that the road from Padcoyo to the highland area was built by mining companies.

The effects of the Chaco War went far beyond improvements in rural infrastructure and the loss of territory to Paraguay. In bringing large numbers of campesinos and workers together in the army, under the often incompetent and abusive command of members of the oligarchy, the war simultaneously strengthened national feeling among sectors of the population that until then had felt little connection to "Bolivia" while undermining general confidence in the ruling class (Hahn 1992:60–62).[12] By the mid-twentieth century Bolivia's landowners and mine owners, the two pillars of the oligarchy, were both declining. This left them unable to ignore the demands of campesinos, mine workers, and the rising urban middle class, whose aspirations found expression in various leftist and nationalist parties during the 1940s (Hahn 1992:60–64). In 1951 the Movimiento Nacionalista Revolucionario (Nationalist Revolutionary Movement, or MNR) won the national elections, but the results were quickly neutralized in a coup engineered by mining interests. The next year a popular revolt in favor of the MNR broke out in the capital, La Paz. After a few days of fighting the government resigned and the MNR candidate of the previous year, Victor Paz Estenssoro, took office promising universal suffrage. In short order the new government found itself forced to reform far more than the suffrage laws: the campesinos of the Cochabamba valley began taking over haciendas and calling for a general land reform, and the mine workers of Oruro called for nationalization of the mines. Paz Estenssoro had little choice but to accede to these demands (Hahn 1992:68–70; Lagos 1994:49–51; see also Zavaleta Mercado 1974).

The campesinos of San Lucas, as far as I could discern, played no active role in these events; rather, the area was "processed" by the Agrarian Reform once the latter was established as a national institution. The government took land from the highland *hacendados* (hacienda owners) and distributed it to the resident campesinos during the 1950s and 1960s; when I was in the area there were no haciendas, and there hadn't been any for quite a few years. This reform had the effect of breaking the power of the locally dominant class, a change which Quirpinis I knew recalled with glee, even though they had never been under the direct control of the haciendas. Most of the old landowners apparently departed for the cities. This left political and economic power in the hands of the San Lucas elite.

This class of people, neither landowners nor campesinos, are in the structural position of those who are called *mestizos*, or *mistis* elsewhere in Bolivia, although in San Lucas they are more likely to be called *caballeros* and do not identify themselves with a 'mixed' position between white national elites and indigenous campesinos. Formerly a junior part of the power structure—merchants, petty manufacturers, and truck owners—they came into power with the disappearance of the upper stratum of regional society. By the 1990s this power was slowly slipping through their fingers; as the countryside lost its attractiveness as a source of wealth, they began moving into the cities and, when possible, into professional careers. It is not yet possible to say what will become of the resultant power vacuum; while I was in the area, the local elite was fighting a fairly successful rearguard action against relinquishing their power, and remained in firm control of regional politics and, to a lesser extent, economics.[13]

San Lucas

Entering San Lucas over a rise, the traveler is greeted by a copse of eucalyptus trees and a sign of painted adobe, declaring: "Bienvenidos a San Lucas: Hogar del Buen Chocllo" ("Welcome to San Lucas: Home of the Good Corncob"). Unlike the other settlements of the region, the streets of San Lucas are lined by houses adjacent to one another. The streets are cobbled, and in the center of town they have cement sidewalks.[14] Nearly all the houses are constructed of adobe, though the offices built by the Government Development Office (CORDECH) being the most prominent exception. Most of the houses have red-tiled roofs and surround inner courtyards in the classic Spanish style; few have windows facing the streets. The town lies on the western bank of the San Lucas River, extending about a kilometer along the river and more than half a kilometer to the west, where the town merges imperceptibly with the small campesino community of San Cristobal. Taxis usually go only as far as the town, but the road continues, leaving town across a dry plain, passing through the village of Yapusiri, and then, a few kilometers downstream, Querquehuisi. After Querquehuisi the road follows the river as it bends eastward and enters a narrow gorge. Here there is little arable land and correspondingly few communities; the condition of the road deteriorates as it descends. On what little land exists alongside the lower reaches of the river, people grow grapes; even farther down, they grow tropical fruit. Below the broad part of the river valley, haciendas once held sway, and even in the 1990s much of the grape-producing land was owned by townspeople, who produced wine. Anyone without a car who wants to continue downriver past the town must walk or hope that a vehicle is heading in that direction.

As in most towns of Iberian origin, the *plaza central* in San Lucas is the symbolic center of the town and, in many senses, of the entire region. It is where the power and prestige of the region's Spanish-speaking elite are most on display. The plaza is about sixty yards on each side and is designed in a style common in the early twentieth century. It has ornate iron railings and a few benches, and is filled with tall conifers, which shade the diagonal cement paths that pass through it and meet in the middle. The town had recently received funding to improve the park and had built benches in a more modern style on the side facing the Catholic Church. The Church, a whitewashed building with a free-standing bell tower, and the priest's residence, a gleaming white, newly renovated complex, occupy the entire western side of the plaza. A large portal, entering one side of the nave, opens onto the plaza. Most of the plaza's south side is taken up by the Alcaldía, mayoral offices, which includes the rarely used town market, and the local court and town archive.[15] Several elite families with houses on the plaza operate stores. The three blocks upriver and downriver from the plaza, and a block and a half to the east and west, contain the houses (and some fields) belonging to the town's richest citizens (although at the time of my stay some upwardly mobile campesinos had recently bought houses in this area).

The town of San Lucas is the region's administrative center and the location of most of its important public institutions. San Lucas is the capital of the eponymous *cantón,* or county, and of the *Segunda Sección* (Second Section) of the *provincia* of Nor Cinti. In addition to the Church, the mayor's office, and the court, the region's only police officer and most other government officials (including the development agency) are located here.

Outside the center of town the houses are farther apart and more likely to be adjacent to the owners' fields. Tile roofs give way to adobe, and fewer houses are plastered or painted. To the west the town opens up into fields surrounded by low adobe walls and peach orchards until it hits the mountain slope, and to the north houses gradually give way to orchards and pastures. The campesino community of Yapusiri is only a short distance downriver from the last houses of San Lucas.

In the 1990s the families of the town elite nearly all owned more and better land than most campesinos and generally had at least one local member who was primarily engaged in a more lucrative occupation, such as working for the development office or another government office, running a store, driving a truck, refining and selling cane alcohol, or teaching; nearly all the teachers in the San Lucas school, and most of the rural schools of the area, were from the town. Some among the town elite held down more than one job. Although the Spanish-speaking elite made up a dwindling minority in San Lucas, perhaps three hundred of the town's one thousand inhabitants in 1992, the central part of town was clearly theirs. Most of them lived there and, unlike the out-of-town campesinos—who walked the streets with a tentative air, showing deference to the members of the elite they encountered—the "San Luqueños," as the elite sometimes styled themselves, acted as if they owned the place, treating one another with an easy familiarity but campesinos with anything from friendly condescension to aggressive bullying or refusal to interact.[16]

The San Lucas elite set themselves off from the campesinos by maintaining an elaborate series of distinctions. Whereas campesinos dressed in tire sandals, or *abarcas*, the elite wore shoes; most women among the elite wore skirts, whereas campesinas dressed in distinctive pleated skirts called *polleras*; and the elite spoke Spanish in their homes rather than Quechua, and it even appeared to me that some younger members of the elite purposely spoke non-idiomatic Quechua in conversation with campesinos. Most among the elite refrained from ever publicly doing manual labor alongside campesinos, preferring to hire campesinos to work their fields and do their housework.[17] Elite houses were uniformly larger than campesino houses, had multiple glass windows (a luxury beyond the means of most rural families), and were organized in a more "civilized" way in that the functions of the rooms were clearly differentiated with spaces of consumption more separated from productive spaces.[18] Although some campesinos claimed kin ties with elite members, I never heard "San Luqueños" mention such relations with campesinos.

During my fieldwork few young members of the San Lucas elite lived in town, as most of them had been sent away to school and frequently never returned, instead settling into professional careers in Bolivian cities or in other countries. Some elite families had virtually disappeared from the town, maintaining no local residence and appearing only a few times a year to farm their land. Although a few prosperous campesinos had purchased former elite houses in the center of town, they had not merged into the elite, maintaining campesino identities and kin ties.

Quirpini

Located about five kilometers upriver of San Lucas, Quirpini is one of the larger campesino communities in the valley. At the time of my fieldwork it was home to approximately five hundred campesinos living in some one hundred households;[19] one elite family owned a house and land there and spent a good portion of each year in residence. Along with the other communities in the valley (Yapusiri, San Cristobal, Tambo Mokho, and Querquehuisi) Quirpini had never been taken over by a landlord; the valley communities successfully resisted all attempts to incorporate them into haciendas (Langer 1989:93). The community is divided into three zonas: Quirpini, Villcasana, and Sakapampa (see Figure 1.4). The largest, encompassing about fifty houses, is Zona Quirpini, which lies along the road between Padcoyo and San Lucas. The school is in Zona Quirpini, as is the new chapel and the cemetery. Across the river from Zona Quirpini is Zona Villcasana, with perhaps twenty houses. Downriver from Villcasana, across a seasonal stream, is Zona Sakapampa, containing some thirty households.[20] The zonas have distinct reputations: Sakapampas are often seen as traditional and proud, even difficult, whereas Quirpinis are viewed as sophisticated and arrogant. Whereas Zona Quirpini is the largest and the site of all the communal institutions, Sakapampa has the best land, and residents there tend to have larger plots to farm. Villcasana, the poorest and least organized zona, has a more humble reputation. The zonas have no formal authorities, as all authorities in the community are either identified with irrigation canals or have a community-wide position. At the periodic reuniones generales, which, in principle, bring together all Quirpinis, the roll is called by zona. Because the zonas are treated as the constituting elements of the community, the community has a three-part structure rather than the more widely known Andean moiety structure.

Figure 1.4. Facing. Map of the inhabited parts of Quirpini, showing the San Lucas River and the road between Padcoyo and San Lucas, as well as the school, the cemetary, the new chapel, the Otondo household, and Miguel Paco's land. Gray areas indicate irrigated/inhabited land. Based on Instituto Geográfico Militar maps: Hoja 6533I (Serie H731) and Hoja 6533II (Serie H731) as well as Instituto Geográfico Militar aerial photos.

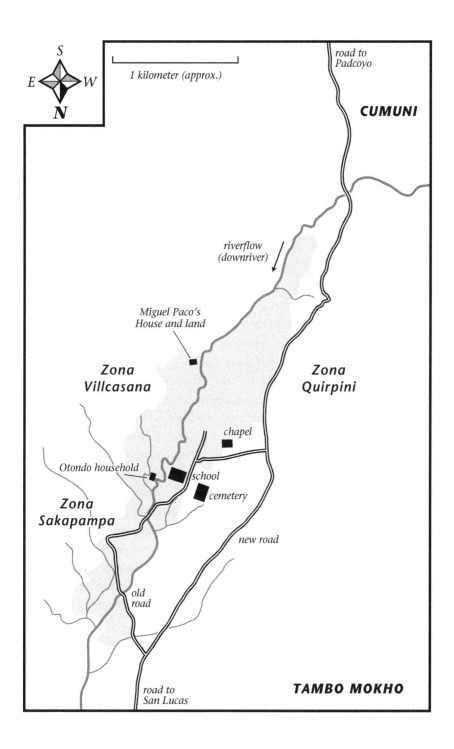

S
E W
N

1 kilometer (approx.)

road to
Padcoyo

CUMUNI

riverflow
(downriver)

Miguel Paco's
House and land

*Zona
Villcasana*

*Zona
Quirpini*

chapel

Otondo household

school

cemetery

*Zona
Sakapampa*

new road

old
road

road to
San Lucas

TAMBO MOKHO

The zonas are a peculiar form of the widespread Andean social form normally called an ayllu in Quechua. The ayllu takes on very different character in different places, and in any single area the word has many meanings; in fact, anthropologists disagree about how to define the term in any particular place (see Rasnake 1988; Zulawski 1995:18; and Platt 1978). What is sometimes taken as the "classic" form of ayllu is the scheme described by Platt (1978) for the Macha, wherein a number of individual households, each called an ayllu ("minimal ayllu," as Platt puts it), together constitute a higher-level ayllu, which has its own authorities. Several of these form yet a higher-level ayllu. This inclusive or recursive structure may involve several levels, each displaying the same internal form as those it includes and the one to which it belongs. At the "top" of this system, what Platt calls the "maximal ayllu"[21] is divided into two parts, the "upper" and "lower." In other words, the ideal ayllu structure is recursively hierarchical (see Turner 1996) and segmentary, in Evans-Pritchard's sense (1969). The other key feature of the anthropological understanding of ayllus is that they combine a territorial basis with kin relations among members (Zorn 1997:83–85, esp. nn. 44 and 45; Arnold 1992; Abercrombie 1998). I explore the nature of Quirpini's zonas in more detail in chapter 5, but here suffice it to say that although they are clearly a kind of ayllu, they do not (any longer?) match much of Platt's model. Today they have no authorities of their own, except in an almost surreptitious sense, and their internal structure does not resemble that of the community as a whole. No one officially represents them, although everyone at reuniones is there as a zona member. The relationship between households and the community of Quirpini is direct, with little mediation through the zonas.

Houses in Quirpini tend to be adjacent to the family's land, and because irrigated land is concentrated in the narrow valley, settlements are not very dispersed. As discussed in the introduction, the school anchored the community's nascent spatial center. In addition to its main educational function, the school was the site of the most important civic and ritual gatherings such as general meetings, authority meetings, and many religious and civic celebrations.

Nearly all the parents I met in Quirpini saw education as crucial to their children's lives and strongly supported the school's main project of making all the children literate in Spanish. Older Quirpinis were effectively monolingual in Quechua, though most men under fifty were bilingual, some even having mastered an Argentine accent for use in Buenos Aires. Only a few young men were not adept at Spanish and almost all were at least somewhat literate, as were most men of the preceding generation. My first impression was that virtually all the women and girls in Quirpini were monolingual Quechua speakers, but eventually I discovered that many were simply embarrassed to speak the unfamiliar language. Most children could read and write in Spanish; in principle, the school was pioneering bilingual literacy in Quechua and Spanish, but few children seemed to be learning written Quechua and their parents placed little value on doing so. Instead, the school was seen chiefly as a place where children could learn the urban "civilized" norms that would help them function in the cities and the town, in politics, and in the wage labor market.

Water, Mountains, and Land

The distribution of irrigation water in Quirpini is complex as well as essential both to subsistence and local social relations. The San Lucas River (usually referred to as *Jatun Mayu,* or "Big River," by Quirpinis) is fed by a number of springs (*ñawi*) to which each of the eight canals (*larqha*) that were in function at the start of my fieldwork[22] had exclusive or shared rights. Each canal starts at an inlet, or *toma,* which is designed to take the water that comes from one particular source. These canals provide water for irrigation as well as most of the water that households use for cooking, cleaning, and various routine tasks.

Sharing the water of a single source, as the three major canals in Quirpini do, requires careful planning and cooperation and is always fraught with conflict. The canal in Cumuni, which shares the waters of Antahawa, has a toma that takes only some of the water. The three main canals of Quirpini divide the water through a complex time-sharing scheme: Quirpini Larqha (which brings water to Zona Quirpini, that is, to nearly half the land and people of the community) gets all the flow during the night, and Sakapampa Larqha and Villcasana Larqha divide the daylight hours.

The major source of tension between households and between those with land on different canals is water. During my time in the area the residents of Cumuni, having recently withdrawn from the community to merge with Mishkamayu, wanted to stop sharing the water from Antahawa with Quirpini, and instead redirect the water out of the valley to irrigate the waterless fields of its new allies. Given the frequent disputes over water, as well as its

practical and symbolic importance, it is not surprising that the most important and effective local political entities in Quirpini were the institutions and
meetings devoted to maintaining the canals and distributing their water.

Quirpinis do not share irrigation water only with one another. All the
water actually "belongs" to the *mallkus,* the powerful spirits who inhabit and
are identified with mountains as well as condors.[23] Antahawa, the mountain
that rises above Quirpini and Cumuni, is frequently spoken of as a person
capable of action; San Cristóbal, a tall hill near the town of San Lucas, is
seen as particularly dangerous. Any mallku is malevolent and frightening to
some degree, and though not considered "evil" in any Christian sense, they
have all the arbitrariness of the very powerful. Another name for these spirits is *yawlu,* from the Spanish *diablo,* or "devil." Like many Andean spiritual
figures, mountain spirits were identified with Christian demons by colonial
Spanish missionaries, an identification that has been revived by evangelical
Christians, who do not make offerings to the mallkus. In all the valley communities, Catholic campesinos perform annual rituals, or *ch'allas*[24] in which
they offer live sacrifices (formerly llamas, now sheep and pigs) to the mallkus
as part of an ongoing relationship that insures continued access to water.
These rituals are organized by the source of the water, where the offerings
must be made, and in Quirpini are held on the first of August.[25]

Quirpinis have an average of less than a hectare of irrigated land to farm,
on which they must grow enough food to live for the year and, if possible,
sufficient surplus to buy clothes, tools, school supplies, and other goods they
cannot grow or make. People plant and harvest only with the aid of animal
power[26] and the help of their neighbors. Families all plow their fields with
ox-drawn plows and use burros to thresh grain. People usually harvest with
the labor available from within the household or employ a system of reciprocal labor exchange, called *ayni,* to recruit helping hands. For planting corn,
a labor-intensive activity, they employ a more elaborate form of reciprocal
labor called mink'a (see chapter 3). Because cash is scarce in Quirpini and
labor is relatively plentiful, there is virtually no labor market among community members, although members of the San Lucas elite frequently hire
campesinos for wages.

Communities in the San Lucas River valley are *originario,* meaning that
they have been recognized as free indigenous communities since colonial
times. As there was no need to give land to campesinos, the Land Reform had
very different effects here than it did in former hacienda communities.[27] But

the Land Reform had more ambitious goals than simply redistributing land. In keeping with the party's bourgeois nationalist vision (Albó 1987:382; Platt 1987:281; Rivera Cusicanqui 1983), the government's land-reform policies had always aimed to turn the campesinos into market-oriented smallholders by transforming collective landholdings into individually titled plots (Hahn 1992:71). Though some communities resisted this change, it was welcomed around San Lucas. My sense was that in Quirpini land was already owned de facto by individual families, and so the Land Reform gave people title to what, in effect, was already theirs.

The Land Reform had another, less welcome effect on land tenure, as it destroyed the long-distance reciprocal ties that connected the area's different ecological zones; the system of "vertical archipelagoes" stood in the way of the program's broader aims by allowing communities to supply their own needs with minimal recourse to market exchange. During my fieldwork a few families maintained ties of mutual prestation with their kin in the lowlands, but most of the circulation of goods between the San Lucas area and the Pilcomayo valley was conducted through barter or purchase at regional fairs.

Apart from the dissolution of these long-distance ties of prestation and the disarticulation of the large ayllus that once dominated the region, Quirpini itself has recently fragmented. Only a couple of decades before my fieldwork, the community had five zonas; since then both Avichuca and Cumuni have broken away. The populated parts of these two zonas were never contiguous with the remaining three, which occupy the bottom of the river canyon. These separations have left Quirpini geographically more compact and, ecologically, a more exclusively valley community.

Migration

In recent decades the long-standing tradition of mobility which I alluded to above has taken on new dimensions and urgency. Few Quirpinis are able to get by on their farming alone, and it is becoming harder to do so, as rainfall becomes less reliable and plots are increasingly divided. The loss of access to highland and valley resources no doubt plays a role, too: traditional Andean forms of mobility have been curtailed. When I was in the area someone from nearly every family in Quirpini periodically left to work for wages, and a cash income of at least one hundred dollars[28] a year was indispensable for a

Quirpini household; some households took in several thousand dollars in a year through migrant labor.

Men's primary destination was Buenos Aires, the Argentine capital. Fewer went to agro-industrial regions in the south of Bolivia or to the several Bolivian cities (for a detailed breakdown of migration patterns, see chapter 7). In the mid-1990s a neighborhood that Quirpinis knew as "La Salada" was fast becoming the center of San Lucas campesinos in the metropolitan area. Based on plots provided for free by the government of the Province of Buenos Aires, this all-immigrant neighborhood in the *Partido* of Lomas de Zamorra was a stopping point for newly arriving immigrants and home to several families from Quirpini.

With few exceptions, migrating Quirpinis took up unskilled or semi-skilled manual work. Just two Quirpinis had completed high school, and both were from wealthy families and had no need to migrate for wages. Agricultural labor at home prepares campesinos for hard work but does not give them skills that are particularly adapted to the urban economy. Some of the more enterprising people I knew had managed to obtain training as construction workers, which put them in a strong economic position. One group of brothers bought agricultural land in Argentina. Most, however, spent their wage-earning careers at or near the bottom of the urban economic ladder.

Between the 1950s and 1990s several factors have driven migration from Bolivia to Argentina. The Land Reform following the Revolution of 1952 had some unexpected effects on the rural highland population, even beyond the severing of intra-regional ties of reciprocity. One consequence of the breakup of large landholdings was, perhaps surprisingly, to free indigenous people and other peasants not only from their servitude to large landowners but from their ties to the land. As one former agriculturalist put it, after the Land Reform it was "as if we had been given a permit of circulation, freedom to go wherever we wished" (Hahn 1992:89; from Rojas 1980:82). Freed from tribute obligations to hacendados, able to take advantage of new economic opportunities, rural people of the highlands could contemplate long-term travel on a level that had not been realistic for decades, if not centuries.

The next factor leading people to migrate from their home communities is the rapid economic growth of the tropical lowlands as a result of postrevolutionary development policies. The most important government move was the construction of a new road between Cochabamba, the second largest city of the highlands, and Santa Cruz, the capital of the Department of Santa Cruz, until then a relative backwater. Successive governments since the first MNR regime have focused on development in the tropics at the expense of the rural highlands (Muñoz Elsner 2000:70, 79; Hahn 1992:91). Santa Cruz has become the major destination for internal migration, as people travel there to work, either permanently or on a temporary basis, on the department's export-oriented agrobusiness-style farms (Stearman 1985).

Another factor encouraging migration is the huge investment in the urban and transport infrastructure under the Banzer dictatorship. In the 1970s Bolivia was flooded with cheap credit, mainly as a result of the vast amounts of cash the oil-producing countries accumulated after the oil embargo of 1973. Banks invested much of this capital in Third World economies, as the developed world offered few advantageous investment opportunities in the post-embargo recession (Bello 2001:126). At the same time prices for tin, Bolivia's dominant export, were unusually high, as were natural gas prices (Muñoz Elsner 2000:78). The military government in power at the time went on a building spree, constructing or improving several important roads and generally upgrading the national infrastructure (ibid.:77–79), while also subsidizing food prices to maintain social peace in the cities. These policies gave campesinos more reason to go to the cities and made it easier for them to do so. Accounts I heard in Quirpini indicate that migration to Buenos Aires only became a common option in the 1970s, when the road was improved, changing the trip from a grueling trek to a few days on a truck or a bus.

The next events influencing migration were the radical changes in economic policy introduced in 1985, along with the coincidental collapse of the tin mining industry. In 1985 a new MNR government was elected, once again led by Victor Paz Estenssoro. This government imposed a neoliberal "shock therapy" on the inflation-ridden economy, which included selling off the greater part of the national mining company created under the first Paz government, and shutting down mines. A few months after this government gained power the international tin cartel ran out of money, and prices began to fluctuate freely, dropping well below the break-even point for nearly all Bolivian mines.[29] Production was cut by half, thousands of miners were fired, and hundreds of thousands of people from the two main mining cities, Oruro and Potosí, were forced to look elsewhere for work.

Many went to the Chapare, the then booming tropical area where coca is produced for the cocaine trade, and thousands of others sought a livelihood in other cities. Although the tin collapse did not directly affect rural areas, it had two indirect effects on rural agriculturalists. First, by depressing the economies of the highland cities (Jetté and Rojas 1999:130–131), the tin collapse reduced the market for their products; second, the flood of unemployed miners displaced campesinos from internal job markets in the cities or in rural agro-industry.

All these changes took place against the backdrop of ongoing ecological decay in the southern Bolivian highlands (Jetté and Rojas 1999:128–130). Rainfall has been decreasing for decades (ibid.: 150); in Quirpini, as in other southern areas, people have virtually stopped farming un-irrigated land. Highland forests are being cut down, resulting in widespread loss of land through erosion. People in Quirpini told me that getting firewood took much more walking than it did in the past—a sign of deforestation. Albó et al. (1981) reports that when migrants are asked why they are traveling, most of them say that, in one way or another, it is because they cannot produce enough food to live in the countryside.[30]

Migration, both national and transnational, has been a key part of Andean campesino strategies for decades. Xavier Albó's series of books on Aymaras in the city of La Paz (Albó, Greaves, and Sandoval 1981–1989) has shown the impact of migrants on the nation's cultural heritage. Migration from the highlands to Santa Cruz, Northwest Argentina, and Buenos Aires has been an important aspect of campesinos' lives at least since the mid-twentieth century (see Stearman 1985; Whiteford 1981; Balán 1990, 1992; Balán and Dandler 1986; and Dandler and Medeiros 1991). Peruvian campesinos have also long depended on migration (see, for instance, Skar 1994; and Turino 1993), and Otavalo people of Ecuador have constructed global networks of entrepreneurial and labor ties (Meisch 2002).

Buenos Aires

The lands we know as Argentina and Bolivia were connected for centuries before the current wave of migration. The Inca Empire maintained fortresses in the mountains of what is now Argentina, and northwest Argentina was a hinterland of the great Potosí mining operation for much of the colonial period. Buenos Aires itself was founded by expeditions sent from what was then called Alto Peru, now Bolivia. For much of the city's colonial history, Buenos Aires was an alternate (often contraband) route for products going to and from the rich mining areas of Potosí and Oruro (Luna 1993). Administrative control of Alto Peru was even transferred to the Viceroyalty of La Plata (most of which now comprises Argentina) in the late colonial period. This link was attenuated only in the nineteenth century, when Argentina's liberation from Spanish mercantile policies allowed it to orient itself definitively toward the Atlantic Ocean, and the new nation's policy turned to the development of the vast *pampas*, the fertile plains that stretch from the Atlantic Ocean to the Andes Mountains.

Argentina is frequently called a "nation of immigrants," and, indeed, the idea of immigration is even more central to the Argentine national imagination than to that of the United States. Although early pro-immigration policies were largely intended to populate the vast plains of the Argentine hinterland (Grimson 1999:21–22), Buenos Aires has always been a prime destination. As early as 1860 nearly half the city's population was from overseas (ibid.:22), and up to the First World War the city's growth was accelerated by an influx of foreign workers. In the nineteenth and early twentieth centuries the government was mainly focused on attracting Europeans in order to "civilize" the country.

After the Second World War Argentina lost its appeal to European migrants, both because rising wealth and redistributive economic policies in Europe made staying home more attractive and because the Argentine economy never again matched the booming days of the early twentieth century. By 1991 only 5 percent of the Argentine population had been born overseas, according to the official census (Programa 1997:124). Furthermore, few of these foreigners were from Europe. Instead, in recent decades, most immigration has been from neighboring South American countries, including Bolivia. As I detail in chapter 7, this change has presented grave challenges to Argentina's preferred self-conception as a nation of immigrants *and* a nation of white people.

But even in the headiest days of European immigration, the newcomers were a challenging presence. Tulchin (1982) points out that one of the major influences on the spatial order of Buenos Aires since the early twentieth century has been the ruling elite's desire to "preserve" the city's center by keeping disruptive presences such as industry and immigrant populations on the outskirts. Even as these outskirts have been expanding, the city has retained its basic structure (Walter 1982).

Research on Bolivians in Buenos Aires began slowly in the 1980s and increased in the 1990s (Laumonier et al. 1983; Mugarza 1989; Grimson 1999). Since the publication of Grimson's ethnography on Bolivians' negotiation of their identities through performance and radio in Buenos Aires, there has been an explosion of research, mostly by Argentines, and largely in the context of the country's new migratory influxes.[31] The dominant themes of this research have been the ways that Bolivians have been succeeding or not succeeding in establishing their own spaces and identities in Buenos Aires, and the impact of cross-border migration on the Argentine nation.

In recent decades government efforts to maintain the public order of the city has led to a shift of immigrants to the departments outside Buenos Aires (Mugarza 1989); about half the people in the areas immediately surrounding the city have come to the province of Buenos Aires from elsewhere (Programa 1997). The immigrant neighborhood La Salada was a direct result of those policies. When I arrived the area had become an important center for migrants from San Lucas only in the past few years, although references to La Salada as home to a concentration of immigrants date to the 1970s (Laumonier et al. 1983). Six families from Quirpini were living there, of twenty from the San Lucas region. The area had recently been reorganized as part of a deliberate policy to settle immigrants outside the city. The blocks and plots that I saw were laid out by provincial authorities, and the latter were given away to anyone who wished to live there. Over the previous few years more services had been provided to residents, from electricity to police patrols to water spigots on each street corner.

This new neighborhood provided a center of sorts for the dozens of Quirpinis spread out across the city. Working in shifting construction sites, in brick factories outside the city, or occasionally in urban factories, many of them lived at their work sites; a few stayed in other slum areas. But nearly all Quirpinis, and many San Luqueños, in the Buenos Aires area gathered in La Salada on weekends or for fiestas, treating the neighborhood as a place to see friends, gather information, and stay in touch with social networks from home.[32]

Connections

In the early 1990s, when Quirpini was less integrated into any system of far-flung kin ties and multi-local ethnic loyalties than perhaps at any time in the past, it was part of many large-scale circulations of goods, money, people and information; these new circuits were in many respects more extensive than any it had been involved in before. Men of Quirpini routinely traveled great distances for work; most had been to Buenos Aires. They returned with money, clothes, and ideas. Routine life in the community was premised on access to a variety of goods manufactured as far afield as China, brought into the area by local shop owners, itinerant vendors, and llameros, and bought with money earned elsewhere. Life was supplemented by development projects that received funds from Holland and the Middle East.[33] Ritual activity required periodic trips to the south of Potosí, to the Pilcomayo valley, and to certain cities, as well as access to minerals from the Aymara highlands and plants from the jungles east of La Paz. Quirpinis increasingly often experienced their world as situated in a larger place called "Bolivia."

In order to portray the places where Quirpinis live, to bring together these many sprawling and intertwined spaces, with their varied scales and deep historical roots, I must write at multiple scales, and give constant attention to the specific linkages and entanglements each locale has with many other places, and how these linkages exist through action. My dual commitment in this book is to represent embodied space, the places in which actual Quirpinis act, yet to do so in a way that does not flatten or elide the way that action happens under conditions that owe their existence to social forces that are present on widely varying scales.

PART 2 ~ FACETS OF A PLACE

2 · Bicycles and Houses

Bicycles—Getting Some Place

My bicycle kept getting Miguel Paco into trouble. Miguel was my host in Quirpini; I lived on his land in a disused house that he had fixed up for me and ate with his family daily. He had no bicycle of his own, having given the family's only, rather old bicycle to his son, and he occasionally borrowed my new mountain bike. The first time the bicycle got him in trouble was with Constantino Paco. Constantino lived across the valley from my house, and we had become friendly over the months I had been in Quirpini. He was relatively well-off among Quirpinis, as he had inherited good land; he also traveled frequently to Buenos Aires and used the money he earned there to buy more land and set up his wife with a small candy-and-soda shop in their house, which was on the one road that passes through Quirpini. Although he shared a surname with Miguel, there was little love lost between them, and Constantino had even told me that Miguel was not a "real" Paco. One day I ran into him and he wasted no time in telling me that he had seen Miguel riding my bicycle at a recent *campeonato,* or multicommunity soccer tournament. Miguel had acted superior, boasting that the bicycle was his own, though everyone knew Miguel's bicycle was old and that I had a brand-new one. Constantino was disdainful of Miguel's lie and accused him of being arrogant based on someone else's property. It would have been all right, Constantino then told me, to show off things he had earned himself, but for Miguel to put on airs with my bicycle was pathetic.

Miguel was not the only person showing off his wheels. On returning from an extended bout of work in a Bolivian city or in Argentina, one of the most important things a young man from Quirpini buys is a new bicycle. Then he might wait until the next fiesta or some other public event to show it off, adorning it with flowers or plastic streamers and riding it slowly and ostentatiously about, dressed in snappy new clothes that to me evoked the image of Bolivian working-class urban youth (tight pants, a narrow-brimmed hat, some approximation of a leather jacket). Having a new bicycle is important in several respects. First, it is a means of travel; with a bicycle a young man can more easily visit friends and kin, and get to San Lucas or Padcoyo, where there are shops and fairs as well as the few opportunities for paid labor in the region. It extends his social and commercial networks, and provides a measure of freedom. At the same time it is a powerful symbol, letting people know that he has traveled and earned money, that he has a good future ahead. In fact, his very mobility makes him an object of admiration.

Much of the display is aimed at young women. A shiny new bicycle, like new clothes, is a good way to show off to girls, as it hints at the rider's sophistication and good prospects, and is simply exciting. Making extended trips for wage labor has almost become a necessary step for a man who wants to establish an independent household, and buying a bicycle is a clear statement that a young man has taken that step. As a symbol of a young man's current mobility and his past (lucrative) travels, it shows him to be a good partner with whom to set up a household. In this respect, a bicycle is a young man's analogue to the common practice among young women in the rural Andes of attending fiestas wearing a carrying-cloth filled with the most beautiful textiles her family can provide as an indication of her supposed weaving skill, and thus her suitability as a wife.

Bicycles are common vehicles for public display: they are expensive, clearly come from elsewhere, and are on display whenever they are in use. Somewhat like cars in many industrial societies, bicycles are viewed by young men as extensions of themselves. Miguel's son, Nelson, once got into a spat with his best friend when the friend said that Nelson's bicycle was "old and worn out" (*thanta*). When people display themselves in this way, they turn local travels into a way of announcing that they have traveled and mastered the ways of distant lands. One of the most important goals of young men in Quirpini is to set up independent households, which they can normally do only when they have accumulated some land and have formed a stable partnership with a woman. Enhanced mobility and the capacity for individual action, which a bicycle represents both as metaphor and index, are important conditions for young men to become part of a married couple, or *qhariwarmi* (literally, "manwoman"), and achieve the spatial stability and locatedness in a household (*wasi*) that being part of a couple implies.[1] Bicycles provide a remarkably elegant image of the importance of mobility for Quirpinis, while at the same time illustrating the complex interplay of mobility with places, social power, and display.

It is important to point out, however, that the household the young man establishes may not be in Quirpini, or even in Bolivia. As I detail in chapter 7, a large proportion of young men leave the region permanently and settle down in a Bolivian city or in Argentina. Often the final step of a man's transition is to sell his land in Quirpini to relatives and bring his wife to live with him. In this scenario, the bicycle is a transition to permanent displacement, to membership in an urban working class, and to a household with a relationship to a physical house and land very different than would be possible in Quirpini.

Showing off with a bicycle, just like any kind of personal exhibition, requires some skill. Although Miguel wasn't trying to attract girls or set up a household, he was still trying to enhance his image through a bicycle. Unfortunately he wasn't very good at these more subtle uses of bicycles, and his attempt backfired on him.

The other time my bicycle caused Miguel problems involved the police. There was only one policeman in the town of San Lucas, where he had an office and a small jail. It was accepted that he was casually abusive of the power he held, as any policeman was expected to be, and that in broad terms he served the regional elite and the national government, not the campesinos. So it was not unexpected that when he saw Miguel in town with my new bicycle, he seized the bike, claimed that Miguel was violating some rule, and demanded a fine in exchange for the bicycle's return. Miguel managed to extricate himself from the police's scheme with the argument that it wasn't his bicycle, but mine, and that he hadn't done anything wrong anyway. He was probably aided by the fact that all this happened on a public street and was witnessed by many campesinos. The policeman was known to routinely seize portable possessions from campesinos and demand fines for their return, whereas he never acted in this way to members of the regional elite nor to me. In this way the policeman would buttress his power by repeatedly demonstrating that he could act with impunity. Though he was a man of humble background, not from the area, this impunity aligned him socially with the regional elite, who enjoyed similar impunity *vis-à-vis* the campesinos. Such casual abuse also served as one of the myriad instruments by which the elite maintained their own dominance over the campesinos. This dominance, and the terms on which campesinos and members of the elite struggled for power, is the subject of chapter 5, but it is relevant here because one of the key terms of this conflict was the control of how people and things moved about. It was hardly accidental that the policeman chose Miguel's bicycle to seize.

The politics of bicycles, then, brings together mobility, public display, power struggles, and the creation of domestic places into one rich and complex image. In the course of the book I move back and forth between descriptions of movement and descriptions of places, but often when I describe movement I am really also talking about places, and vice versa. The two are inextricable, and any attempt to separate them would only lead to confusion.

A common Andean cosmological principle is that the entire world is interconnected and animated by the ceaseless movement of liquids that fall from the sky (*janaq pacha,* or "upper world") as rainwater and arise from the mountains as springs, then flow into rivers and down into the sea, from where they evaporate and return to the sky or rise through the interiors of mountains. Water channeled into irrigation brings this dynamism to plants, while body fat, seen as a liquid that flows through the body, gives people "force" (*kallpa*), or the bodily capacity to act and to move (Orta 1996:569–571). In Quirpini loss of fat, such as to an attack by a *lik'ichiri* (a person believed to steal body fat in order to sell it), leads to increasing weakness and usually death. Loss of the ability to act, through loss of the fat moving through one's body, is tantamount to loss of one's being. Even semen, widely treated as a substance closely related to fat (Abercrombie 1998:66; Salazar Soler 1991:10; Kapsoli 1991; Orta 1996:569), is part of this general movement of fluids, imparting its energy to a woman's body, much as rain and irrigation water do to the soil (see Arnold 1987). The world, then, is fundamentally dynamic, and although sacred places, resting spots, houses, fields, and other sites may divert or suspend that movement, they never negate it. Indeed, such places, as I will demonstrate with regard to houses, are the products of patterns of movement caused, for example, by people, goods, water, saints, and spirits.

The verb *puriy* is, after *riy* ("go"), the most common Quechua word for human or animal movement; it is often glossed as "walk" or "travel." The word's denotations are many, however, and it can refer to the "functioning" of a machine as well as the movement of water in canals and rivers. The term can even refer to a condition of being, treated as an active process (Mannheim 1987:282). In keeping with the dynamic view of people and the world, an active state of being can be treated as a kind of movement. Seen through the movement of water and the verb *puriy*, "being," "doing," and "moving" become difficult to distinguish.

Movement is so interesting to Quirpinis not only because movement is life but also because of places—where people are going, where they are coming from, and what is being created by the movement. Ultimately, at stake when people and things move about is the place they are going. Mannheim (1987:282) argues that the verb *puriy* presupposes the verb *tiyay*. Usually glossed as "sit" and "reside," *tiyay* is used not just for the act of sitting but also when people want to say where they live. Mannheim argues that the term denotes "existence in a location" and covers such specific meanings as sitting, residence, sedimentation, and the calming of one's spirits (ibid.:280). When used to denote residence, the word always has a predicate denoting a place, normally a community or a house. In other words, traveling—which is itself a mode of active being—presupposes the places in which the movement begins or ends.

The bulk of this chapter, for instance, is about houses, but in order to address houses I must discuss place-making spirits and political struggles over locality, and, less obvious, the movement of water, the circulation of goods, the patterns of movement that characterize people's life courses, and struggles over knowledge. From here on, bicycles will fade into the background, as I alternate between describing the life of houses and vignettes that enrich those descriptions and clarify the mutual implication of locality and movement.

Like the bicycles, the places I talk about here have provisional importance—at some point each will fade in and out of focus or will appear in different guises, and at times will seem to disappear. Places always exist in relation to other places (their own internal parts, the larger social and geographical elements that contain them, as well as places that are simply elsewhere) and also in relation to people's ever changing concerns and projects.

As a result, and as I emphasized in the introduction, they have a permanent kaleidoscopic quality, and we can only approach them if we allow them to be elusive.

Houses and Households: *Wasi* as Articulation

NAMING HOUSES

Around the San Lucas region, as in many Quechua-speaking areas, the most common word for household is *wasi,* a Quechua word with a broad range of meanings. In reference to physical structures, wasi can refer to a single room, a building of any kind, or indeed any structure that encloses something. In toponyms, wasi denotes a place habitually occupied by something or associated with it, as in the village that used to be named Khuchi Wasi, or "Pig Place." When followed by a possessive suffix, it often takes on the connotation of the English word "home," as in *wasiy,* "my home." The term also refers to the collection of rooms, usually surrounding a central patio, that houses a group of people, usually kin, who participate in a single domestic economy. In many circumstances it can refer to the residents of such a complex or a person acting as the residents' representative. A wasi, then, is both a physical space and a group of structures as well as the people that occupy them. It is the Quechua term that comes closest to the anthropological concept of "household," although, as in English, any technical term fails to do justice to the breadth and multiplicity of the colloquial term. The most striking ways in which it exceeds the strictures of the English term are in its recursion (it can refer to a room, a building, a complex, and also the land that contains these) and its use to refer to a certain kind of place, without reference to people or buildings. In keeping with the semantic range of the term, as well as the other terms I discuss here, I will shift between talking about the physical spaces and buildings of houses, and domestic social groups or households.

In Quirpini, houses fit into the complex of movement and locality in several ways. As the most frequented and complex places in the community, wasis are significant points in most local and long-distance travel. Households are sites in complex patterns of circulation: of people, seeds, money, goods, and information; these patterns are manifest at many spatial and temporal scales. Finally, households are themselves the sites of many of the secrets that Quirpinis keep and the object of much curiosity, gossip, and prying eyes.

Accordingly, much curiosity among Quirpinis about what their neighbors are up to focuses on houses and the comings and goings of people around them.

Households, not individuals, are considered the main actors in most public situations in Quirpini; for example, communal labor obligations are calculated by households; attendance and voting at *reuniones generales* (see chapter 5) are reckoned in terms of households; and the various authority positions said to govern communal institutions—the *kurajkuna* (political authorities), the *junta escolar* (school committee), and others—are in many senses filled by households. Most reciprocal labor debts are incurred between households;[2] no such debts are incurred among the members of a single household. As Orlove and Custred (1980:32) and Harris (1978) argue, the household is the basic social unit of an Andean community; Platt (1978) treats it as the most elementary form of ayllu. The conflation of households and acting subjects is taken to the point that not only do Quirpinis routinely refer to households by the name of a person (usually the senior resident male), but not infrequently they also refer to people by the name of the land on which their house is built, as when Miguel Paco, whose land was called Cancha Loma, was sometimes referred to as "Cancha Loma Miguel." Like the larger ayllus, wasis are defined both through the land they control and the people who inhabit them.

Another word that includes some of the same semantic space as "household" is *kusina,* from the Spanish *cocina,* or "kitchen." Kusina refers primarily to the room, often freestanding, in which most of a household's cooking and eating takes place. Kusinas vary in makeup, but each has a simple unbaked clay stove in one corner with three holes for pots, placed below a smoke-hole in the roof. Normally they have low benches or other places to sit, but little other furniture. When Quirpinis talk about a household as a source of food (as in collective work parties, where each household provides food), they may well refer to it as a kusina. Ideally the kusina is controlled by a woman, and the identification of kusina with wasi is tied up with the marked tendency for each wasi to be home to exactly one woman of childbearing age and for a general identification of domestic reproductive spaces with women. This is in contrast to exterior productive and public spaces, which are more masculine in their associations. This usage is commonly heard during fiestas, when people remark on the presence or absence of certain kusinas; here they are referring to households in their reproductive capacity.

A household can also be designated through the patio or courtyard, which is its defining spatial feature. The term *pátiyu*, from the Spanish *patio*, is most often employed when people are talking about the house as a physical space. The ideal household layout, which most families achieve over a period of years, consists of at least three freestanding rooms surrounding a central patio. In principle, every household enjoys the presence of a named *wirjin*, or Virgin, a manifestation of the Pachamama, to whom offerings are buried in the center of the patio.[3]

Finally, the word "ayllu" may be used, in its sense of "family," to refer to the members of a household, insofar as they are close relatives. In Quirpini, most households contain nuclear or extended families. Only four or five have members who are not descended from a common living person or married to someone so related to the other household members. The term "ayllu," however, also has many other meanings, as mentioned in the introduction. It can be used to denote kinship of any kind; to say that someone is *aylluy* ("my ayllu") means that the person is one's kin. It can also refer to a hamlet of related households, although I never heard it used this way in Quirpini; a sub-section of a community, such as a Quirpini zona; a village such as Quirpini; and a nested series of territorial/ethnic groups comprising multiple villages such as Kellaja, the moribund ethnic group that once united Quirpinis with the members of several other villages.

Many of these terms have fuzzy edges, and all refer to slightly different entities or to the same entities differently characterized. For instance, Cirilo Paco, the elderly bachelor uncle of Miguel Paco, lived on the same land as his nephew but occupied a couple of rooms around a different patio, about fifty meters from the large patio around which Miguel and his immediate family lived. Part of the land had once been Cirilo's, but he gave his land to Miguel and partially merged his domestic economy with Miguel's family. He normally cooked for himself but obtained foodstuffs from Miguel's domestic supply. Because he owned no land of his own, he was counted, for purposes of communal labor obligations, as part of the same wasi as Miguel, yet in many social senses he occupied a different wasi. He was undoubtedly of Miguel's ayllu (in the sense of family, they were kin and lived on the same land), yet he did not share a pátiyu. I, too, was a marginal member of the household: I ate nearly all my meals with Miguel, Emiliana, and their children, and my labor in collective and reciprocal projects counted as work done by the household, but I lived in a room on yet another pátiyu on Miguel's land and was definitely not of his ayllu.

I encountered the fluid nature of wasi membership when I conducted a household survey. The most common area of vagueness arose when I spoke to the parents of adult children; in most cases, when I asked, "How many people live in this house?" they would list all their children, including those with independent households of their own and even those who had been living in Argentina for years. In a few cases the parents claimed all their children for their household, but, in surveying one of the children's houses, I was told emphatically that the two households were separate.

Another generational ambiguity lies with parent/child households that have only partly separated. When I surveyed twenty-six-year-old Panfilo Puma and his nineteen-year-old wife, Epifania Colque, in their newly purchased house, for instance, Panfilo told me that they still lived with his father Esteban; they were in the process of setting up their new household, and Panfilo appeared uncertain about claiming complete autonomy. Genaro Mamani lived with his wife, Jacinta Santos, in a house directly adjacent to that of his father's parents, Fabián Mamani and Augustina Ibarra. The two families held separate fields and separate kitchens and patios, but they owned adjacent plots of land and worked them together. When it came to labor obligations, rights to water and political participation, there were two households: Genaro's and Fabián's.[4] Children who stayed in Quirpini and lived near their parents most commonly separated gradually from the parental household; in these situations a young couple usually maintained close ties only with one set of parents, generally the husband's. If the child moved farther away or if one of the parents died, the remaining parent and one of the children's families would end up living in the same house.

The nature of a house, then, has everything to do with the way that the house is incorporated into circulations of people, water, goods, and information, and how it is connected to other houses and places, whether neighboring houses, the community as a whole, or future and past houses. Even the terms by which Quirpinis refer to the constellation of features I call "houses" depends on the feature and how they are engaging the house. There are broad consistencies across the different situated ways that houses exist; I am not suggesting that there are different houses for community meetings versus preparing dinner but rather that houses are always partially manifest and that this is reflected in the terminology and practices around houses. Stephenson

(1999:79) refers to Andean houses as "dense texture of . . . signs"; to this I would add, perhaps redundantly, that they are dense textures of possibilities for action and signification.

This richness of potential significance and association that households encompass can be found trans-locally as well. Abercrombie (1998) shows that houses in K'ulta, on the Bolivian altiplano contain cosmic models, whereas Arnold (1992) sees houses in nearby Qaqachaka as structures of memory. Stephenson (1999) finds resistance to modernizing and assimilationist programs in Arnold's Qaqachaka material on house building. Although I did not find any of these possible aspects of houses to be highly developed in Quirpini,[5] I have little doubt that here we are dealing with differential realizations of some broadly similar ideas and practices related to houses.

LIFE OF A WASI

It is useful to see a household, in its physical and interpersonal sense, as a series of transformations. Over a period of years and generations, the physical and human makeup of a wasi changes, and these changes follow a broad pattern. Houses become different places in response to both external and internal concerns and events, and many of these events, and the possible responses, are similar for different households.

The physical space of a house undergoes transformations according to the household residents' phase of life. I was told that, normally, the youngest son of a family inherits the house and the largest plot of the land and the elder brothers receive parcels of land as they enter into families and each build a house on his own parcel. Daughters are supposed to receive smaller parcels, on the assumption that they will move to their husband's house on the husband's family land. These new families ideally start out by building simple houses (a room and a kusina are the minimum form of a wasi) gradually adding rooms, walls, and animal pens as time allows and the family and its material possessions grow. While I was in Quirpini, Bernaldino Alvarado built a one-room house to live in with his pregnant wife. Initially the kitchen was only a lean-to. When he had the time, he intermittently worked on a low adobe wall about seven meters in front of the door of this house, which, he explained, was to create a patio, and indicated that he had already planned, in a general way, where several other rooms were to go around it.

One effect of the traditional inheritance pattern is for groups of kin to concentrate in more-or-less contiguous stretches of land. Often these areas are named after the family that currently is, or historically was, predominant in the area; for instance, I lived in an area called "Ibarra" after the many Ibarras who lived there; the southern part of the Zona Sakapampa was inhabited almost exclusively by people named Puma, and was routinely called "Puma" or "Pumakuna" (Pumas). In these areas the ties between kin, between neighbors, and between friends tended to be combined, resulting in a dense web of ties of reciprocity and affection, characterized by the intensive circulation of goods, reciprocal labor, and people. Although there are no communal or zonal exogamy rules in Quirpini, people generally marry out of such areas because of incest prohibitions: most of their neighbors are also their kin.

In practice, inheritance rarely works out in the ideal way described to me. It probably never did, but by the 1990s some specific factors had led to new patterns of land transfer. First of all, for a couple of decades at least, rather than simply moving off their parents' land, most sons had been moving permanently out of Quirpini, migrating to cities such as Santa Cruz or Buenos Aires, where wage labor was plentiful. Many land parcels in Quirpini were so small that it was not practical to subdivide them further; the lack of land was aggravated by the lack of rain, a long-standing problem throughout southern highland Bolivia. Most commonly one son migrated temporarily, as his brothers moved away permanently. He then bought the land that his brothers had inherited, eventually reconstituting a holding based on his parents' lands, and sufficient to support a family. This is one of the reasons why long-distance travel had become a key step for men on their way to setting up a house. Even a young man very committed to migrating would most likely marry locally and receive his inheritance of land. He would then build a small adobe house where his wife and children would live and farm while he made periodic trips for wage labor. His wife would farm his land as well as any she had in her own right, perhaps using the money her husband brought home to hire male neighbors for occasional help. Should the couple eventually decide to make a permanent move out of the region, they would sell their land (including any land she held), ideally to a brother or other close relative; the house they had built might then be abandoned, or become the nucleus of another family's growing household, or even be maintained as a storage room or field-side shelter should the land's new owner not live nearby.

The other main factor that had changed the way land and houses are transferred across generations also arose as a result of migration. Parents often used the prospect of inheriting land to keep control over their children, particularly their sons, and as a means of keeping them physically nearby. Couples, and particularly men, who managed to keep their sons or sons-in-law in close proximity were that much more powerful and respected in the community. With the rise of migration in the last few decades, however, many older men's efforts to exert this control had become self-defeating. For one thing, most adult men eventually left to settle permanently elsewhere, thus moving definitively beyond parental control. The remaining son had usually earned enough money in his travels to buy land and build a house of his own rather than stay under the parental roof once he had established his own family. I describe one such intergenerational power struggle in the conclusion to this volume.

Eventually most houses are abandoned. Either they become too old for continual repair or the people who inherit them choose not to live there—perhaps having moved to a city or to a spouse's land elsewhere, or simply having built another house already.[6] The old house might be used as a storeroom, or the family might remove the wooden doors, lintels, and roof beams to use in a new house, leaving the adobe structure to erode back into the ground. If no one builds on the site, it eventually returns to farmland and the remaining adobe bricks are ploughed back into the soil.

A house in Quirpini is an object of action, a destination, a goal, a way of realizing oneself. Young men ride bicycles in part to impress girls, which they do because occupying a house and land as part of a qhariwarmi is a necessary element of independence and full personhood in Quirpini. Houses and land are objects of intense desire, and this desire drives men to migrate, as well as to return.

BUILDING A WASI

One reason why people and families can be so mobile is that it is so easy to build a house in Quirpini. The primary building material is mud bricks, and the clay soil of the San Lucas valley is both ideal for making bricks and plentiful. Apart from mud, building a house requires rocks for the foundation (also not hard to find), wood for the roof beam, and cane and grass, which are needed for building the roof. Cane comes from the lowlands and the grass from mountains, but they are easily acquired or collected. Roof beams and lintels are made of wood. The oldest houses in Quirpini, perhaps fifty years old, were built before eucalyptus trees were widely grown in the area and so have roof beams made from the twisty *mulli* tree. These houses are not at all rectilinear in outline, and their walls were often made entirely of stone. I was told that with the advent of the tall, straight eucalyptus tree, rectilinear houses became more popular, as did adobe for walls, as square houses and adobe construction were seen as more urban and "modern" than the older style of houses. Certainly the newer houses do more closely resemble the houses of San Lucas town. The biggest monetary expense involved in building a house is acquiring the doors. The major restraints on most families' ability to build are temporal: the seasons and the availability of time. Adobe bricks can only be made in the spring and fall; in the warm rainy season they do not dry well, and in the winter they freeze and crack before they dry. In addition, making adobes and putting up walls are slow jobs, which men normally do alone or with minimal help. During planting and harvest there is rarely enough time for this sort of work, so it gets done in the available interstices of time. Building a single room can take more than a year of occasional labor.

The most complex and labor-intensive part of building a house is putting on the roof, or *wasi urqu*. This job requires the coordinated efforts of many people, both to put the roof beam into place and to properly put down the necessary layers of cane (twined together to form a rigid base for the mud roof), grass (for water resistance), and mud (also for water resistance and to hold all the materials together). Most families call a mink'a—a kind of labor party also used for planting corn—to put up a roof, inviting a number of male neighbors, friends, and kin to do the work in a single day, while some women cook for the men and serve them food and drink. The family that owns the house must reciprocate the labor that they receive from each family. Putting up a roof is a considerable expense, and more because of the cost of entertaining the labor force than of buying materials.

Once a house is built, it remains a house in every sense only thanks to constant effort. The roof must be recoated with mud every couple of years and periodically remade. Hinges must be fixed, cracks caulked with adobe, eroded walls repaired. Apart from repairs, families are constantly rearranging things—filling in a window hole with adobe bricks, moving a doorway, raising a doorstep to keep out water. In addition, the house must be *ch'alla-d* (blessed by prayers and offerings of corn beer or other alcoholic drinks) every year at Carnival to maintain the Pachamama's blessing. In addition to all the work it takes to keep a house from decaying, people are also constantly altering their wasis, adding rooms, moving animal pens, and so on. I have already described the way houses evolve in the normal course of a family's development, but a family also might decide to raise chickens and build a house for that purpose, or might lose their ox and decide to use the land where the cattle pen stood for planting or to build a new room. A man might want a workroom in which to practice handicrafts,[7] or a woman might decide that she needs a larger kitchen. The only houses on which relatively little work is expended are old ones used for storage; these houses are generally left to a gradual process of decay, slowed by a rare bout of maintenance. Even abandoned houses are transformed, as their owners remove their wooden elements such as doors, roof beams, and lintels to reuse in a new house.

Houses in and around Quirpini are plastic almost to the point of being fluid. Unlike the wood, steel, and cement dwellings in which most people live in industrial societies, houses in rural San Lucas are not built first and then inhabited. Rather, they are built and inhabited at the same time, constantly repaired and transformed as part of the life of a household. The state of a house reflects the state of the household, because it is the product of the endless creative efforts of the household. Indeed, a wasi can be seen as a temporary "fixing" of soil (hallpa) by the removal of water.

Here I should underline that not only are houses the ongoing product of people's creative efforts; everyone is aware that this is the situation. People in well-established households occasionally remark that they might put in a new wall or rebuild the kitchen. As far as I could tell, there was no house in Quirpini whose construction was not remembered by someone; people did not often talk about when or how wasis were built but could easily explain a house's origin when asked. The malleable nature of people's homes is a given, so much so that it is never remarked on except when people are contemplating a specific change. This is reflective of the way that places of all kinds are seen as the products of actions.

Houses, Places, and the Pachamama

Quirpinis treat houses as dynamic, as restless; they project them into time through transformation and produce them continuously. We can better understand this dynamic quality of houses by more closely examining their connection to the Pachamama, a figure I have heretofore mentioned only briefly.

The Pachamama is probably the supernatural figure with whom Catholic Quirpinis[8] have the most frequent contact. She is an ancient Andean object of worship; yet to think of her as a mythic character or even as a character at all would be to misunderstand how she works. She rarely turns up in narratives; in Quirpini there are no tales of what the Pachamama has done in the past or regarding her impact on the landscape, and no one told me of encountering her except through a medium. These narrative absences differentiate her from many other figures in the spiritual world of Quirpini, such as saints, mallkus, *chullpas* (the half-dead skeletons of ancestors who lived on earth before there was a sun, and who can still make people sick), Jesus Christ, the trickster-fox "compadre Antonio," and so on; the Pachamama is unique in being absent from all but the sparest narratives.

She comes up, instead, in rituals and in people's projects. Quirpinis attribute to her the power to let crops grow or fail, control over the success or failure of any major undertaking such as building a house or bridge, and also significant influence over the health or well-being of people, livestock, households, and physical possessions. As a result, people constantly carry out rituals intended to invoke her and win favor. These include various kinds of libations, or ch'alla, *q'uwara* (a burnt offering of animal fat, coca, and incense), whole or partial animals offered as burnt sacrifices, and various buried offerings of products from the subsistence practices which depend on her for success.

There are no major rituals devoted solely to the Pachamama, as there are to the mallkus, to the souls of the dead, to various saints or to Jesus; instead she turns up in a variety of activities as an ever invoked presence. At all fiestas people offer part of each drink to her as ch'allas; during corn planting they ch'alla to her and give her a q'uwara as well, and sometimes a plate of food. No house is completed until it has been ch'alla-d with corn beer splashed on its walls and roof; many people also incorporate small bottles of liquor into their roofs as an offering to the Pachamama. All the civic construction I saw in Quirpini, such as school buildings or bridges, was accompanied by a burnt offering for the Pachamama, and was ch'alla-d, too. She receives an offering of wine during the early August irrigation canal rituals, even though these events are primarily focused on the mallkus, owners of the irrigation water (see chapter 1).

Twice a year people's actions are more focused on Pachamama than usual: August and the subsequent corn-planting season; and the week of Carnival, which usually falls in February. August is when it is most appropriate for a family to mark the ears of their livestock, a form of branding. Household members, perhaps with some friends and kin, gather in the animal pen while one house member notches the ear of each new animal. The pieces of ear are mixed with coca leaves, sprinkled with alcohol, and buried as an offering to the Pachamama. During corn planting she receives several offerings in the course of each day's work. Carnival, at the opposite extreme in the annual calendar, is the ideal time to ch'alla one's house and other major possessions. People understand Carnival ch'allas to be directed to the Pachamama, intended to ensure that the objects so blessed will last. At the same time, in the course of their house visits, the Carnival dancers perform around a pot of chicha in the center of each patio, an offering to the Pachamama.

The name "Pachamama" tells us something of her role. As in many languages, *mama* means "mother," but as Harris (2000) points out, it also can refer to a lady and to unusually shaped tubers or pieces of ore.[9] Harris concludes that the term might mean "source of fertility" as much as simply "mother" (211–212). *Pacha* is a rich and complex word. At its simplest, it can refer to land and overlaps somewhat with *hallpa,* the word for soil and agricultural land. But it can also refer to space in a more abstract sense—something like extension over a terrain. Quirpinis might use the word, for instance, when discussing where to erect a new building and whether there is room for it; Harris glosses this sense as "place" (213). It can also denote a delimited period of time, such as a season or an epoch. At the same time it refers to a world as a whole: *kay pacha,* or "this world," is the full extent of the cosmos we inhabit, both in space and time. It is different from *janaq pacha,* Heaven ("upper world"), or *ukhu pacha,* the Underworld ("inner world"), but it is also related to *ñawpa pacha* ("ancient world" or "before-world") when the chullpas occupied the land where Quirpinis reside. Andean cosmological time is famously punctuated by *pachakuti,* or "world-turnings," dramatic transformations that ended one epoch and began another. *Pacha,* in other words, can refer to a-space-and-a-time as a single whole. Some anthropologists have rendered her name in English as simply "Mother Earth" (Bastien 1978; Allen 1988), but this translation is misleading. Although she is identified with the soil (and with creatures that live in the soil such as spiders), there is more to her. As reasonable—and as limited—a translation would be "Earth Mother," "World Mother," or even "Space-Time Mother."

As a term for land, for open space in general yet specific places as well as entire worlds, the word *pacha* parallels the spatial uses of the Pachamama. She is always potentially nearby—anyone can make an offering to her at any time just by pouring liquid on the ground, burying objects, or burning incense, yet she is present in a much more concrete sense in certain places that she articulates through her presence. That presence is marked by people's convergence, as on a patio during Carnival or on a field during planting.[10] The Pachamama is always potentially present as part of the background but is also available to articulate a specific moment (the start of a project) or location (a house or a field).

I suggest that the Pachamama is generative not only of crops and animals but of certain kinds of places, things, and actions— perhaps not the material presence of crops, livestock, and places but their dynamic potential, their continued existence, and specificity. Her role is not to preserve them; she does not ensure that things will remain unchanged so much as that they will continue to live and go on doing what they do. This idea is not problematic for crops and livestock—fields that remained always unchanged would not really be fields nor would static animals be animals—but it might not be such an obvious approach to the continuity of a house, an irrigation canal, or a truck. Invoking the Pachamama for inanimate places and objects is a way to ensure that the house will continue to shelter people, to undergo repairs, additions, and sundry transformations, and to articulate the movement of its residents and others; that the canal will continue to effectively channel water to the fields; that the truck will continue to function, carrying people about and generating income for its owner. In other words, people call on her to ensure that things will *puriy*. In relating all these things to the Pachamama, Quirpinis are treating them like *chajras*, as generative, as objects or events defined in some important sense by their dynamism and potential for being part of a larger pattern of movement.

And they are also treating them like houses are treated, as objects of desire. The Pachamama not only keeps things working, she underpins their specificity and projects them into the future. In giving a house its name, in the way she is invoked at the start of a trip or at planting, she establishes an object or event—a house, a trip, a field and its crop—as something that will continue to be what it is (i.e., to do what it does, to unfold properly, to satisfy the desire to which it corresponds) in the future. Invoking her invokes the fusing together of being, identity, action, and duration. She unites space and time. She presides over the transition from potential to actuality, from the general to the particular. In concrete terms, she projects plans into a completed trip, seeds into a harvested crop, a collection of structures into an inhabited house, open land into a productive field, a bicycle that exists now into a bicycle one can ride next year, space into a place, animals into one's own livestock.[11] This is why she is not a character in narratives—she is the basis for narratives. She is unlocalized because she is the condition of locality. She has no fiestas because she is the blessing invoked in fiestas. Insofar as the Pachamama marks places such as houses, she marks them as dynamic, generative centers, and actively projects them into the future.

Household Activities and Spatial Structure

In approaching a wasi, a visitor traverses its outer boundary. This outer boundary has the effect of sorting people according to their relationship with the household. For someone who is not particularly well known in the household, it is rude and intrusive simply to enter a patio unannounced. The visitor should stop some feet short of the edge of the patio and call out a greeting. If there is no answer, he or she should, ideally, leave, and even if someone answers the visitor should not enter the patio unless invited. Many conversations take place either just outside a patio or with a visitor standing outside talking to a household member inside. The more familiar a visitor is with the household, the farther into the patio he or she can advance without causing offense—members of the household do not normally call out a greeting when they enter the patio, and close relatives who visit often can refrain from announcing themselves until they are approaching the doorway to a room or, if the patio has a gate, until they arrive at the gate.

One way to grasp the way Quirpini households work is to examine their characteristic spatial schemas (Hanks 1990), which imply certain activities and prohibit or impede others. A schema is a series of constraints and possibilities built into the landscape, people's minds and memories, and their bodily habits and language. It is shared, although everyone operates differently within such schematic space.

From the viewpoint of someone approaching a house not their own, a wasi constitutes an increasingly exclusive space the farther into it one proceeds. The area outside the walls of the various rooms is open to all but the most threatening or strange passersby; in the early days of my stay in Quirpini, I could alarm people just by passing near their houses, and, similarly, strange people who appear to be crazy or troublesome can be driven out of a household's fields, even out of the community. In the patio, the space is reserved more for those who are familiar to the household or have been invited in. If there is an all-purpose room, that is generally the next most accessible place and where guests will be invited. The kitchen is more private still, but a known person of equal status, such as a neighbor, will be invited into the kitchen if they are being asked to share a meal. The sleeping rooms can be the most private, and few people who are not part of the household enter them, unless these rooms also serve as work rooms, in which case visitors may well be invited in. This schema is transformed during fiestas and work parties (mink'a) when, first, the whole domestic space is turned over to production (of corn-beer and food), and then parts of it are opened for entertaining. One of the characteristic features of festive and collective occasions, in fact, is the way they transform domestic space, making it relatively public.

Although there are broadly common schemata governing the space of wasis in general, for members of each household these schemata are differently centered; their own homes are rich in possibilities, full of distinct yet multifaceted spaces that lend themselves to different activities and form part of various ways of moving, whereas the houses of their kin and friends are simpler, more filled with spaces of entertainment and collective work. Distant houses, and houses of people they are not close to, appear simple indeed, made up of spaces governed mainly by rules of politeness such as those detailed above—when you can enter the patio, how far you can proceed, and so on.

A wasi is the prime multipurpose space in Quirpini; most other spaces are more clearly dedicated to single purposes—fields, irrigation canals, or school, paths, for example. As such, the wasi is a key site for the transformation of things; wasis, and the rooms that comprise them, are spaces into which things enter and then are different when they emerge. They are places where many different paths of circulation meet. These activities and patterns of movement also contribute crucially to the nature of the domestic space in which they are situated. Here I focus on the household I knew most intimately, that of Miguel Paco and his family.

When people spoke of Miguel's house as a place or destination, they usually called it "Cancha Loma," the name of the parcel of land on which the various patios of the household stood. But when speaking of the domestic unit consisting of Miguel, Emiliana, and their children Nelson, Javier, Geronimo, Alicia, and Waldemar, as well as Miguel's uncle Cirilo and (for a while) myself, they called it *Miguelpa wasin* or, less often, *Emilianajpa wasin* ("Miguel's house" or "Emiliana's house"). In the roll call of Quirpini's monthly reunión general, the household (which could be represented by any adult resident) was referred to by Miguel's name.

Miguel's land contained four different groups of house structures. He, Emiliana, and their children lived in the largest, a collection of three one-room adobe buildings accompanied by a small stone cattle pen, a chicken house, and a small pen for sheep or goats, all perched on a rise at the southern edge of the cultivated part of Ibarra. To the east Miguel's uncle, Cirilo, occupied a single room among several storerooms surrounding a smaller patio. About fifty meters north of the main house, between the lower cornfield and a well-traveled path, stood a small three-room house on a diminutive patio, which Miguel had built when he was a teenager. He lived there with Emiliana until his parents died, and as their only son he took over the house. I lived in one room of this house and used another to store my bicycle. Between "my" house and the main house stood the eroded walls of a long-abandoned house; I never knew who had lived there or how long it had been abandoned. Miguel's land was traversed by a well-traveled path connecting the Ibarra with Zona Quirpini and the main road, on the far side of the river. This path wound between several small fields, passing by the main house near where the principal irrigation canal for Ibarra emerged from the river gorge. This canal provided most of the household's water, in addition to watering the fields.

Every morning Emiliana would fill a bucket from the irrigation canal and sprinkle water on the patio to keep the dust down. A rough rectangle of packed dirt, the patio was about seven by ten meters and was bounded by the bedroom (*puñuy wasi*); the workshop/public room that Miguel called his "salón"; in other houses a room devoted to entertaining might be called the *aqha tumanapaj wasi,* or "room for drinking corn-beer"; the kusina; and the *kancha,* or cattle pen (see Figure 2.1). The kancha opened to the wasi's exterior, but the three rooms for human use had single doors letting onto the patio, as in almost every house in Quirpini. Behind the kusina were some enclosed pens for goats, sheep, and chickens. The east side was open, facing toward the hill

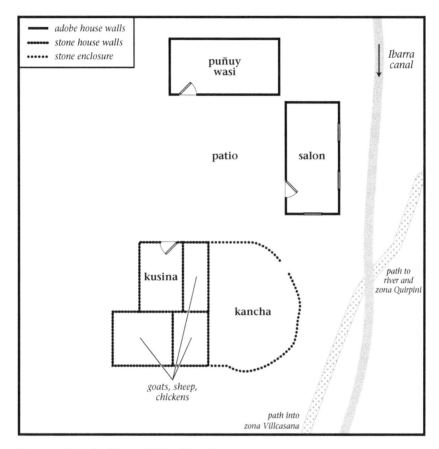

Figure 2.1. Main buildings of Miguel Paco's wasi.

that dominates Ibarra and a barren area with some small trees. Nearby was Cirilo's house, partly dedicated to storage for the entire household; across a nearby quebrada, one saw Felix Villcasana's house and the huge mulli tree that stood over Victor Condori's, some two hundred meters away.

Wasis do not have a single center but several areas that could be called their centers for different purposes or from different perspectives; the patio is one of these and is the most multipurpose area of houses which themselves are distinctly multipurpose in all their parts. In Miguel's house, this was where many visitors were entertained, particularly unfamiliar ones, and where the family slaughtered goats or sheep and where Emiliana washed the children. It was also the part of the house that is most "outside"; when the weather was fine (as it usually was) Miguel could often be found on the patio repairing tools or a musical instrument or making a hat, perhaps while the children played nearby.

The layout of Miguel's house is not atypical, apart from the two outlying semi-independent residents that his uncle, Cirilo, and I occupied. Some of the wealthiest households have more than one patio; some have several *puñuy wasi* or no workroom. But all are oriented around a patio, onto which all rooms open, and all have animal pens on the margins of the residential rooms.[12] Some patios are walled in, and others are closed by a gate. Some households have extensive storerooms around the main patio, whereas others, like Miguel's, make use of nearby buildings. All houses are situated near an irrigation canal whose water is crucial to many aspects of the domestic economy. Most have an earthen oven, not very far away, for making bread and, on rare festive occasions, roasting meat.

The patio is a public center of the house; it is the part of the house's interior (*wasi ukhu*) that is most open to visitors and public events. Any goods or people entering the house pass through the patio, although hardly anything stays there. The exception is the ceramic container of *chicha* that is buried in the center of the patio as an offering to the Pachamama. She herself is, in a way, resident in the center of the patio, although she is everywhere else as well; here is where offerings are made to her by or for the household. The patio, then, serves as the wasi's ritual center. Yet going from the patio into any of the rooms is to go *ukhuman* (inward); of all the spaces within the walls of a wasi, the patio is the most *hawapi* (outside). Its public character, in a sense, makes it the house's exterior when compared to two other rooms.

The kusina is also a kind of center of the house. Like the patio, it lends its name to the entire household because it is the hearth, the center of domestic reproduction. This is where families gather to eat and talk. It is a woman's space and is most closely identified with the woman of the household who is of childbearing age, as she normally is in charge of the cooking. Close kin and friends are invited into the kusina. In Cancha Loma, Emiliana spent several hours there each day, cooking, preparing to cook (though sometimes she did her preparations on the patio), eating with the family, and cleaning up. Some kitchens are large enough to store food, although Emiliana's was not; it was a stone structure too low to stand up in and barely large enough to fit seven people seated on the floor. Kusinas are where most of the family's food is brought together and transformed into meals that the family members will eat and that will be shared with other households at work parties and fiestas.

The ingredients Emiliana used for cooking came from far and wide, and represented just about all the ways that a campesino can acquire items in rural Bolivia. Corn, fava beans, and wheat, as well as tomatoes, herbs, and other vegetables, were homegrown and came from the family's fields around the house. Occasionally a chicken or lamb, raised by the family or acquired from a neighbor, would be obtained. Water, necessary for cooking as well as for washing dishes, people, and clothes,[13] came from the irrigation canal to which the family retained access by joining neighboring households in maintaining and running the canal. Peppers, and rarely fresh fruit, came from the hot valleys, and can be purchased in fairs or acquired by barter. Noodles, rice, vegetable oil, sugar, salt and other dry goods came from the cities; either Emiliana or Miguel would buy them from one of the elite-run shops in town or from the traveling vendors who occasionally turned up and sold goods cheaply from their trucks. They collected various herbs, as well as firewood, from the plants in the area, particularly on the un-irrigated hillsides.[14] In the kusina all these items are brought together and transformed, by women's work, into actual consumable food; the kusina is the heart of the wasi as the space where potential values are realized.

The puñuy wasi constitutes yet another center of the house. If there is only one puñuy wasi, as in Miguel's house, the entire family sleeps there, often in a single bed. For a period of time Emiliana told me that she was sleeping in the salon with her new baby, mainly to avoid having sex with Miguel, and thus more babies. If the household is constantly being situated and resituated in relation to what is outside by many kinds of movement, the puñuy wasi is the house's still center, where things move the least. Generally this is where people store or hide personal possessions. Money is usually kept here, hidden in some nook, as are important papers. This is where people conceal *trago* (cane alcohol) and also store clothes and textiles. Keepsakes and small ritual objects, such as the miniature clay cattle with which people ask saints for livestock, are concealed in the puñuy wasi as well. The room, then, is normally filled with trunks and old suitcases, locked boxes, as well as items hanging from the rafters. As in the kitchen, the objects in the puñuy wasi represent a tremendous variety of patterns of circulation and are acquired in myriad ways. The difference is that most of these things are not used or transformed in the room; instead, they are stored, kept out of sight, and preserved there until they can be put to use, usually elsewhere, when the trago is drunk or when a legal crisis necessitates the use of a land title or simply when the clothes are worn. The room is a place of rest, for objects as well as people. Nonresidents almost never enter here except during fiestas or preparation for fiestas.

A room such Miguel's *salon* may or may not be distinct in other Quirpini houses. Miguel's workroom, one end of which was dominated by a wooden structure he used to prepare felt for hats, also served as a room for entertaining small groups of guests. This was the room to which he would invite distinguished or intimidating outsiders, such as the priest, a government official, or a newly arrived gringo anthropologist. It was fitted with benches along two walls and a locally made table. (In many houses, a single room serves both for storage and for visitors.)

During fiestas this schema is transformed. The outer boundaries of the house practically disappear, and most of the private spaces become open to general visiting. This is especially true in the preparation for fiestas, when the various spaces of the wasi, patio, puñuy wasi, and kusina are turned into women's work spaces. The wasi becomes, in effect, a single large kusina devoted to the reproduction not of a household but of public social relations. What also changes is the way the wasi articulates movement. In many celebrations, such as an individual work party or a fiesta passed by one of the kurajkuna, rather than providing a crossing and transformation point for various circulations a wasi becomes the convergence point for many visitors. It becomes, for a moment, a center for some group of people, whether they are the members of the household's networks (say, for a house-roofing party), a zona (for a saint's day), or the entire community (for a major fiesta such as Navedad or Carnival). The disappearance of boundaries and the refiguring of the entire wasi as a center are not unrelated; the wasi is transformed from a bounded, contained space where a family may work, or *tiyay*, into the provisional center for a much larger entity, defined through those who gather there.

The nature of a wasi as a geographical and social phenomenon largely lies in its capacity to influence the movement of people and things: drawing people close only to make them stop outside the patio; containing a site that attracts raw foodstuffs, firewood, and water, and in which they are transformed into food; attracting fellow Quirpinis during Carnival. Having an impact on movement is central to the nature of places, but it is also a key feature of politics. Wasis are manifest not as the mute structures I saw on my first walk around the silent village but in the ways that they structure the movement of people, goods, and information. In this sense, wasis are manifestations of power; they exist through the power they exercise over people and things, and to inhabit them is to realize them by creatively responding to, and even taking advantage of, the way they structure action.

Movement, Places, and Vision

Every three months the San Lucas valley sub-central of the national campesino union (CSUTCB, also commonly called the sindicato) holds a meeting that is supposed to be attended by a representative from every family in all six communities of the valley. The meeting rotates from one community to another but is never held in San Lucas, and no one from San Lucas is allowed to attend the meetings or join the union. In March 1994 the meeting was held in Quirpini, and I attended.

The morning meeting was comprised of three concurrent sessions, where people discussed different issues and proposed resolutions; the afternoon meeting would be a plenary gathering, for final discussion and voting. I walked about from session to session, listening to the discussions. For the first hour or so my presence provoked some curious looks but no strong reactions. I did not personally know any of the officials; most of them were from Yapusiri, a community some eight kilometers downriver. Eventually a young sindicato official who was running one session called me up to the front of the small group he was addressing, wanting to ask me some questions. When I agreed, he proceeded to ask increasingly accusatory questions, suggesting that I was up to no good and that my very presence in the valley was an injustice. When he asked if a Bolivian would be allowed to go to the United States and conduct a study like the one I was doing, he was quite taken aback when I said probably yes, although the person would have to find the money.

Whether or not I thought a Bolivian could get the necessary permission, I knew what was at stake in the question, and immediately realized which answer would work for me and which would cause me problems. I could easily have lied, as the man had no access to information that would allow him to catch me in a lie. It was his awareness that he had no way to check on what I was telling him that seemed to bother him. I was secure in the knowledge that whatever I said could not be verified or disproved. For instance, one rumor went around that I worked for the Central Intelligence Agency. Could anyone find out whether that was true? Did any of them even know what a CIA agent is or does? Even I am not sure what a CIA agent does or how to recognize one.

The question session soon turned into a lecture, with the union official and a colleague claiming to all present that people like me did not belong in the area and comparing me to the "gringos" who had conquered Bolivia. They demanded that I leave Quirpini and were only grudgingly satisfied when I told them that, in fact, I was planning to depart soon.

I was told that the plenary meeting that afternoon adopted a resolution demanding that I leave Quirpini immediately. A letter to that effect was supposed to be signed by the residents of Quirpini and then delivered to me. A similar resolution was adopted regarding the Peace Corps volunteer who had been working in the area for several months and lived in Yapusiri, where the union was particularly strong. As far as I knew, no one in Quirpini ever signed the letter, and I never heard anything further about the matter beyond rumors. The Peace Corps volunteer, on the other hand, was obliged to leave Yapusiri on short notice and move into San Lucas. He managed to substantially restore his position at the next sindicato meeting, which he attended, by pointing out that he was bringing considerable material goods to the communities where he worked. This showed that he was well-intentioned and able to help, that he responded to the authority of the sindicato, and that the sindicato could influence the path of the goods he was bringing to the area.

This incident illustrates how the peasant union depends for much of its authority on its ability to control movement and land, for the sindicato rose to prominence around the issue of land reform and is most powerful in communities that were once haciendas, where the land was given back to the campesinos after the revolution of 1952. The territorial nature of the union is underlined by its recruitment principle: anyone in the region who lives and has land outside San Lucas can join. By excluding people from San Lucas and holding meetings anywhere *except* in the regional political center, the sindicato combats the spatial element of San Lucas's regional power.[15]

The sindicato is just about the only powerful institution not located in town and not dominated by the town elite; on the contrary, its organization is premised on a critique of San Lucas's spatial dominance, an effort to decenter the town and disperse power into the rural communities. One of the sindicato's main raisons d'être was combating the way the town controlled how people and things moved in the region and exerting its own control.

The union leaders were in a sensitive position because they had been unable to influence my entry into the region. When I arrived in the area no one in San Lucas or Quirpini had suggested that I contact the union for permission to reside in a community, and I had had little contact with the institution. Quirpini's own union leader, Constantino Paco, had told me on a few occasions of his complete lack of confidence in the union. He only took up the position as a *cargo,* an obligation that all adult men share to fulfill a political role in the community, but he had no interest in the sindicato's role. My presence was an indication of the sindicato's weakness in the San Lucas valley. In the highlands, where the sindicato effectively constituted the local government, I could never have taken up residence in a community without the sindicato's permission.

Instead of going to the sindicato, I sought permission to reside in the area and conduct my research from various governmental and semi-governmental agencies and officials. Yet here I was not only in the area, but in the space of a union meeting, and moving around freely. Without realizing it, by going to the meeting I was flaunting my ability to elude the sindicato's control of my movement. I was able to move about without asking their leave or giving them much information about myself; they could not determine my "ends," or where I was going.[16] Seen in this light, the sindicato's effort to expel me and the Peace Corps worker was a way to reassert its ability to control movements in space.

The sindicato's anxiety about who I was and its inability to influence my behavior fed into each other, making my presence a threat. People compensated for this lack of knowledge with a proliferation of rumors about me, all of them efforts to explain why I had come to the area and why I was asking so many questions. These rumors accused me of being a miner in search of "white silver,"[17] a capitalist planning to expropriate peasant lands, a CIA agent or a fat-stealing lik'ichiri. Similar stories circulated about the Peace Corps worker.

These rumors were an effort to develop at least some vaguely comprehensible framework within which people could account for, and to some extent anticipate, my actions. Each of these narratives in which people roughly placed me implied some future action, as well as a past. I found that people who knew me best were more confident constructing my story in a more personal way, in which the particulars of my character played a larger part than generalized narrative models.

The insights I gained at the sindicato meeting gave a new dimension to my understanding of the relationship of place, movement, and power. Part of what is important about mobility for Quirpinis is its connection to knowledge: they learn about their social environment by keeping tabs on people's travels; they are intently aware that their own travel puts them on display, even as that travel constitutes an ideal way to gather information. The ability to control movement is a basic element of power, but this in turn depends on understanding people's intentions and capacities. Houses play a central role in struggles over movement and knowledge; they do not just articulate the movement of goods and people. Houses are also organized to facilitate control over the movement of information. They are key vantage points, as well as prime sites for strategically hiding and revealing information about oneself. The spatial strategy of the sindicato, as well as the planning and realization of the chapel (see the introduction), show that the politics of movement and control operates at multiple scales, and at different scales it is the means by which very different struggles are carried out.

The layout of houses is sensitive to the interplay of people wanting to know as much as they can about what is going on around them while maintaining control of what others know about them. Although nearly all the houses in Quirpini broadly follow the schema outlined above,[18] a wide variation is seen in the arrangement of rooms, and the absence and presence, and size, of the walls that run from structure to structure and enclose the patio. Some houses, especially those in Villcasana that are across the river from the main road, have several rooms separated by open spaces; the overall effect is a roughly delineated and relatively open, visible, and accessible patio. In contrast, most houses have at least low walls between the exteriors of the several structures, and some are enclosed by walls too high to see over and a wooden gate that can be locked. This last kind of patio is completely unobservable from the outside and presents the most clearly marked boundary between the inside and outside of the household. It is also difficult to see out from these patios, particularly as most houses have no windows, only slits for ventilation.

The most desirable location for a house is near the road, a location that affords easy access to transportation and to the *mercadería* trucks that periodically passed through the area selling dry goods at low prices. For some, this created the opportunity to open a small store to sell candy and soft drinks to passersby. The relatively high number of passersby meant that a household by the road had better access to information. While I was in Quirpini, I could already see the process of many families in Zona Quirpini rebuilding their houses close to the new road; many of the houses in the zona were lined up along the route of the old road. The trade-off was that many more people could see into the house, and more strangers passed by. Houses near the two roads passing through the community—the newly derelict one in Sakapampa and the main road in Zona Quirpini—generally have walled-in patios. With so much movement around the house, it is easy to see what is going on (just by sitting outside the house for a few minutes every once in a while, for instance), whereas keeping control of what the many passersby see is more challenging. In such places as Villcasana and Pumakuna, on the other hand, there is no automobile traffic, and most houses are noticeably open—some have almost no walls around the patio, and the few walls they have are generally low and can easily be seen over, though the patios of wealthier families are generally walled in.

Everybody conceals some possessions in their houses, particularly in the bedroom. People in Quirpini hide their money, the amount of food they have, legal documents, ritual objects such as miniature ceramic cattle that are used in petitioning the saints, and more. Indeed, wasis can be used to hide all sorts of things; for instance, once when Miguel's son Nelson was at my house during planting season, he saw a neighbor walking down the path toward our houses. He quickly retreated into my patio where he was hidden from the passing neighbor. When I asked why he had done this, he explained that had they seen each other the neighbor would have invited him to work at his corn planting the next day, and Nelson would have been obliged to accept, although he had no intention of going. Lying and accepting the invitation would have been one way to avoid the problem; however, hiding himself in the patio was an even better solution.

One of the most important realities about movement is that someone is always trying to control it. The regional elite of San Lucas maintain their position in part by exercising multifaceted control over the movement of people, goods, and information. The Sindicato Campesino is engaged in combating elite power on the very terms in which it establishes itself, namely, by taking control of space. The apparent success of the Church's chapel-building project came both when they made the concessions necessary to mobilize Quirpinis to come and build the structure, but, more profoundly, when Quirpinis incorporated it into their own spatial practice. Part of the price of this success was that the priest had to allow himself to be influenced by the chapel's proposed existence and promise to come to Quirpini more often. A central medium of the exercise of power is the ability to control other people's movement, or the movement of things that affect them, such as goods and information. A wasi is itself an instance of control applied to movement.

In talking about a lived space such as a wasi, then, it is not enough to describe the patterns of movement within, through, and around it. We have to understand that just as these movements presuppose and realize the schematic organization of the wasi, the organization of the house presupposes all sorts of potential movements and intentions, which it invites, repels, influences, or resists. It also presupposes certain possible changes in its own structure, according to the life stage of its inhabitants. People's actual movements are the product of their potential movements and the imposition of representations of those movements—the rooms, beds, stoves, doorways, and other physical features of the house impose such structuring representations of how a body might move. At any stage in its life, a wasi is progressively transformed by its inhabitants and places different constraints on people's actions; the schematic organization of houses itself follows a schematic development.

"Lived space," as I employ it here, is inspired by Lefebvre's use of the same term. For him, lived space is a synthesis of action and representation in a kind of contemplative residing (Lefebvre 1991, esp. 33–46; see also Shields 1999). Lefebvre posits a three-part dialectical dynamic to social space. "Spatial practice" is the physical, schematic, and enacted spatial reality of a society. "Representations of space" are the images of that spatial practice produced by (in modern societies) social scientists, planners, and bureaucrats. "Representational space"[19] is an interpretive response to these representational efforts, a synthesis of action and representation. It is space fully imbued with symbolic, often artistic, meanings that are, he implies, subversive of the representations of space. He also refers to representational space as "lived space."[20]

Opinions differ on how to interpret Lefebvre's dialectical analysis, but here I read it in a light that is most productive for my analysis of spatial practice in Quirpini. I conclude that "representational space" must in turn inform "spatial practice." Hence the dialectical interplay of movement and control is open-ended yet recursive. The way in which people actually inhabit a lived space such as a house is partly a response to the structuring representations that make up the physical and schematic order of the house. This order incorporates multiple influences, on multiple temporal scales. The most prominent influences include Quirpinis' actual subsistence conditions, the available technology and resources, and the demands of people's conception of themselves. Among these is the notion that to have a house without a wirjin to ch'alla at Carnival is, in some sense, not to have a house at all; that a decent family must have space in which to offer hospitality to guests; and that a house by the road without patio walls would feel exposed. Houses in Quirpini also incorporate a specific history, which includes multiple efforts to transform domestic space. So, for instance, the arrangement of rooms around a central patio owes more to historical Iberian household organization than to a pre-Colombian tradition; it is a colonial imposition. Also, the Bolivian Land Reform transformed the relationship between houses and land, as it severed non-market links between families and communities in different ecological zones. Such exercises of power continue, as in the government program to eradicate *chagas*, disease, in the name of which officials encouraged campesinos to separate human and animal living spaces, and to install ceilings. These efforts at control presuppose certain habits and practices on the part of their subjects; they are themselves interpretations of those practices, albeit interpretations that will put new constraints on them and are intended to transform them. This is why I call them "structuring representations" of spatial practices. Quirpinis' adaptive and creative, often resistant, responses to these structures are what produce lived space—a rereading of the structuring representations. The resistance to modernizing pressures that Stephenson (1999) identifies in Qaqachaka house-building practices is one example of "representational space" being transformed as it is lived. Lived space incorporates spatial practices that are in turn subjected to new structuring representations, which are in turn realized through creative and mobile responses.

The same dialectical progression plays out in the realization of various spaces and incorporates various struggles. The priest's plan to build a chapel, for example, was part of a long-standing struggle between the town and the highland communities. Here the process of creating new lived spaces is clearly historical. Similarly, the sindicato's refusal to allow anyone from San Lucas to join its organization, or its recurrent acts of what could be called "circulatory warfare," such as the 2003 roadblock on the one road into the San Lucas valley, enacts a struggle over the interpretation and control of the space in which people act.

At one level, a wasi is a structured collection of what Gibson (1979) calls "affordances," potential actions implied, even invited, by a situation. Yet a good part of the activity that a house invites is focused on the house itself—a house is the result of people's intentional action and is an object of desire. Beyond that, a good deal of the activity related to houses is focused on other activity that is in turn focused on the house. The spaces that make up a house are already represented in terms of what can move through them, and the movement through them is itself already represented by the doorways, gates, and walls through which people move.

A wasi, then, turns out to be a dynamic and reflexive site of multiple kinds of movement and processes. Each of these processes gives rise, at any moment of observation, to an apparently static configuration of rooms, houses, and so on. Yet these configurations are only provisionally, if at all, separable from the activities that produced them and continue to do so. For a wasi to be a wasi in the full sense, it must be implicated in all these processes, each one reflecting the intentional activities of the ever changing cast of people living in the house and those connected to them. Without recurrent movement, people coming and going, goods and information circulating, unless it is always being built, rebuilt, expanded, and improved, and were it not incorporated into the multigenerational movement of residences, a wasi would be still, or *ch'in* ("silent"), as people say of sleepy villages and unoccupied houses.

3 · *The Geography of Planting Corn*

Planting, Repetition, and Reciprocity

Corn-planting season struck me from the first as a moment when people in Quirpini were engaged with their social world in a particularly intense fashion. The long sequence of work parties followed by drinking sessions, the tremendous number of meals people shared, the repetition of everyone's shared activities, and the sheer level of attention that everyone around me was paying to the logistics and ethics of giving and receiving, meant that everyone was absorbed, mind and body, in their social relations. Planting corn is crucial to all Quirpinis' livelihoods, as corn is the main crop of the San Lucas valley and the largest single component of Quirpinis' diets. The planting, called *sara llank'ay,* is done in large work groups, recruited by each household through a form of labor reciprocity called mink'a. In mink'a, people gather to spend a full day working for one household, whose members feed the visitors and throw them a party. The household recruiting labor in this fashion is said to "mink'a" the invitees. Often, but not always, the inviting household is obliged to reciprocate the person-days of labor received, when the recruited households plant their own corn.

When Quirpinis plant corn, there is, of course, no immediately useful product—no visible product at all, in fact; the material result of planting will not be available for several months.[1] Nevertheless, a productive process is started and will continue until harvest as the corn sprouts, grows, and matures, and the members of the household weed, irrigate, and care for the plants. In corn-planting, households are situated in both a social and spatial geography. Planting reaffirms a household's relationship with the Pachamama, and at the same time reenacts and re-creates relationships with other households and individuals in an extended network of kin and friends.

Corn planting intersects with a number of different kinds of activities and movements, including irrigating, brewing, cooking, visiting, fetching firewood, drinking, eating, and playing music. The key space of intersection for these activities and movements, and their object, is a cornfield, or *sara chajra*. At the same time people's labor in planting corn temporarily transforms the relationship between fields and houses. During most of the year the chajras around a house are the house's appendages, the places where crops are grown to be taken into the house where they will be made into food (*mikhuy*). At corn planting this relationship is reversed, and the chajra becomes the final focus of all related activity; the work going on in the chajra becomes the justification for everything that has been done over the preceding weeks.

Each time people mink'a to plant corn, everything they do presumes and implies the times that their neighbors will plant corn or have already done so, both in that same year or other years. The people working in one field on any given day may well be working at another in a day or two, and probably were at yet another shortly before. Corn-planting season is a period of extremely intense work and socializing, all of which people share with a loosely defined mutual-aid network.

Because people plant corn every year, indeed many times every year, putting too much emphasis on what happens at an individual planting can be misleading. The various roles and elements of corn planting have names, and when people talk of these and partake in them their emphasis is clearly on the similarities the plantings share. Planting corn, then, can be understood as a regular activity whose elements are *textualized*, or *scripted*; in other words, whenever a household plants corn, the household members are doing the same thing they did the last time they planted corn, the same thing as their neighbors are doing when *they* plant corn.[2] The script of each of those activities, whether social, manual, or culinary, is itself made up of a series of scripts. There is, then, a way to plow, make chicha, invite people to your corn planting, and comport oneself when at someone else's corn planting. These techniques were all foreign to me when I began my fieldwork, and so each corn planting took on the character of a transformative event, at least in the sense that it represented a leap in my knowledge. As I learned how to do what had to be done at the plantings, however, they became more similar, more repetitive, and less like events in themselves, and in this my thinking came closer to that of people in Quirpini.

Corn planting is repetitive, of course, and people in Quirpini plant corn in a way that emphasizes its repetitive aspects, thus encouraging the similarity of one corn planting to another. It is repetitive not only in the sense that planting occurs many times every year, but it is also largely requires repetitive actions. Plowing, covering furrows, grinding peppers, stirring corn beer—all are actions that take effect only gradually through their own repetition. The planting season, more than other times of the year, is when the generic, or iterative (Derrida 1971), nature of Quirpinis' actions is most manifest. This minimizes the event-quality of what people are doing and emphasizes its resemblance to similar activities, as opposed to its contiguity with different activities. Their actions become relatively paradigmatic, that is, people's actions are focused to a considerable extent on the form of those actions rather than on their connection to previous or subsequent actions.[3] The "ethnographic present tense," which I employ frequently in this chapter, is particularly apt for narrating a situation in which Quirpinis act as if they are working from a shared script of actions that they have done before and will do again, rather than taking part in unique events.

The Sara Chajra through the Year

Planting is just one moment in a yearlong cycle of activities involving and transforming cornfields. An agricultural field changes constantly as a place; it evolves throughout the year in terms of what it is good for, what Quirpinis can do in and to it, and how they need to move in relation to it. Our starting point, then, is what people do to and around sara chajras over the rest of the year.

Some time during planting there is a change of seasons, from *chiri timpu*, or "the cold season," to *qumir timpu*, or "the green season," as the nighttime frosts of winter end and daytime temperatures become warm. Deciduous plants throughout the valley begin putting out leaves, grass sprouts everywhere, and with the start of rains in November, becoming heavy in December, agricultural areas start to become verdant. By late November all the corn plants have sprouted, and, aside from the fields planted in wheat and other late grains, the land is thoroughly green. Weeds also start growing, and all members of the family devote time to the endless task of keeping them at bay. After corn planting many families put in smaller crops of wheat or barley. None of these crops is very large, and rarely, if ever, are they planted using mink'a in Quirpini.[4] Until the rains begin, everyone is concerned with negotiating for as much irrigation water as possible.[5]

The rains start tapering off in late January, by which time the corn plants are fairly high. How tall the corn grows varies dramatically; depending on the quality of the soil and the amount of fertilizer a household acquires for its field, corn can grow nearly two meters high or may never grow above a single meter. The richest households can afford to buy fertilizer, whereas the poorest families have only the manure produced by their animals and whatever natural compost they can find.[6] In December and January people begin talking about one another's corn; they remark on corn that is particularly tall and healthy-looking or, less often, on fields of notably sad-looking corn.

By mid-February the first ears of sweet corn can be harvested. This is one of the great culinary treats of the year; harvested and boiled immediately, it is the tastiest corn I have ever eaten. Potatoes and the first sweet fava beans are also ripe around now, in time for Candelaria, a scarcely observed first-fruits meal. People told me that in times past, before it became possible to buy food like rice and noodles, the months before the early harvest were known as *yarqhay timpu*, or "hunger season," because food stores were running low. But February still marks the start of a month of truly delicious eating. Because the months of rain give rise to plentiful grass, sheep are producing enough milk for cheese and the animals are fat enough to slaughter for meat. By the end of February the first peaches become ripe.

The months of February and March are when people pay the most attention to corn and corn plants, for several reasons. People go into the fields to pick ears of corn at least once a day, and corn on the cob (*chuqllu*) reappears in people's diets. The cornstalk, or *wiru*, can also be eaten once the ears are gone; it is sweet, and people cut off a length and chew on it like sugarcane. Also, the cornfields are at their most beautiful now; everyone delights in the fields of green corn plants. And late February or early March is the time of Carnival, the huge and all-embracing fiesta that incorporates corn and various parts of the corn plant as important themes. People eat sweet corn, may steal stalks of corn from their neighbors' fields, they dance with corn, and they adorn their Carnival offerings to the Pachamama with flowers and cornstalks.

After March the remaining corn is left on the stalks to finish ripening and to dry. The only major work remaining is harvest, from early April to early May. Quirpinis normally harvest a field with the labor of their own household; if the field is too big for the household to harvest quickly, household members might hire a neighbor for *jornal*, a standard daily wage. When the corn is dry, some members again come to the field to remove and husk the ears of corn. These are taken into the house, where they finish drying and then are stored in a back room until they are needed. The cornstalks and leaves are carried off to be fed to cattle. At some time during the winter the adults in the family go through the dry corncobs and select the best kernels for next spring's planting.

Once the harvesting is completed, the field is once again bare. Goats are pastured on the stubble for as long as it lasts. With the subsequent harvests of wheat and other grains, and as the wild vegetation dies back in the fall, the terrain becomes open, bleak, and uniform. The field lies unworked and inactive through the winter months of June and July, until preparations for planting begin again the following August, near the end of winter.

Preparations

CALENDAR AND TIMING

Early August is the period that Poole (1984) calls the start of the calendar. It is the end of the coldest and driest time of year. Little vegetation is apparent in winter, as most of it dies back or is eaten by livestock in the fall. In late August the freezing night temperatures begin to moderate, grasses start growing, the first buds appear, and wild trees and plants throughout the valley come to life. The Pachamama is at her most active now, and the mallkus are walking about in the mountains. In many parts of the Andes, August is the time when "the earth is open" (Isbell 1985:164, 1974:117; Arnold 2006:145). This month, along with Carnival, is one of the two best times to carry out ritual libations (most notably to the mallkus for continued irrigation water) and is also when people mark their animals. It is a dangerous time as well, for the mallkus and the Pachamama can be very destructive; anyone who ventures into the mountains at night will likely be driven mad by the mallkus. August is a time of transformation and renewal, but it is not a good time for certain beginnings, such as marriages.

Quirpinis begin planting corn shortly after the local fiesta of Santa Rosa, on August 30, and end by the time of the regional fair celebrated for San Lucas's patron saint day, October 18. It used to be that the planting season in Quirpini could only start once the Otondo family, the only elite family resident in Quirpini and the community's biggest landowners, planted their corn. Adolfo Otondo still planted early in the season, but in the 1990s others might plant before him. There is a general movement of planting mink'as from the lower lands to the upper lands because the frost ends earlier at lower elevations. Households in the lower part of Quirpini, then, begin preliminary preparations—irrigating their fields and doing *barbecho*, or initial plowing[7]—in mid- to late August.

When preparing to plant corn, households must pay close attention to timing; each household keeps tabs on the families nearby to make sure it isn't planting on the same day as its neighbors. There are bound to be more than one hundred mink'as in about forty-five days during corn-planting season in Quirpini alone, and many people's mutual-aid networks extend to other communities, so there is always a likelihood that two families that would normally help each other might plant on the same day. This is unavoidable partly because the exact timing of a planting is fixed by processes that everyone has to initiate several days in advance, and whose progress cannot be perfectly predicted.

By the same token, households must decide which corn plantings they will attend. Large households have considerable flexibility, as they can send different members to different places. Often Miguel would go to one planting, perhaps with one of his older sons, while another son went to another planting, perhaps with his mother. In this way the family could spread its labor around fairly widely.

Mutual observation, always a key part of social life, becomes particularly intense during corn planting, as people need to coordinate their activities across households. Preparations for planting are largely public in nature and, as such, offer many opportunities for observation. When people begin preparing chicha, their neighbors for more than a kilometer around can tell from the continuous plume of smoke that they will be planting in a few days.

When household members repeatedly head up the mountainsides, returning with large bundles of firewood, anyone who sees them can anticipate that they will soon be making chicha. People pay the same sort of attention to plowing, a visit to request water from the water judge, taking corn to the mill and back, and so on. Each of these activities, which involve people moving about the land and provoking further circulation of objects and labor, is also a display, and sets information in motion. This movement of information informs people of the best time to invite others to their fields, ensuring that they will be able to attract their neighbors' labor when they need to, as well as to plan where they will take their own labor. I first became aware of this when people began to mention, casually, that a certain person would be planting in, say, three days. When I asked how they knew this, it generally turned out not that the person in question had told them but that the smoke of their fire indicated that the household was making chicha or the person was seen plowing across the valley. This information gives someone as good an idea of when members of a household will be planting than if told by the members themselves.

MUTUAL-AID NETWORKS

Each household in Quirpini maintains a loose network of family, neighbors, and friends to whom they turn for help in work, borrowing goods, support in conflicts, and so on. These networks are structured in two ways: first, some members are closer and others more distant; and, second, certain relationships are best suited to certain kinds of reciprocal exchange. The outer limits of any such network are undefined—no one could give an exhaustive list of the people they turn to for help. Seen from the outside, these mutual-aid networks form a dense and unbounded mesh of relationships. Yet rather than relating households as parts of some delineated or corporate whole, networks relate them as pairs of households with mutual obligations. They are made up of reciprocal actions, of people and things recurrently and predictably moving between and within households. Network relations are the stuff of a different sort of sociality than the community as a whole or the people who share an irrigation canal: such groups have a fairly clear membership, which looks the same from anyone's perspective, and members' mutual obligations are generally expressed in relation to the whole rather than to other individual members.

Unlike similar phenomena in Yura (Harmon 1987) and Chuschi, Peru (Isbell 1974, 1985), in Quirpini mutual-aid networks have no name and are never experienced as wholes; the relationships that comprise a network are referred to by terms such as ayllu (family) or *compadre/comadre* (ritual co-parent), by Spanish terms like *amigo* or *cuate* (friend), as well as by a host of individual kin terms, but there is no specific term for the aggregate of relationships. Networks are made up of the kin, neighbors, and friends of the members of the household, and, even more clearly than other social institutions, exist insofar as they are enacted, mainly through acts of mutual aid. Exchanging favors, visits, goods, and especially labor, as in corn planting, is the real substance of these social ties.

The relationships comprising a network are quite variable. For instance, Emiliana could always call on her sister, Satuka, for help because they were family, but they did not actually get along at all; they often fought and bitterly criticized each other when they were apart. Constantino Paco and Justiniano Cruz were not related to each other, but they had always been neighbors, were about the same age, and constantly helped each other; they were friends. Many friends formalize their relationship by becoming compadres, or co-parents, when one friend becomes godfather (*padrino*) or godmother (*madrina*) to the others' child.[8] Godparents and co-parents have specific roles and rights, in addition to the obligation to help one another; for instance, Anisa Villcasana, madrina of the marriage of Miguel Paco and Emiliana, frequently came over to mediate when they fought. When I first arrived in Quirpini, Genaro Mamani and Miguel Paco had terrible relations even though they were close neighbors. At some point they suddenly reconciled, and the two families began helping each other with work and making periodic visits. Because they were neighbors, and shared many close allies (such as Anisa and her husband), they did not need to have a strong friendship in order to cooperate regularly. The relations that make up networks within Quirpini invariably involve some element of reciprocity, and are enacted as relations between equals.

One kind of relationship that is not normally enacted in corn planting is the patron-client relations many Quirpinis maintain with members of the San Lucas elite. Adolfo Otondo, for instance, was an important ally of many people in Quirpini, but he rarely worked at anyone's mink'a, and on the few occasions that I saw him do so, he made it clear that he was doing it as a favor, not because he was obliged. Had he entered fully into the reciprocity underlying corn planting, he would have undermined his elite position. The networks of people who migrate frequently also include many who will never be anywhere near Quirpini or directly involved in corn planting there.

Mink'a is the most involved form of labor reciprocity practiced in Quirpini.[9] Within a household, no debts of labor or other matters are calculated; instead, these are organized through clear but rather flexible roles based on gender, age, and status. Close relatives of household members, as well as close friends, can be called on for small favors, which are also only calculated in the loosest sense. People who are fairly close usually *ayni* each other, that is, they exchange the same amount of the same kind of labor. People might employ ayni for roof repairs or to alternate doing a task with someone else. Ayni is a straight exchange of equal amounts of labor, with no additional payment or hospitality necessarily involved.

Mink'a is more complex, and in some versions seems to be a variation of ayni. The term refers to an arrangement whereby a person or household arranges to have a number of people do some work together (in Quirpini, it should be one day's work, the smallest unit for calculating labor time). People mink'a in order to do tasks that require a lot of work all at once, like re-roofing a house or planting a large field. In exchange for the work received, the host gives those who are helping a generous meal, and all the chicha and *trago* they can drink. In Quirpini the host always joins in the work; when a member of the San Lucas elite invites campesinos to work for him "in mink'a," he himself never does so. A striking feature is that in Quirpini, as in many parts of the Andes, one term designates both a situation in which this exchange of work for hospitality completes the exchange, and one in which completion comes only when the relationship is reversed, and the host of the first work party helps those who helped him, receiving their hospitality in exchange. The San Lucas elite, needless to say, engage only in the first kind of mink'a. Among Quirpinis, no one marks the difference, and when I asked how the work was organized, people always told me that the labor in sara llank'ay mink'a was reciprocated.

Mayer's (1974, 2002) analysis of Andean reciprocity suggests, and my experience confirmed, that different forms of reciprocity are not always clearly distinguished. The second, balanced, kind of mink'a shares something of the logic of ayni (Isbell [1974] even refers to it as "ayni-minka"). The dividing line between mink'a and ayni, as they are understood and practiced in Quirpini, is somewhat hazy. On one occasion a woman told me that she had mink'a-d a friend to pasture her goats. Puzzled that she should use unequal exchange for pasturing goats, I asked what the arrangement was, and it turned out that the women had alternated pasturing both of their herds together. "But isn't that ayni?" I asked her, to which she replied that, sure, it was ayni. Clearly the lexical difference mattered little to her. Ayni and mink'a, then, are apparently treated as differentiated versions of one practice more than as two different kinds of interaction. During my first corn-planting season in Quirpini, I found it difficult to ascertain the common name for the work relation people employed. I had expected it to be "mink'a," but when I asked, most people told me it was "ayni." The next year (when I knew people better, and my Quechua allowed me to more easily follow other people's conversations), I heard only references to "mink'a-ing."[10]

At times Quirpinis will hire labor for a wage instead of using ayni or mink'a. A household might pay people to plant a secondary field or to help with a small piece of work. Women whose husbands are migrating, and who are thus cash-rich and labor-poor, might hire men to do some work in their fields. There is an implicit tension in such hiring among Quirpinis, because wage labor is understood as an inherently hierarchical relationship. While I was conducting my fieldwork, the existence of wage labor had not dramatically changed the prevailing ethos of equality. No one, however, hired people to plant corn in the main field near their house; to do so would have represented a dramatic break with the terms of social life in the community.

When households mink'a each other, when those who share networks work, eat, and drink together, the egalitarian parts of a household's network are manifested in their fullest form. At any one mink'a this sharing takes the form of an unequal exchange of work for food and drink, but in the corn-planting mink'a, the most common form, the work received will in principle be returned, and the network will manifest itself as a group based on relations of balanced reciprocity. In corn-planting mink'a Quirpinis enact overlapping sets of reciprocal relations centered on single households.

MAKING CHICHA

Among the Catholic families of Quirpini, preparing, offering, and drinking chicha is one of the most important elements of the hospitality so central to mink'a-ing. A family must offer chicha in order to engage in any circulation of labor beyond the simple exchange of ayni.

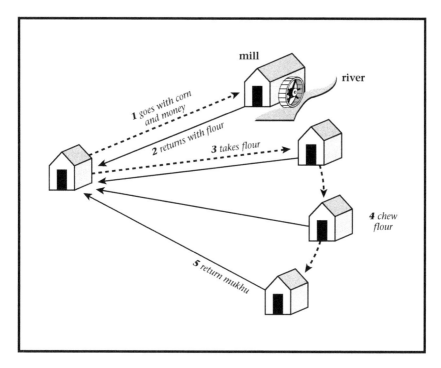

Figure 3.1. Diagram of the circulation of corn and mukhu for chicha.

Making chicha is a complex socio-chemical procedure that can only be accomplished with the help of the household's networks, and involves the household in several kinds of circulation. The preparation work largely takes place in the house patio, and all the ancillary labor results in products that are taken to the wasi. Most of the preparation is done by women or children.

To start with, the household must collect enough firewood to keep a fire going for several days. This means turning to a number of close members of the household's network and asking them to get the firewood; usually this is done as a favor or in ayni. If it is done in ayni, the favor will of course have to be returned.

The corn for chicha must be ground into flour at one of the water mills in Cumuni, whose position at the head of the valley guarantees that river water will always be plentiful there. Most people have no burro, so either they carry a large bag of corn in a poncho on their back or, more often, borrow a burro.

I was told that borrowing a burro, like asking someone to fetch firewood, incurs a small, vaguely calculated debt. Unlike exchanges of labor, the loan cannot be repaid in kind. Getting corn milled generally takes the better part of a leisurely day; the mill grinds slowly, and it is necessary to stay and keep an eye on the process.

The household then calls on kin and neighbors to chew some of the flour into a paste called *mukhu*; the enzymes and yeast in people's mouths begin the fermentation process. The women of the household divide it up into small bags and send their children to the houses of several close kin to ask for help in making the mukhu. There the women and children (and sometimes the men) of the house will spend a few hours chewing on wads of meal, each wad for a few minutes, until the bag is entirely empty. (See Figure 3.1 for a diagram of the movement of the corn during its transformation into meal and mukhu.)

When the meal is chewed and the firewood collected, chicha brewing can begin. This takes two days, during which time the chewed meal is boiled in water carried from the river, mixed with the other meal and boiled some more. When all the cooking is done, it is poured into large clay pots and left for two to five days to ferment.

Few households have all the many containers needed to prepare a big batch of chicha (a vat made from an oil drum to boil the chicha, a number of clay pots of varied sizes for fermenting and storage), so one element of preparing chicha is borrowing the needed pots. Many neighboring households routinely exchange such pots or else the borrowing just becomes part of a more general exchange of favors.

The start of chicha making determines the approximate time when a family can plant. Once household members begin preparing chicha, they have set a frame of about four days in which they will have to plant.

Other preparations include acquiring the food needed to feed the guests, and arranging for oxen and drivers. Any decent corn-planting mink'a in Quirpini includes a midday meal of *pikanti*, a dish of chicken, rice, and potatoes flavored with hot peppers. All these are favorite foods in the area, none easily available. Rice does not grow anywhere near the San Lucas region and can only be acquired in stores in town or from traveling dry-goods sellers. Most families raise chickens, but they are a valued resource and parting with them is a significant expense. Those who do not have enough chickens to offer a piece to each guest have to buy some. Usually the potatoes must be purchased or obtained by barter from a highland household. The sauce is spiced either with powdered peppers bought in San Lucas or with peppers from the Pilcomayo valley.

The competition for status implicit in mink'a leads to a kind of food inflation. I was told that until only a few years earlier the standard planting food was a corn dish called *sara pila*, but that as people acquired increasing amounts of money through migration, chicken became a must. In my experience, only Victor Condori, a relatively poor widower, mink'a-d without offering chicken (instead, his daughter made a spicy dish of *chuñu,* or freeze-dried potatoes). His mink'a was held the same day that a wealthy and respected neighbor was planting, and hardly anyone turned up at Victor's. He dejectedly commented to me that people went elsewhere because "they want chicken."

Although all the food and chicha is prepared in the house, the focus ultimately turns to attracting people to the chajra on planting day; until the field is planted, the food and chicha are consumed only in the chajra. By keeping these goods in controlled motion, each household is best able to influence the movement of other goods and of people, bringing them to the chajra. Chicha, in particular, is the fruit and concretization of the productive relations and the patterns of movement that go into making it. It is also, as we will see, treated as the ultimate end product, and the necessary condition, of corn planting.

FINAL PREPARATIONS

People invite others to their planting only a day or two in advance. They do so by sending children to visit each household they want to invite to announce that there will be a planting the next day. The invitations rarely come as a surprise, for by now everyone pretty well knows who is planting when, and also who is likely to invite them to the planting. Sometimes an uninvited guest will join the work; this might be a friend who wants to lend a hand, someone who wishes to form a relationship with the planting household, or a passerby. Indeed, it would be rude if a passerby did not join in the work for at least a few minutes, and accept a cup of chicha.

In inviting people, a household must primarily consider how much work needs to be done based on the size of the field(s) to be planted. Any work done in mink'a must be completed in a single day, so if there are too few men, they will have to work especially hard and into the night. On the other hand, too many attendees might require an unwelcome expenditure of food and drink, or mean that there is not enough to go around. Every person who comes to help is also a potential debt of labor, so inviting too many people can create awkward situations later on. The household must also arrange for a sufficient number of teams of oxen, and people to drive them. One team of oxen will do, but it is better to have at least two. In mink'a-ing, I was repeatedly told, the oxen are always borrowed, never hired.

Within the temporal frame set by chicha preparation, a household can do its final plowing and irrigation. A few days before household members expect to plant, they do another barbecho and then irrigate again. The timing of irrigation depends on the availability of water and is arranged with the water judge. This makes it less likely that close neighbors will plant at the same time, as they often share a single canal.

After the irrigation, usually done by youths or older children under adult supervision, the field will be dry enough to plant in two to three days, a judgment that is generally clear by the day after irrigation.

By the time planting begins, the house, the field, and the planting family have already been firmly situated in a geography of circulating water, people, favors, and goods. The same people making the channels for water have offered ch'allas to the mallkus every August, and have served, or will serve, as the yaku alkalti, not to mention having repeatedly dug out the local canal. Multiple elements of preparation for planting have already placed each household in mutual-aid networks connecting them to their closest allies.

Planting Day

The culmination of all this movement and work is planting day. On this day everything is focused on the chajra: all the prepared food and drink is eaten and drunk in the field; relationships cultivated over the last year and longer are once again realized as people come and work in the field or prepare food; and the field itself is plowed and watered and make ready for planting. The corn will be planted, and the sara chajra will be transformed.

PRELIMINARIES

Shortly after sunup, someone from the planting household goes from house to house reminding people to come. The bulk of those attending start out at *las diez* (ten o'clock) or *p'unchayña* (daytime now); at that time the sun is well above the high ridge that marks the eastern wall of the valley. Whoever is lending oxen to the planting household brings them early in the morning and stays around while they are fed grain mash—a special treat for their hard day of work ahead. The women who will help cook lunch and dinner begin arriving now and head directly into the house. The plowmen start to appear as well, to barbecho the field before planting. The field has been untouched since it was irrigated a few days before, and the soil is hard and caked together. The other invitees turn up one by one during the final barbecho, as the male head of the household greets them and offers them chicha. Some stand around to one side of the chajra to drink, chat, and inspect their tools for a few minutes, while others, often youths and children, stroll out to the field to break up clods, or *khuliyay*,[11] with *kullpanas*, the tools that will later be used to cover the corn furrows.

PREPARING SEEDS, *Q'UWARA*

After the final barbecho is done, a couple of women, usually of the planting household, bring out the seeds. These they carry to the middle of the field in large bags (usually purchased) called *costales*.[12] The women sit by the bag and break up some boughs from the *mulli* tree, an evergreen that grows all over the valley, and place these boughs in the bag. Mulli has a pine-like fragrance, and I was told that it kept bugs (*khurus*) away from the germinating seeds. Then they put some of the seeds into smaller bags for the sower to carry later on.

After these women leave, another woman, usually a senior woman of the planting household, comes out carrying a potsherd in which she has placed some fat (*untu*), a resinous substance called *q'uwa*, and incense. These ingredients have several sources: the fat comes from local cattle or pigs, the potsherd is household detritus, the other ingredients are acquired by trading with llameros. The whole substance is called *q'uwa* or *q'uwara* and will be burnt as an offering to the Pachamama, the female deity or presence who, as discussed in chapter 2, governs fertility, the earth, and many human endeavors. In this case I was told that the q'uwara would help insure a good crop. The woman sets the q'uwara down in the middle of the field, ignites it, and leaves once she is sure it is burning. A burning q'uwara is dangerous, especially for men, and I was repeatedly warned to stay away from these offerings. One man told me that since the Pachamama was drawn by the odor of the smoke and came to eat it, she might eat anyone else she found nearby as well. Generally the

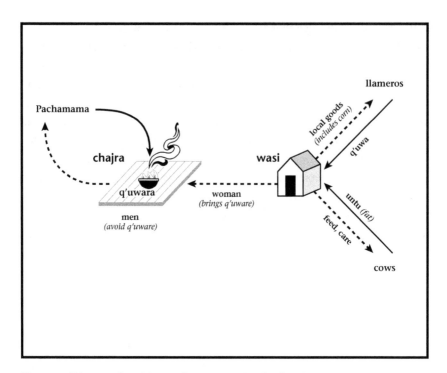

Figure 3.2. Diagram of positions and movements involved in q'uwara.

men pay little overt attention to all this, and no one begins working until the offering has finished burning. The Pachamama is the final element that must be present in the field (Figure 3.2), and her presence completes the displacement of the center of domestic space from the buildings around the patio (the usual locus of the house's Pachamama) to the field, while at the same time highlighting the dual gendering of the chajra.

STARTING THE PLANTING

Now everything is in place for the planting to begin: the oxen and their drivers are ready to begin making furrows; the seeds are sitting out in the chajra; the women are cooking in the house; one or two women are in the field to drop the seeds in the fresh furrows; the many pampirus are present, ready to enter the field and begin covering the seeds in their furrows; and the Pachamama has come and consumed her offering.

Now starts most of the men's work, although the women in the house have already been working for more than an hour. Once a few furrows have been plowed, however, everyone present must ch'alla. The field's owner, the *wasiyuj*,[13] is very insistent and peremptory in calling everyone over to drink, repeatedly urging the men to put down their tools and pressuring those who are slow to respond. This is the only situation in a mink'a where I saw the host ordering people around in this way. For most of the day, the wasiyuj is markedly low-key with his guests, rarely giving direct instructions to anyone. Since all the men fully understand all the roles they and their fellows perform, they can work with little or no instruction.

The women come out from the kitchen and sit with the men in a circle in the field just beyond the area that has already been planted, and someone serves chicha all around, a cup or two for everyone. Before drinking, everyone ch'allas, pouring a small amount of chicha on the ground. This is understood as a way of returning corn to the Pachamama to ensure that the corn will grow so that it can be made into chicha again next year. It is this ritual that led me to understand the extent to which planting is focused not on what is ultimately produced—corn as a source of sustenance or as the staple of regional cooking—so much as on the next planting. In one sense, people act as if the point of planting is so they can plant again next year. As one man told me when I asked why we were drinking at the start of planting, it is "to drink next year."[14]

PLOWING AND PLANTING

The most common plowing technique is for one team of oxen to break a furrow across the lower end of the field, followed by a woman who drops seeds into the furrow from the small woven bag she carries. She is called the *iluri*[15] and is usually from the planting household. The plow, always driven by a man, is pulled by a team of oxen. The furrows should be straight and parallel, and as close to one another as they can while allowing room for the corn to grow. The plowman (*llank'aj*) and his team make a furrow across the field, following the contour of the ground so that rain and irrigation water will not run off and erode the soil.

The plowman constantly urges the oxen on with cries of "Wiy! Wiy!"[16] and occasional flicks of the long switch he carries in his free hand. When he reaches the edge of the field, he turns the plow around in an arc off the edge of the field, and then begins the next furrow in the opposite direction from the first, proceeding in this way back and forth for the entire length of the field. A few feet behind him walks the iluri, dropping seeds in the furrow at short intervals.[17] She follows him on each pass, waiting while he turns the plow around at the end of each furrow. From time to time she goes to the costál of seed in the middle of the field to replenish her small bag; as the planting nears the middle of the field, someone moves the bag farther into the unplanted area.

Most of the men who attend are needed to *pampay,* or flatten, the furrows. As the llank'aj and iluri pass, these *pampirus*[18] come into play. Each carries a kullpana, which can be a pickaxe or a stick about three feet long with a thick piece of wood attached perpendicularly at the end to form a T. Swinging the kullpana across the new furrows in a back-and-forth motion, the pampirus advance in parallel down the field, each covering the seeds and smoothing the soil for his designated section, or *surqu*. A *surqu* can vary from 1.5 meters wide to 4 or even 5 meters, depending on how many pampirus there are and the field's dimensions. The pace and timing of this work is determined by the speed and number of plowing teams. By the end of the day, each pampiru will have gone the length of the field in this fashion, covering and smoothing a section of each furrow. Pampay is exhausting work but requires little skill. It was the only work in the field I was allowed to do at planting. The plowman/planter and the pampirus work perpendicularly to each other, covering the field completely with their two motions.

This is how most of the day is spent, the planters going back and forth across the field behind the yoked oxen as the pampirus rhythmically beat and smooth the planted furrows. Although fields vary dramatically in size and shape, it became clear to me, as people explained the process or drew pictures of fields for various purposes, that their basic concept of a chajra was square in shape. The largest fields require well over twenty pampirus and two or three pairs of oxen to plant them in a day. At irregularly shaped parts of a field, a man or boy may go and dig furrows with a pickaxe, dropping and covering the seeds himself; this is the only situation in which men put corn seed in the ground.

From time to time as the planting continues, a couple of people, often young men and sometimes the male household head, go about serving chicha to all those in the field. Each person takes a quick break to drink and then goes back to work. As always, the drinker first pours a small amount on the ground for the Pachamama, returning the corn to the soil.

COOKING

While the men and the iluri are planting, the rest of the women cook in the kitchen. During the day they prepare lunch and a smaller dinner for everyone present, and also supervise the serving of chicha to the men all day long. Whereas the men's work is relatively simple and repetitive, involving just a few roles, the tasks of the smaller number of women require much more careful coordination. First, the dishes are not always the same. The standard meal is pikanti, but it can be prepared in various ways and accompanied by a number of side dishes; some initial decisions have to be made about the overall meal. Second, cooking pikanti involves multiple preparatory steps. Ideally these are done simultaneously, so the available labor needs to be carefully allocated, and the work must be timed. For instance, the sauce for pikanti involves *uchu* peppers cooked in oil and salt. Someone has to grind the large number of peppers used, which are then fried with the other ingredients. At the same time the chicken must be cooked. It is preferable to put the sauce on the chicken while both are still hot, so timing is important. Others must prepare the rice and potatoes, necessary side dishes. At least one woman spends much of the morning washing dishes and pots.

All this joint work means that the women talk much more than the men do in the field. The women's work requires greater coordination, as they are in much closer physical proximity, all gathered together in a patio. Whereas men working in the fields might be silent for minutes at a time, each absorbed in his own task and physically separate from those around him, women in the house constantly interact, exchanging instructions and advice, talking to their children, and chatting about whatever topic is at hand.

In addition, the coordinating role is more meaningful in cooking than in planting. Whereas for men, the male head of the landowning household makes his authority felt as little as possible, and spends much of his time serving his guests, the coordinator of cooking work has a more demanding task. She need not be the female head of the household. On the occasions when I was able to get a good sense of who was in charge of the cooking, it was often a middle-aged woman respected for her intelligence, responsibility, and cooking ability. Certain women would find themselves in this position repeatedly. I never heard the position given any name, and I was not able to establish how a certain woman would be selected for the role, but it was clear that this position was granted along with certain other kinds of status. In this it was the opposite of the role of the wasiyuj outside—any man with land can be wasiyuj for his household's corn-planting. While every pampiru can expect to be a wasiyuj sometime as a matter of course (either during the same season or later in his life course), some women dominate the coordinating role, and others take it up only rarely, or never.

This also means that, as Gose (1994) has pointed out, the wasi is ruled by a very different ethos than is the chajra. Among men in the field, hierarchies of power and status are minimized. In planting, the field is dominated by a male, public, egalitarian sociality, whereas the house is the place of female, domestic, hierarchical relations. Insofar as mink'a has a message, this difference plays a part in it: nearly everything about the mink'a is focused on the men in the field rather than the women in the house. The event is not called "cooking" or even "sowing" but "plowing": it is named after a male role. In addition, the men are outside and very much on display. The men will call any passerby over, as I described above. In contrast, the women are hard to see from outside the house and do not interact as much with those outside. The public face of the corn-planting mink'a is one of equality, while hierarchy is kept behind the scenes, in the house.

LUNCH

Lunch is generally served in the early afternoon. The exact time depends on when it is fully prepared, and when the men have completed enough of the field—usually just less than half. When the women start bringing out pots of food, the plough stops and each pampiru finishes his furrow, puts down his tool, and strolls over to where the women are gathering. Lunch is eaten in a part of the field that has not yet been planted, usually at or near the center—not far from where the seeds were placed in the morning. The men kneel or squat in a rough semicircle facing the women, who sit in no particular order among the pots, their legs tucked under their skirts. As always when Quirpinis share food within a group, a cloth is put down in the middle of the circle, and on it are piled boiled corn, toasted wheat flour, and boiled fava beans. The women fill the enameled metal plates, passing them from one to the other as each adds something from one of the pots—rice, potatoes, meat, or pepper sauce. When each plate is ready, someone, often a young girl of the planting household, takes it to one of the men. The women eat after the men have all been served, and chicha is served continuously, usually by a youth. There is always a second course, which in my experience was a corn dish called *sara pila.* The two dishes are normally too much to eat, and many people end up carrying corn home, perhaps along with some of the grains and beans that were placed on the cloth.

When everyone is done eating and the excess food has been packed away, the drinking contest begins. To start it off, the man and woman of the house stand next to each other just outside the circle of people, each bearing a *pulu,* a long, curved gourd with a hole in one end, filled with chicha.[19] They both begin drinking from their pulus, racing to finish first, while everyone watches with great amusement. Everyone I asked about this contest said that it could predict how the corn would grow, although no one seemed to be sure or even very concerned about how to interpret the augury. In any case the contest is repeated many times, as all the adults present are expected to take part. Everyone sees it as tremendously amusing and vaguely suggestive; the men and women are matched up by ad hoc designation, so the whole thing ends up looking like an extended joke about inappropriate sexual behavior.[20]

At lunch, the gender dualism that is so central to planting is made manifest but inverted. During the productive part of the day—when the men (and the single iluri) are sowing and the women are making food, everyone observes a fairly strict gender segregation. This is maintained even when the women bring out the q'uwara, since the men must get away from the burning offering. At lunch, the men and the women come together as complements, the women serving food and the men eating. They come together again as opposed parts of a whole in the drinking competition. In other words, they come together to consume the fruits of their labor, but instead of eating and drinking indoors or in a patio, as Quirpinis usually do, they eat in the field, the space the men have been working in. This is one of many indications that in mink'a the normal relationship of production and reproduction, and of male and female realms, are inverted.

By now everyone is stuffed and a bit drunk. They sit or lie on the ground for a few more minutes, chatting and joking, until they arrive at a sense that it's time to get going again. The women begin carrying the pots back to the house, where they will prepare dinner, while the men and the iluri slowly make their way back to the plough to begin planting again. Then they take up the same rhythm as in the morning, the pampirus advancing slowly while the planters crisscross the field. This continues until the field is completely planted; work may be over by mid-afternoon, but sometimes it continues until nightfall.

SUPPER, DRINKING, AND THE NEXT DAY

The plowmen and iluri finish work first, and the plowmen immediately lead their teams off to one side of the field, unyoke them, and give them something to eat. The iluri usually goes inside, while the pampirus finish covering the last furrows. By the end of the day everyone is quite tired, sometimes exhausted. The pampirus head to the house, leaning their tools against the outer wall as they enter. Everyone drifts into the largest room in the house, or sometimes the patio, and sits down on whatever chairs or benches are available, if any. Hardly anyone leaves at this point, before eating. Some women will already be in the room, while others are preparing to serve plates of food. As is the custom, the men sit on most of the available seats or benches along the side walls of the room. The women primarily sit on the floor, close to the entrance. People do not usually talk as much as at lunch because they are tired, but there is some joking. Dinner is simple, one or two plates of boiled wheat, called *riku pila*. Everyone eats fairly quickly, and when dinner is done, all begin to ch'alla.

First, the male head of the household brings out large ceramic containers (*cántaros*) of chicha and presents one each to the men who drove the plows. This is called their *t'inka* (a gift in recognition of a favor). Each plowman then designates a *kamachi*, a man who serves chicha from his cantaro. In effect, the household is giving to the plowmen the privilege to serve chicha to others, to play host in a small way. Giving the chicha to the plowmen to offer to the others again identifies the corn seeds that have been going into the ground with the chicha that they will become.

Presently some other people designated by the field's owners begin serving *trago*, diluted (but still powerful) cane alcohol, from bottles. Trago is served in little cups, which make their way around the room like the larger mugs of chicha. When the initial cantaros of chicha are finished, some women continue serving from other containers; the drinks are no longer served via the plowmen. The ideal way to drink in a group is to alternate between chicha and trago. Chicha is associated with women, and trago, also called *qhari aqha* or "male chicha," is considered masculine. The reasoning for this gendering, I was told, is that chicha is made by women, whereas trago can only be bought from the still in town with money, something men acquire in their travels for labor. As a general rule, ceremonial events should contain a multitude of male/female pairings, a complementary duality that indicates completeness.[21]

At this point, with everyone eating and drinking inside the house, and with gender dualism restored to the interior space, the inversion of chajra and wasi that was effected during planting has been negated. Once again the house is the transformative center of this particular homestead, the surrounding fields an exterior space that generates the material to be transformed. The next day, and the day after, another house's domestic geography will be inverted and restored in the same manner.

After dinner some people slip away to sleep, usually in the face of their hosts' strenuous objections. As the drinking proceeds, more people leave, often using some pretense such as having to go to the bathroom. Those who remain become increasingly talkative and festive as they drink, which they may continue doing for the next few hours; sometimes someone pulls out an instrument and plays. As the night proceeds, some begin to fall asleep, either in the main room or in a side room, and others just become extremely drunk. One of the most succinct descriptions of the celebration I heard was: "After work we eat, then drink until we fall asleep. The next day we drink until there's no chicha left."

In Sakapampa, the celebration after planting takes a slightly different form. Most of the musicians in Quirpini are from Sakapampa, and the music of Carnival in particular is almost entirely dominated by men from this zona; in addition, Sakapampa is seen by everyone in Quirpini as more traditional than the other zonas. Here, at the end of planting, several men appear in the field playing the long flutes associated with Carnival, on which they play the unique Carnival tune of the current year (see chapter 4). The flautists lead everyone into the house, where they play the Carnival tune and dance in a circle for much of the night. In the morning they play again. Everyone I talked to about the music in Sakapampa told me that it used to be the custom throughout Quirpini to play music and to dance after planting, but in Villcasana and Zona Quirpini people had forgotten this custom.

A few women of the house rise early the next morning and prepare breakfast, often a whole-wheat porridge. Some men are usually still awake, and others begin stirring. Everyone eats, some of them leave, and those remaining begin drinking again; a few more visitors may drop by. The mood is quiet, as people are generally hung over and tired. A few people will stay around for most of the day, eventually leaving when the chicha is finished; by now many have already gone off to attend another planting, while others have gone home to rest or work.

The pattern of activity I have described in this section takes place, with some variation, at least a hundred times in Quirpini alone during the planting season, as every household plants corn, and some hold more than one mink'a if they have fields in separate locations. Many nonresidents have land in Quirpini as well; those with local kin ties generally employ mink'a to plant corn. This is also one of the most intensely social times of the year, as most of the work people do is for other families, and much of it they do with members of other households. The intense social character of corn-planting season is matched only by Carnival, which is in many ways its opposite, or complement.

All the adults and young people in the community spend this time crisscrossing the land for work visits, in a kaleidoscopic forming and reforming of household networks. Everyone will be part of a hosting household, and will be guest repeatedly, each time in the company of a different cast of characters, often a variation on the cast of the previous day's work. This is the time when people exert the most continuous and vigorous shared effort. In one stretch Miguel Paco and Emiliana spent three consecutive days working, interspersed with three nights of drinking. An adult can expect to attend ten or more plantings in a year.[22] By the time the fiesta of San Lucas comes around, people are exhausted and ready for the slower pace of planting less labor-intensive crops.

What Has Been Produced?

Here I elaborate on the role that sara llank'ay mink'a plays in three creative processes. The first two are the production of a network of relations and of corn; both of these turn on the third—the production of the chajra as a place, particularly in relation to, and in contrast with, the wasi.

The crucial social form through which planting is done are networks, through which people bring others to their houses and fields on planting day as well as during the weeks of preliminary activities. Each household maintains a unique set of relationships with other households, enacted mainly through visits for reciprocal labor, lending (*mañay*), and socializing. These patterns of visits vary in their intensity and content according to the kind of reciprocity they involve.

Unlike among the Yura of Harman's (1987) account, mutual-aid networks in Quirpini do not correspond to, or constitute, any clear territory or bounded group, such as the community, the zonas, or the irrigation canals do. Instead, the geography they define is a terrain—an articulated collection of locations and features within a larger space. In talking about corn planting and mink'a, it is somewhat misleading even to refer to the people doing the work as Quirpinis, since this is a time of year when people do very little *as* Quirpinis, beyond calculating when they may start planting. In practice, people's networks mostly include fellow community members largely because the many social events that do bring Quirpinis together tend to create a multiplicity of ties among Quirpinis, and partly because the community is internally contiguous but separated from nearby communities by uninhabited areas. Yet nothing that people in Quirpini or, as far as I know, in other campesino communities of the area do in planting presumes or alludes to the community or the zonas. They do not invoke them ritually; they do not visit any sites that would relate them directly to the community (such as the school). Quite the opposite happens—the school owns some fields, and the members of the junta escolar, the school's governing committee, must organize a planting mink'a as if they were the field's owners. During this time of year, the school becomes, as much as possible, just another planting household.

Planting season in much of the rural Andes is a defining social moment, but in Quirpini it forms an opposite social pole from Carnival, which involves the enactment of large-scale corporate social groups. By mink'a-ing, everyone makes the greatest use of the network of kin, neighbors, and friends that throughout the year comprise the core of their own social world.

In Yura, over the course of a planting season, mink'a enacts egalitarian relationships, since everyone in a given rancho attends everyone else's planting, and so the unequal relations at one are reversed later on (Harman 1987). In Quirpini people do not necessarily return the labor they receive, nor are they expected to. There is an ideal way of mink'a-ing, in which two people exchange attendance at each other's plantings, but I was told on several occasions that this was not necessary. Not everyone seemed to have the same sense of what they were owed—I heard a few men mention that they would not go to so-and-so's corn planting because he had not come to theirs, but occasionally I asked someone if a person whose planting he was going to attend had come to his planting and was told no, with no apparent concern. I counted the mink'a visits made by members of Miguel Paco's family during the planting season of 1993; they worked more than forty person-days at other people's corn-plantings, although only twenty-two people came to theirs. Nearly everyone they invited came, so they were clearly aware that they were giving more labor than they received. Insofar as I could tell, they were motivated by a combination of the desire to help their neighbors (and to be seen doing so) and by the prospect of free food and drink. The social bonds enacted in corn-planting mink'a can easily become non-egalitarian in nature, although they are always characterized as utterly equal.[23] Even the ideally egalitarian networks enacted in corn-planting mink'as, then, reproduce hierarchies.

In extending invitations and asking for favors in the course of preparing and completing a planting mink'a, members of the inviting household enact a number of fluid groups, such as "those who will *mukhu* for us" and "those who will help us plant"; those called on enact the inviting household as a momentary center of their separate activities when they respond to the call. That the wasi/chajra is the defining center of their shared role is clearest for those who come on planting day, as they spend the day working together. In a given year these groups are ephemeral; but when the same invitations and convergence are performed over and over by a similar group of people, the relationships gain a certain persistence and become attributes not only of the whole of the bilateral relationships between households but also of the mass of common relationships that all the parties to a household's network share.[24]

Although activities in corn planting are fundamentally dedicated to the production of corn through the planting of corn seeds, corn hardly makes an appearance. It is particularly absent from the male, public part of the planting, remaining instead under the control of women and thus under wraps to a certain extent.

In the public part of planting, the actual corn stays almost entirely out of sight to most participants—it is kept in a bag in the middle of the field, where only the women handle it. The corn seeds follow a course from storage inside the wasi, to a costal in the field, to the iluri's hand, and then to burial in the chajra; they are never on display.

Corn that is not intended for planting does make a limited appearance during the event, but here, too, it is controlled by women. The most marked public appearance of corn, then, is the chicha that the men drink all day and that everyone drinks at the start of plowing. The chicha is treated as a transformation of corn, returned to the earth, to the Pachamama and to the men and women working, in order to ensure the next year's supply of corn. Boiled corn is also a central part of the lunchtime meal; in the past it was apparently the major component of the meal. People also used to bury the contents of a plate in the middle of the field as an offering to the Pachamama, just as they still offer chicha.

All this is to say that the corn being planted, which is in effect all potential generation, remains nearly hidden as well as under the control of women. Last year's corn, however, which has already been realized as food after passing through the wasi and being transformed by women's work, is available for everyone to see and consume. This year's corn will appear out of the ground presently, gradually becoming a topic of people's conversation, and will reach the height of public attention in February around Carnival, when people are eating sweet corn on the cob, stealing plants, and dancing with them. Corn will remain in the public eye until harvest, when it will then disappear into people's wasis to appear only as food and chicha.

In planting, people do not produce corn; rather, they produce a hidden, potential generation. This is part of why they connect planting more to future plantings than to the apparent final product of their planting—in fact, they reverse the obvious relationship of corn planting to food, acting on planting day as if boiled corn and chicha were good mainly to feed those working in the field, and as an offering to ensure the growth of future corn. I mentioned earlier that in planting some aspects of the relationship of wasi and chajra are reversed. What is achieved through this spatial reversal is the inversion of the ordinary relationship of the production of people versus the production of things (Turner 2002; Graeber 2001); while everyone's attention and activity are usually focused on the house, where agricultural and other goods are realized as things that people can use (i.e., the consumption of things for the production of people), on this day everyone's focus is on a chajra, and the creation of the potential that will be realized later in the agricultural cycle, starting in February.

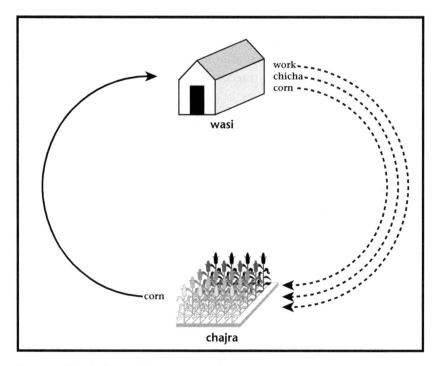

Figure 3.3. The ideal circuit between wasi and chajra.

The chajra, however, is created as part of a domestic productive space, and once the planting is done, the chajra withdraws from center stage and returns to its proper position as a place subordinate to the patio and the rooms of the wasi. In Carnival, which focuses on wasis almost to the exclusion of chajras, the Pachamama is again located in the center of the patio. The chajra, in other words, is never fixed but is part of a dynamic circuit that defines the productive life of a household.

This transformation is effected through a complex pattern of circulation between the field, the house, other houses, and more distant places; the main things circulating are men, women, seeds, and money. In order to think more clearly about the repeated movements that are performed and invoked in corn planting, I adapt the term "circuits" as developed by Roger Rouse (1991) to talk about transnational Mexican migration. Rouse calls the relationship between his subjects' home community, Aguililla, and Redwood City, California, where many Aguilillans live and work, a "migrant circuit." He uses the term to indicate that although Redwood City and Aguililla are two distinct places, there is a constant movement of people, money, goods, and information between them, to the point that each place, and the path between them, becomes inhabitable as a single social space for Aguilillans. Here I suggest that "circuit" is not just a useful concept for characterizing transnational spaces, such as that of migrants, but can be usefully employed to understand the constitution of all sorts of places of many different scales. For instance, the constitution of the productive space of a house and its surrounding fields happens through a variety of predictable movements of people and things between houses and fields—this spatial relationship can as usefully be called a circuit as that between Aguililla and Redwood City (or between Quirpini and La Salada in Buenos Aires, a circuit we will encounter presently) even though it is much smaller, and the only 'border' it crosses is the distinction between the house and field (see Figure 3.3). Similarly, Quirpini and San Lucas are connected by a circuit, as Quirpinis constantly go to the town to buy food, baptize and register their children, attend church, and take part in various regional celebrations.

In planting, and especially in the ch'alla at the start of planting, people act as if there was a simple and closed annual circuit between house and field. Corn's ideal path is into one's own chajra (as seed), from the land into the house, where it is transformed into food or chicha (some of which is consumed and some poured on the ground of the chajra as a libation to the Pachamama), and then back into the household's chajra as seed. Every household's ideal is to plant corn with seeds from the corn they planted the year before.

This dyadic relationship between house and field dominates corn planting and is constantly invoked during the work, mostly in an inverted form. De-centering the wasi in favor of the chajra invokes this dyad as central to planting, as does the ritual treatment of food as if it served mainly to insure further planting, thus treating reproduction as a step in production. The invocation of the Pachamama in the field rather than the patio also invokes and inverts a dichotomy between house and field.

This duality is also played out in an elaborate gendering of space, enacted in sara llank'ay as the interaction of a subordinate, domestic, and hierarchical house and a central, public, and egalitarian chajra. The dominance of the chajra in the gendered pair house/field is also manifested in the way the field contains the entire pair: while on planting day the house is an entirely feminine place, the male chajra subsumes both genders, providing a location

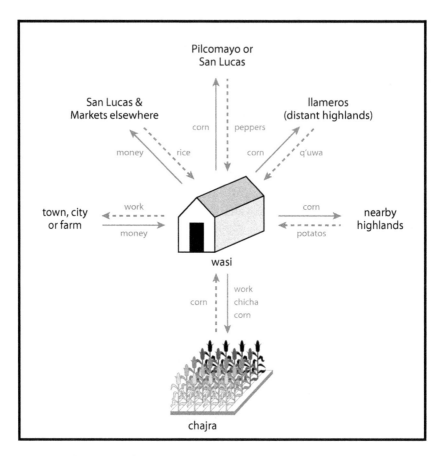

Figure 3.4. The circuits of corn planting;
the invoked geography of a chajra.

for the Pachamama and incorporating women in planting and serving food. In fact, on planting day, when it becomes the center of domestic activity, the chajra takes on a key structural feature of wasis: a feminine center to which the Pachamama is invited. Consistent with the usual gendering of public and private, exterior and interior space, this center is marked by things that are in some sense hidden: the q'uwara, which men must avoid; and the corn, concealed in a bag. In corn planting everyone enacts the dominance of men over women, and its justification: the men's work is public and egalitarian, and they are creating the potential off of which the household lives; the women's work is domestic and hierarchical, and they are merely realizing the potential already produced by men. In this moment, when men's work could be seen as adjunct to women's (providing the materials that women will make into food), everyone acts as if the entire pattern of circulation initiated for planting, centering on men's work in the chajra, is an end in itself.

But growing corn, or even planting it, is not as simple as this dyadic circuit suggests. Those (such as Miguel Paco) who do not have surplus seed in the fall have to buy from other households with more corn; this is one of the factors that leads poorer Quirpinis to migrate, since there are few sources of cash available in San Lucas to those who do not produce an agricultural surplus. These households amend the wasi-chajra circuit with migratory travel and the circulation of money and corn.

But even for households with plenty of corn, the wasi/chajra circuit is implicated in extensive patterns of circulation, both practically and ritually (see Figure 3.4). The q'uwa, for instance, comes from distant highlands, and is brought to Quirpini by llameros, who trade their goods for corn and other agricultural products of the area. Where the midday meal may once have reinforced the closed chajra/wasi circuit, when it consisted mainly of corn, today it involves products from multiple ecological and economic realms. Rice is grown in the eastern lowlands, and can only be bought from a store in San Lucas for money, which is gotten mainly by traveling to distant labor markets in Buenos Aires, various Bolivian cities, or the commercial farms of Camargo. Similarly, hot peppers can either be bought from stores in town or acquired by trade with agriculturalists from the Pilcomayo River valley to the east. Potatoes can sometimes be purchased in San Lucas, but they are relatively scarce in the spring, and the most reliable way to obtain them is by trade or purchase with kin living in the highland areas immediately surrounding the San Lucas valley.

The materials brought together in the field at planting follow circuits that implicate the entire household in a multi-scaled geography that can extend as far as Argentina and incorporate multiple forms of exchange. The geography so invoked, and the varied exchanges that move across it, correspond to a major part of the geography that Quirpinis actually inhabit. From one perspective, all these circuits are centered on the wasi, as the creative/transformational center in which corn is made into food, chicha, and money, and in which food is turned into *kallpa,* or the capacity to act, which is what enables them to work, in the fields and in distant labor markets. And, normally, as discussed in the last chapter, the house is the center that articulates all these circuits. But when this geography is invoked with *q'uwara* and lunch foods, the circuits along which move the *q'uwa,* rice, peppers, and so on only make sense in relation to the chajra and the cycle of corn produced for the sake of corn.

Methodological Reflection

The geography enacted through inter-household reciprocity is spatially far more restricted than the circuits traveled by corn and other crucial ingredients in corn planting, but at the same time these ties are far more useful when it comes time for people to travel to Buenos Aires. Unlike the circuits that integrate wasi and chajra in the production and consumption of corn, these relationships are portable; as we will see in chapter 7, they are essential to households' migratory plans. Corn planting, then, is characterized by the coordination of activity and movement on many different scales. A key technique I am employing in this ethnography is always to pay attention to the different scales at which people are acting, and on which their actions have consequences.

Another theme of this chapter is the form of actions and the spatial forms those actions imply. This is why I have made so much use of the terms "script," "text," and "circuit"—all refer to kinds of schemata, in the sense that they are what results from focusing on the ideal or aggregate form of action, rather than its particularities. This chapter and the following one, largely concerned with Carnival, are to a great extent taken up with a spatial poetics of repetitive action, considering what the spatial and social fruits of repetitive action can be.

I have also made considerable use of the idea of invocation as a way to talk about the implicit geography of actions, and begin showing how very large-scale phenomena can be encapsulated in local action. This idea I derive from Weber's (1999) "acting in relation to." For Weber, this sort of deictic action even serves as a definition of "social action," which he defines as action "in relation to" other people. Here I am fashioning the concept into a more precise tool, which lets us examine the way that people incorporate people, places, or ideas that are not present into their actions. This idea is crucial in chapter 6, when I consider the ways in which he Bolivian nation makes itself present in Quirpini.

4 · *Carnival and the Spatial Practice of Community*

Up to this point I have held 'Quirpini'—considered both as a place and a context for action—in a kind of suspension. I have done this in order to highlight smaller-scale spaces, and to emphasize my point that community is not a given, nor is it always present to actors. But if it is not always part of people's actions, how is it lived? What sort of a place is it? Like any place with the depth and persistence of a community, with such a powerful capacity to locate people and actions, it is lived in many ways and in many different situations. Certain places take on richness and permanence by turning up as an organizing framework or meaningful reference point for many different activities and by providing a container for the projects of many actors in which multiple scales of activity can be articulated.

If anthropologists have had a habit of treating space as a prefabricated container or stage-set for action, this is largely because places persistently present themselves in just this way—as the background that gives significance to what people are doing. Paul Ricoeur (1974:85) remarked that "language seeks to . . . die as an object," which is to say that it tends to make itself transparent, to disappear in favor of what it is being employed to say. Similarly, we could say that places seek to die as products: places have a strong tendency to appear as if they are prior to action, as if their existence is independent of action.[1]

Many approaches to places identify them with territories, and therefore put a great deal of emphasis on their borders as the defining feature of places

MISHKHAMAYU

CUMUNI

QUIRPINI

San Lucas River

KHOCHA

AVICHUCA

TAMBO MOKHO

S

E ✧ W

N

1 kilometer

Figure 4.1. Map of the borders of the old ayllu Jatun Kellaja (Quirpini), indicating the approximate borders of Avichuca and Cumuni, the two communities that have broken away. The shaded areas represent the arable land along the river. Based on the map "Plano General de la Propiedad 'Jatun Kellaja'" in the Office of the Reforma Agraria, Sucre.

(see, for instance, Verdery 1994; Appadurai 1996a). Accordingly, in approaching Quirpini, I begin with aspects of the community that can be identified with its boundaries. In the process I will show that talking only about borders would leave us with a rigid and impoverished notion of what Quirpini is for Quirpinis. I then go on to talk about the spatiality of Quirpini that is not contained by borders. The most effective way to grasp that spatiality will be to consider the main fiesta in which people act in relation to Quirpini as a whole, and enact themselves as Quirpinis. This is Carnival, a complex, multiday celebration that encompasses the space and nearly all the people of Quirpini, the surrounding communities, and San Lucas.

Quirpini in Its Borders

In principle, the territory of Quirpini is surrounded by a continuous border, much like a nation-state, a city, or a province. My very first encounter with Quirpini, before I had visited it, came from looking at a map in the Agrarian Reform office, which represented the communal boundaries, some property lines, and a farcical representation of the community's geography.

On the Agrarian Reform map, made in 1971, the border of the ayllu Jatun Yucasa constitutes a neat and unambiguous line enclosing the territory of the community (see Figure 4.1). But this map does not describe the border of Quirpini. The entire eastern part of Jatun Killaja, called Avichuca, broke away from the rest of the community in the 1980s and formed a separate community. There is now a border between Quirpini and Avichuca, drawn to divide fairly the excellent grazing lands of the Pampa of Avichuca. In addition, as mentioned above, the southwestern part of this delimited area, at the head of the valley, had recently broken away from the reduced Quirpini and was in the process of joining the neighboring community of Mishkhamayu. The resultant border between the two communities was a point of contention when I was there, as we will see presently.

Furthermore, although the line on a map is continuous, the edges of Quirpini have different significance in different places. In some areas, under certain circumstances, people cross the border without encountering it in any way (for instance, when riding in a truck along the road from the main highway to San Lucas); in other situations it matters a great deal. In the valley bottom, as well as in the grassy parts of the highlands, the border delimits where Quirpinis may pasture their livestock; the interior borders that mark off the zonas of Quirpini are supposed to serve the same purpose. In the past, when individual communities had the responsibility to maintain the road running through their lands, the border marked the ends of this work obligation, carried out at Easter. If a stranger is expelled from Quirpini, he will often be chased as far as the border, no farther. In what follows, I present situations in which borders matter, and why and how they do so.

I once traveled with some Quirpinis to the neighboring community of Avichuca, on a high plateau to the east of Quirpini. The path from Villcasana goes up the side of the valley and across a high grassy plateau, crossing a disused landing strip. For a short way the border between the communities runs along the path and is marked by a series of low stone markers, or *mujun* (from Spanish *mojón*, "border marker"). At the point where the path finally crosses into Avichuca, there is a pair of larger mujun. As we passed these markers, we stopped and scoured the area for stones to add to them. Someone explained that you should generally add stones to a mujun when you pass it. This gesture has two effects: it is a way to mark a transition—a rite of passage—but it also maintains the physical mark of the border, which regulates access to grazing lands.

When I arrived in Quirpini in 1992, there were no mujun marking any border between Quirpini and the neighboring community to the south, Cumuni, because, until recently, Cumuni had been a part of Quirpini, one of what were then five zonas; over the previous two decades Cumuni had separated itself and joined with another community on the highland plain to the south of the San Lucas valley. The change was gradual, but by the time I was in the area Cumuni had its own school and communal authorities, held its own community meetings, organized work parties, and levied school fees; it was in most senses separate from Quirpini. One crucial step that had not been completed was the establishment of a border between the newly separated communities—in fact, there was disagreement about where the border should lie.

The Quirpinis decided at a communal meeting in August 1993 to put up boundary markers. A large part of the community, joined by some teachers from the school, went up the road to where the putative boundary crossed it. Someone pulled out three Bolivian flags and planted one by the road; two school authorities took the others, and each led a group of people along the boundary, in either direction up the valley sides and away from the road. At various points along the new boundary, established by discussion, the people stopped and gathered stones to pile into a mujun, while the authority waved the flag. At each end of the newly created boundary the authorities waved their flags and lit sticks of dynamite. Miguel Paco, who did not take part, later told me that lighting the dynamite was an aggressive act and could lead to trouble.

I heard that the next day the Cumunis came and pulled apart all the mujun as soon as we left. They would not accept the new border partly because some Cumunis thought they had a claim to more territory, but mostly because they were concerned that if the border were plainly marked they would lose the right to pasture their animals in the high grazing lands to the east and west of the valley. At a meeting between the two communities a few weeks later, various solutions to the border problem were discussed. One proposed solution that stood a good chance of being adopted was to place mujun to mark the intermediate part of the boundary while leaving out the final markers, thus leaving the mountain pasturage undivided. The border dispute was not fully resolved when I left.

Here part of the problem was a clash over the sort of space that borders create—for the Quirpinis, putting up the border was recognition that Cumuni had separated itself from Quirpini; it was a way to finalize the break while forestalling any land claims by Cumunis. The Cumunis were not looking at the land as territory that had to be divided between two communities, so much as productive terrain; they were thinking about what they could do with the land. Where the Quirpinis were trying to restore and preserve their community's territorial integrity, the Cumunis were mainly concerned with preserving their access to grazing lands.

When I arranged to join Nicanor Huarachi on his trip to Argentina in late 1993 I was surprised to learn that we had to be careful, when setting off, not to talk to a woman between leaving our houses and catching a car on the road that runs through the community. If you do meet a woman, Nicanor told me, you might as well just go home and start on another day. The only other option is not to greet her; if you run into a man and woman together you can talk to the man but must not acknowledge the woman in any way (in Quirpini this would be flagrantly rude behavior). This prohibition joined another I had already heard about: you should start a major trip only on an even-numbered day because trips started on odd-numbered days would end badly. When we were setting off in a truck on the main road, Nicanor did what I had seen others do when starting a trip: he crossed himself; his wife, Luisa, who had joined us this far, did the same.

Here, the borders of Quirpini, seen as the place where a journey begins (past which the traveler is "away"), run right through the heart of community lands. For anyone setting out on a trip, the road is the point at which they leave Quirpini and set off for another place.

Rouse (1991) and Kearney (1994) distinguish "boundaries" as lines that demarcate the outer limit of some place, and "borders" as the social spaces in which different social groups or political systems encounter one another. Rouse (1991:17) argues that the spread of immigrants through the U.S., along with laws making employers responsible for their employees' legal status, had spread "border zones" throughout the U.S. In Quirpini community boundaries do not involve the sort of categorical distinctions that the U.S.–Mexican border does, nor are they policed to the same extent. There are clear border zones, however, which, though clearly "placed," do not correspond at all with the community's boundary. The main border area is the road running through the community. The prohibition on meeting women, like crossing oneself, has to do with the transition from being at home to being "on a trip." The road is the area from which outsiders normally appear in the community and where encounters with outsiders generally occur. Although houses are clustered around the road insofar as is practical, those on the road have a far more closed plan than ones farther away, and houses across the river generally have an open plan. The closure of houses on the road is a response to the inviting but threatening openness of the border zone.

Other border areas follow secondary paths—a key annual work party is dedicated to maintaining Quirpini's portion of a path running from the distant hot valleys through Avichuca to the town of San Lucas, on which traders carry hot peppers and other tropical products to local fairs. Some, like the mujun we repaired on the way to Avichuca, lie at the intersection of boundaries and roads. Meetings between Quirpini and Cumuni to discuss their conflict—border activity par excellence—were held on the main road, at the point where it crossed one disputed boundary between the communities; during the discussion the Quirpinis stood in a semicircle on their side of the boundary, and the Cumunis formed the other half of the circle on their own side. Clearly a spatial transition between "inside" Quirpini and "outside" Quirpini can take place in a number of locations and not just on the perimeter of Quirpini's territory.

From the accounts above, clearly the borders of Quirpini do not primarily keep things out. They can be mobilized for this purpose, but that is by no means their main effect. Rather, they mainly force people to orient their actions to the border or to the place the border surrounds. That it is a bounded entity makes Quirpini a "place"; because people have to acknowledge it in some way as they move about, they must defer to it. The rites and negotiations I have described are gestures of acknowledgment, or deference. They invoke the community as the thing being acknowledged, and they do so specifically through acts that concede the transition point between being in the community and outside it. The borders of Quirpini regulate where people pasture their livestock, particularly those of different communities, because the borders allocate rights to land. They provide an outer boundary for certain proprietary concerns that Quirpinis share. By concentrating the encounter with the community as a whole into small places, they intensify awareness of Quirpini and the separation between Quirpini and neighboring communities.[2]

The borders of Quirpini are spaces that consistently elicit gestures recognizing that there is a significant difference between what is within the border and what is outside. In thinking of the borders of Quirpini as part of a spatial schema, we can see that the practices noted above are not as ephemeral as they might appear. Some, such as building mujun, physically inscribe the border in the landscape; or, rather, they inscribe an index of the border in the landscape—encountering a pile of rocks in the middle of a plain for someone unfamiliar with mujun would say little about borders, territory, or much of anything else.

The mujun itself indexes this mass of spatial knowledge, recurrent practices, memories, and possible actions, which are not evenly distributed, in space or through the population, by localizing them, turning them into the demand for certain specific gestures right here, right now. Mujun are, in other words, places where parts of the community's spatial schema are realized. Most elements of this schema are realized through some form of movement, as in the examples given above.

What are Quirpini's border zones? To start with, they are made up of the spaces where people's gestures of acknowledgment must take place. The gestures are localized—they occur where mujun are situated, where paths cross the border or the main road. The gestures that invoke and create the borders of Quirpini, whereby people acknowledge that Quirpini is a place, simultaneously define a number of lesser locations. These are places that constrain people's actions, but they can do so only because they have a specific relation to the whole of Quirpini. Although the borders of Quirpini are realized in these areas, they are significant only because of the community they outline. It is the clustering of certain kinds of places that makes something a border, even though it is the border that seems to make a place. In areas where there are few paths and no grazing land, the borders of Quirpini are fairly notional. They are there, and a few people probably know the landmarks that define them, but where they do not affect people's actions much, they exist mostly for their potential.

There are, of course, many boundaries in Quirpini apart from those that enclose it—the internal space of Quirpini is divided by multiple bounded territories. The three zonas have precise, but unmarked, boundaries, which do little besides locating households and property; grazing rights on the mountain slopes are only notionally distributed by zona; and, on the valley floor, grazing rights go with household property. Since the Agrarian Reform reached Quirpini in the 1970s, every family has held its agricultural land as private property, bounded by commonly understood and precise lines.[3] This sort of territory is the most common cause of dispute between Quirpinis, either because the lines are not as precise as they ought to be, or because of long-running disputes about who owns particular plots. Such disputes are regularly renewed when a landowner dies, and the heirs jockey for as much land as possible. Although most families have a single name for the contiguous land on which their house sits (e.g., Miguel Paco and his family lived and worked on "Cancha Loma," Demetrio Condori on "T'uru Pampa"), in fact every small field that makes up a landholding has a name, which the owners of the field and others in the area know. Both the named parcels and (less often) the larger holdings are usually called *chajra* (a term that also denotes "countryside" or "rural land"). Generally, when people sell land or inherit it, it is these named parcels that change hands. Sometimes they are divided, in which case each new field will be given a name and the new boundary marked with a path or some similar break in the cultivated area, or *pampa*. Outside the cultivated fields, either on the mountain slopes or among the dry areas of the valley floor, every place one might be appears to have a name, and is a *chiqan*, a place. Such named places do not necessarily have clear boundaries at all, as people seem to use them mostly to orient themselves. Once, while traveling to Qhocha with Miguel, I asked him about toponyms along our route, and he was able to name more than thirty in the course of a two-hour hike. Most of these places carry names that refer to some actual or remembered feature of the terrain, such as *cienega pampa* ("marshy plain") or *telegrafo mukhu* ("telegraph hill").

Wasis themselves are bounded territories, with borders that must be respected. The territory of a field and of a house work very differently—no one who is not close to a household may enter the space of a wasi unbidden, but paths through the inhabited parts of Quirpini normally cross people's land, winding between chajras, and I never heard of any individuals trying to prohibit someone from crossing their land. Property boundaries are good mainly for claiming exclusive access to productive resources, whereas household boundaries mark more thoroughgoing spaces of exclusion.

There are a number of other bounded places in Quirpini, such as the cemetery, surrounded by a high adobe wall and a locked gate. Every year someone is named to keep charge of the key and open the gates for funerals or fiestas. The school is partly surrounded by walls and a gate, and although the school, as the most public and collective entity in the community, is never really excluded space for anyone, it is always clear whether one is inside the school grounds or outside, and the passage from outside to inside is marked by a clear transition (passing through the gate, when it is open, ascending the riverbank, or, as a last resort, climbing the wall). The chapel was built with a locked door, windows, and a roof, and so it, too, became a bounded space, to be entered only with some sort of authorization.

In sum, the territory of Quirpini is itself crowded with territories. Many of these contain other places (rooms in the school and in wasis, tombs in the cemetery, chajras in a landholding), some of which are marked by boundaries and others are not. Even seen through its borders alone, Quirpini has complex internal structures.

This discussion of the borders and bounded spaces of Quirpini brings up a more general point: in trying to grasp the nature of Quirpini as a place, just how much should we focus on borders? Already they seem to be escaping themselves, revealing their own incompleteness as a way to approach a place. Everything about borders—being crossed, containing action, organizing names and people—presupposes a larger and more complex space within which they are situated, as well as richer internal space than the borders themselves can tell us about. Borders are very good for defining territories, but, as I pointed out at the start of this chapter, a place is much more than simply its territoriality. I would go so far as to say that territories in general are only comprehensible as one aspect of a space that contains multiple territories, which themselves often contain territories. In other words, although borders imply a uniform and undifferentiated space on their inside and outside, that space can only be understood as a space of action and significance if we approach it as complex and structured, with its own hierarchy of spaces. I call such a space, the complementary other side of a territory, a "terrain."

In order to clarify the distinct ideas of place I am employing, I make an argument that is parallel to one Rouse makes about the identity of Mexican immigrants to the U.S. In his article, "Questions of Identity" (1995), Rouse argues that migrants between Aguililla, Mexico, and the U.S. do not just take on a new identity when they come to this country: they take on "identity" for the first time. Social relations and people's sense of "who they are" in Aguililla, he argues, are not structured through identity-based categories whose members take themselves to be broadly similar to one another so much as through networks of relationships that establish every relationship in a unique way. Whereas in the U.S. the privileged form of public self-designation involves including oneself in a group whose membership is supposedly the same in some important way, and whose boundaries are clear, Aguilillans, says Rouse, trained in public action based on the cultivation of personal contacts and alliances, are more able to act publicly through coalitions rather than through essentially defined identity groups. The distinction Rouse draws between identity and networks is analogous to the difference between the space of Quirpini as manifested in the construction, crossing, and ritualizing of borders (which surround a space that appears uniform in that its distinguishing feature is that it is contained within the border) versus Quirpini's space as a collection of places and people potentially related to one another in various ways through people's activities and movement. The kind of place created by borders consists of a uniform space—what I have been calling a "territory"—surrounded by boundaries. The other sort of place is a space with internal distinctions, structure, and some kind of texture—what I am calling a "terrain."[4]

Rouse opposes identity-based and networked social relations as different kinds of social relations; in discussing the space of nations, Appadurai similarly suggests that the superimposition of bounded national territory and structured, hierarchical internal national spaces is "bizarrely contradictory" (1996:189). I suggest that, at least when we are talking about places, territory and terrain are complementary aspects of the same thing. Quirpini can look like a territory or like a collection of interconnected places, depending on what is being done in it, how it is being lived. These two ways that places can be understood can themselves be understood as two mutually implicating aspects of one thing.

From certain perspectives and for certain purposes Quirpinis live in a community with a uniform undifferentiated internal space. When I first began asking about toponyms, for instance, several people flatly denied that the land was subdivided in any way, insisting that "it's all Quirpini." Similarly, when they put up the boundary with Cumuni, they were enacting a place that did nothing more than exclude Cumunis and include Quirpinis. Although such a place is protective of its inhabitants and serves to articulate egalitarian sentiments or exclude a pesky anthropologist, it does not work very well as a space of action. It implies no internal places in which or on which anyone can act. In practice this is not a concern, because the border/territory image of place is entirely focused on the border and on the relationship between the place and what is outside it. In other words, the perspectives that treat Quirpini as a homogeneous space surrounded by a border are not concerned with action within Quirpini so much as with determining what is outside the community and what is inside.

For other purposes, Quirpini is a space of places—with destinations, routes, and areas of greater or lesser familiarity. It is a terrain of specific and differential possibilities. If we are to understand Quirpini as a place, we cannot just look for gestures of exclusion or containment but must explore more subtle aspects of how people move about.

We can get a privileged view of how Quirpini works as a terrain, I argue, by closely examining the way people move about in the community's most complete moment of self-enactment: the annual fiesta of Carnival. Just as corn planting was a moment of extraordinary social importance for the people I worked with, it was during the weeklong celebration of Carnival that I felt people most thoroughly inhabited Quirpini. In other words, during Carnival Quirpini is a reference point for people's actions, to a far greater extent, and for a longer period, than at other times. Carnival is an event that brings together the "whole" of Quirpini, and in which people act out some of the social and spatial relations that define the community and relate the community to the larger region. It has a similar role in other rural Andean communities (see, for instance, Medlin 1983).

I turn, therefore, to the annual celebration of Carnival, and the version of Quirpini that is enacted in it.

Carnival: Enacting a Community

The fundamental relational act of Carnival, its basic element, is the visit. In talking about Carnival visits, I mean a person or a group of people going from one house to another, where they can expect to be welcomed by one or several hosts and offered chicha and other drinks, which the visitors and host(s) ideally share. At the level of where people go, the entirety of Quirpini is constituted by a highly organized series of visits. Over the course of the multiday celebration these visits are organized into various patterns, each constituting a different image of the terrain (but not the territory) of Quirpini, and its relations with the town of San Lucas as well as other communities. The sum of the visits (by the end of the celebration several hundred of them have been enacted in Quirpini alone) is an embodied collective terrain of relationships, which together make up a version of Quirpini.

I attended two Carnivals while I was in Quirpini, and they followed the same basic form. The community's celebration starts on the Tuesday before Ash Wednesday (this day in the Catholic calendar is the "Fat Tuesday" celebrated in New Orleans as Mardi Gras), which usually falls in late February. The most intense celebrations in Quirpini take place over the four days from Tuesday to Friday; they are followed by two days of inter-household visiting and quieter drinking, culminating in the Sunday of Tentación, which everyone refers to as the "end" of Carnival. In the town of San Lucas, the celebration mainly takes places from the previous Sunday through Ash Wednesday; by the time Carnival starts in Quirpini, it is half over in town. As with all Catholic religious celebrations in Quirpini, the few evangelical Christian converts do not take part. In the mid-1990s they were not so numerous that their absence had a noticeable impact on the celebration's ubiquitous pretensions to encompass the whole community.

Carnival loomed large in people's imagination; as soon as Christmas and Reyes (January 6) had passed, people began talking about preparations for the event, speculating on which of their migrating kinsmen would return and asking if I would be present to "dance" the fiesta. Carnival and planting season are the two times for which Quirpinis make a special effort to be present; although few people return from Buenos Aires just for Carnival, many hasten their return or delay their departure in order to participate. Weeks before the fiesta starts, young women and the men who play the Carnival flute start making sure they have their dancing costumes, and households ensure that they have the resources they will need: corn to make chicha, money to buy alcohol, and hard candies, called *confites*, that they are expected to pelt at their house guests. The kurajkuna also have to get peaches and enough food for dozens of visitors, as well as lining up help from their mutual aid networks. Even those who play no central role in the dancing wear their finest clothes.

A few weeks before Carnival, someone from the community (usually Tiburcio Puma) sets off on a several-day journey by foot to the community of Tapchukira in the region of Toropalca, nearly one hundred kilometers to the west, in southern Potosí. There he finds someone from whom to "buy" a new melody for Quirpini's flautists to play during the fiesta. People from all the neighboring communities go to the same area[5] to get new Carnival tunes, which people in Toropalca claim to learn from the sound of streams. Tiburcio told me that the traditional way to learn is to play the tune over and over as you walk, so as to have it memorized by the time you return and be able to teach it to the other flute players; nowadays, however, you can just bring a tape recorder and record the tune. When the new tune arrives, all the men who are planning to play flutes that year gather in someone's house for several nights and learn the tune together. During the four days of Carnival they play the community's unique melody incessantly; and during the following months they play it at some fiestas, and then it is put aside, to be replaced by a new tune the next year. Nearly all the flautists in Quirpini are from Sakapampa; I sometimes heard Sakapampas complain that people in the other zonas could not be bothered to learn to play the instrument, instead lazily insisting that Sakapampas play for them.

The last week before the Tuesday of Carnival is a swarm of activity. Most households entertain at least a few guests, so women throughout the community make chicha and cook. Women with marriageable daughters iron all the traditional weavings they can find, so their daughters can dance with them in a carrying cloth over one shoulder, showing off their weaving skills.[6] The families of the communal authorities, and to a lesser extent the school authorities, are expected to entertain visitors more elaborately, and so have more preparations to do, getting peaches and confites, and preparing meat to grill for visitors, along with a variety of dishes. The authorities have to call on those in their mutual aid networks for help, even as these are busy with their own preparations.

The heaviest burden falls on the family of the *corregidor,* for whom this is the most important fiesta of the year; as we will see shortly, he is expected to entertain a large part of the community in his house. For the corregidor, the fiesta is the culmination of months of preparations, saving, borrowing, and calling in favors. It is also the pinnacle of a man's public career in Quirpini.

When I asked people in Quirpini what they do on the first day of Carnival, most often they told me, "We go to the corregidor's house." The corregidor's house is the culmination of a complex pattern of visits that includes the houses of all the kurajkuna.

On the Tuesday of Carnival in 1993 I went in the morning to the household of my neighbors, Felix Villcasana and Anisa Ibarra. That year Felix was Quirpini's *alcalde mayór,* the fourth-highest of six ranked positions that make up the community's formal political authorities, or kurajkuna. When I arrived at about 8:30, Anisa was serving chicha to a small group of visitors seated around the patio, all from the Ibarra section of Zona Villcasana. The widower Daniél Ibarra was playing a drum, and Tiburcio Puma was playing the previous year's Carnival tune on a large flute. Vidal Mendez and his wife, Tomasa Paco, were there, and their teenage daughter, Nazera, was dancing in the courtyard, wearing black wool *almilla,* and carrying a full load of brightly colored and carefully ironed weavings in a carrying cloth she wore over one shoulder. She carried a white flag on a stick, which she waved as she danced. Felix himself was not there; he was working in Argentina and had designated his younger cousin and godson, Gregorio Villcasana, to take his place for the fiesta. Over the next four days Gregorio would be called "tata alcalde" (father alcalde) as Felix would have been called, and would do everything the alcalde mayór would normally be called on to do, although the obligation being fulfilled was Felix's.[7] Gregorio's wife, Satuka, was there, along with several of their children. Today he was seated behind a table, and from time to time someone would come up and ch'alla to him. Anisa, the "mama alcalde" (mother alcalde), was busy serving the guests and preparing bread babies for a household ch'alla later in the week, and she rarely was able to sit down for long.

I joined the guests in the patio, and we sat and chatted, drinking slowly while the late summer sun rose above the ridge to the east, waiting for a few more neighbors to turn up. At one point Gregorio and Anisa went to each guest, kneeled down and asked for our pardon. When Anisa felt that everyone who was coming had arrived, we got up and set off, heading to the house of the *cacique*, the second-highest-ranking position of the kurajkuna, who lived downriver in the Puma section of Sakapampa.

Tiburcio and Daniél played the previous year's Carnival tune as we walked among the verdant cornfields, Vidal occasionally joining in on a smaller flute. Carnival comes at the greenest time of year, when all the trees and bushes of the area are in leaf, and there is grass on the ground; the landscape looks much softer now than during planting, and despite occasional torrential downpours, the warm weather is generally fine.

When we arrived at the cacique's house we just walked right into the patio, with no announcement beyond our music. No one else was there apart from the cacique, his wife, and their son. Tiburcio, Nazera, and Daniél began to dance and play around the pot in the center of the patio, while the rest of us sat on benches and on the ground at the patio's edges. The *mama cacique* and her son served us chicha and trago, and we drank and chatted some more. A short while later a group of Pumas arrived, led by Pablo, a senior member of the extended Puma family. Their musicians joined ours at the center of the patio, and the others sat down with us to drink. Not long after, as it became clear that no one else was arriving, everyone in the house stood up, and, led by our flute players and several young girls dancing and waving flags, we set off for the nearby house of the corregidor Alejandro Copa, to join the groups coming from other authorities' houses.

This series of visits is part of one year's instantiation of a cascade of visits through which the Catholic Quirpinis make their way from their houses to the house of the *corregidor auxiliar*. People start the day, usually late in the morning, by congregating in small groups at a neighbor's house; often this neighbor is an authority. Each group of neighbors makes some effort to insure that there will be at least one man to play flute in the group, and one woman dancing, carrying a flag of colored cloth, and wearing traditional woolen clothing, called *almilla*, which consists of an *ajsu,* or long black woolen dress with embroidery at the sleeves and hem, a bright woven cloth on the back held on by a woven belt around the waist, and broad flat hats of wool felt. The flautists ideally wear an outfit called *traji* (from the Spanish *traje,* or "suit

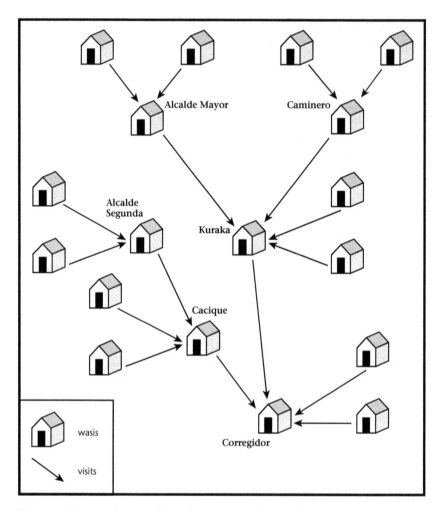

Figure 4.2. Synoptic diagram of cascading visits to authorities' houses
during Tuesday of Carnival in 1994. This pattern differs every year,
depending on the relative locations of the authorities' houses.

of clothes"), consisting of white homespun shirt and trousers embroidered
at the cuffs, a locally made poncho, and an embroidered white woolen hat.
When everyone is gathered, they set off to the wasi of the nearest member of
the kurajkuna, the flautist playing last year's Carnival tune, and the dancer
waving her flag. This group is called a *pantilla*.[8] The flautist and dancer are
often called *karnawalkuna* ("carnivals"), a term that also refers to the whole
of the carnival dancers and musicians.

Eventually the decision is made to move on, and most of those present form a loose procession to the home of the next-highest authority located between the starting point and the house of the corregidor auxiliar, the highest communal authority. The same pattern follows at the next house, until, by late afternoon, all the pantillas have followed a cascading pattern to the corregidor's house.

On the first day of Carnival in 1994, the pantillas followed the pattern I depict diagrammatically in Figure 4.2. The *caminero* (Panfilo Puma, occupying the lowest rung of the kurajkuna hierarchy) and the alcalde mayór (Angel Bautista) lived in Sakapampa, so the tata and mama caminero and their visitors first visited the house of the alcalde mayór, and then the combined groups went up to Zona Quirpini, where the corregidor, Justo Cruz, lived. The *alcalde segunda* (Gregorio Villcasana, who the year before had fulfilled his older cousin Felix's role as alcalde mayór) and the *kuraka* (Felix Ibarra, son of Daniél) lived in Villcasana, so the segunda visited the kuraka, and they traveled together across the river to the corregidor's. The cacique lived above the corregidor in Zona Quirpini, so he and his visitors came directly to Justo's house.

That year I skipped the preliminary visits, as I was occupied by preparations for the later days of the fiesta, and in the late morning I headed directly over toward the corregidor's house, on the opposite side of the valley, near the main road. Before I had even reached the river, I heard the familiar sound of Carnival music, and joined up with the pantilla coming from Felix Ibarra's house. The group was ten people strong, with one adolescent girl in almilla, waving a flag. The only flute in the group was a small one played by Vidal Mendez. We crossed the river and headed through some fields, resplendent with green corn plants, on the way to the corregidor's. When we reached the main road, we saw and heard the pantilla from Sakapampa, with its many flute players, approaching from below. They were a larger group, many of the musicians in homespun traji, and several young women in almilla, waving flags. We paused to wait for them, and when the two groups met, everyone in each pantilla greeted one another, as the musicians and dancers joined into a single group and briefly danced in a circle, much as they would around a house's pot of chicha. Now merged, we headed up the road to the corregidor's. The musicians and dancers entered together at the head of our pantilla, and joined the musicians and dancers already surrounding the flower-bedecked and half-buried pot at the center of Justo's patio. Gregorio and Felix joined Justo at a table from which he was presiding, and their wives went into the kitchen to help serve the guests. The rest of us greeted everyone we encountered and took seats along the edge of the patio.

Justo's house was not very big, and with forty to sixty people in the patio, the dancers often bumped into other revelers, and movement was difficult. As was usual, the six tata kurajkuna sat along one wall, behind a table laden with bowls of food, including grilled meat. People frequently came up to the table to help themselves, and to ch'alla the men and their staffs of authority, or *varas*. The mama kurajkuna were seated in a group on the ground nearby; while the men stayed seated, many of the mama kurajkuna bustled about, helping to prepare and serve food.

The dance at the corregidor's house was a moment of intense display for everyone present. The musicians and dancers wore home-made and self-consciously "traditional" *traji* and *ajsu*. Most of the other participants wore their best and showiest store-bought clothes. I had returned from Buenos Aires a few weeks before, and had given new shirts to Miguel, Emiliana, and their children. I had been slightly surprised that they never seemed to wear them, but that was explained when the family turned up at Justo's, all wearing their new Argentine clothes. Young men also tended to show up in the sort of city-style clothes and bicycles I described at the start of chapter 2, although young women were more likely than young men to wear traditional clothes and carry weavings on their backs.

When I talked with people about these visits, they often said that "everyone" went to the corregidor's. It was clear, however, that not everyone was there, and I interpreted these statements to indicate that Carnival represented the coming together of the "whole" of Quirpini (or *Quirpinintin*, as it was sometimes put).[9] The times I attended, nearly seventy men, women, and children converged on the house, some joining the musicians and dancers circling the center of the patio, others sitting and drinking, and the children playing or sitting and watching. There might be five or ten women singing and dancing in a ring around the flautists, who faced one another in a tight circle as they played, surrounding a ceramic pot full of beer. They freely came and went as they played, periodically stopping to drink. One year a man even decided to dance as a "woman," carrying a blanket on his back tied with a rope in place of the fine weavings in a carrying cloth, and waving a cornstalk for a flag. People get very drunk at the corregidor's house, and the mood is extremely festive, although I was told that there were often fights. Getting drunk is very much part of the point of Carnival. The authorities sit behind their table and receive food and obeisance; a number of women help the corregidor's family members prepare and serve food and drink. Many people stay there drinking until late at night, and anyone can sleep over.

The visiting on this first day of Carnival is entirely focused on the internal space of Quirpini. The sequence of visits enacts Quirpini as a hierarchy of relationships articulated through the structured set of authorities; Quirpini actually comes together through the houses of the authorities. Whereas the mutual visits that define reciprocal relations between households enact a space between two households, which in turn is the building block of each household's mutual aid network, the sequential visits on the first day define a field of relationships that incorporate the many Catholic households of Quirpini as well as the households of the authorities. This field is structured by the convergent pattern of the visits. Visitors converge in increasingly large (and thus increasingly inclusive) groups as the visits ascend the authority hierarchy, culminating in "everyone" gathering at the house of the corrégidor auxiliár, the pinnacle of the authority structure specific to Quirpini. Although the physical location of each successive convergence, including the final one, is different each year, depending on who fills the annually rotating authority positions, the structural locations (kuraka's house, corregidor's house) remain the same. In any given year the specific order of the convergent visits also varies according to the relative locations of the authorities' houses, but over time the underlying pattern is evident.

From any household's long-term perspective, there is another progression going on. Most couples can expect to pass several authority positions in their lifetimes, and in the normal course of events they will start as caminero and proceed up the authority ladder. This means they will be sponsoring progressively larger and more expensive celebrations over the years, culminating, ideally, in entertaining "everyone" as the tata and mama corregidor. In practice, relatively few families combine the resources, respect, and desire necessary to complete the authority positions through corregidor, but nearly all families take on several of these positions over the years.

Wednesday is the most un-centered day of Carnival; in Quirpini and San Lucas people travel about in multiple trajectories, making visits and offerings in many different patterns. People told me that it was generally the day the authorities and Carnival dancers (i.e., the karnawalkuna) went down to San Lucas to make their visits. Most Quirpinis, however, do not join in these visits to the authorities and notables of the town. Instead, they spend the day ch'alla-ing their houses and possessions or their livestock, or attending the cha'alla of a friend or relative; Carnival is one of the ideal times to insure the well-being of a wasi and its contents through offerings to the Pachamama. Many others simply carry on with household tasks or prepare for the festivities to come on Thursday and Friday. In San Lucas most of the elite townspeople are done with Carnival, but the town is a hubbub of crisscrossing visits by pantillas from communities throughout the San Lucas valley, as well as dance groups (called *comparsas*).

The first year I attended Carnival, the authorities and dancers left the corregidor's house late on Tuesday afternoon, and spent the night in town before making their visits on Wednesday morning. The next year they all spent the night in their own homes and went into town the next morning. I ran across one group of dancers on the way into town, and learned from them that the authorities and dancers (and anyone else who wants to come) normally gathered by zona; the three groups met up where the old road through Sakapampa joins the new road. Although no one remarked on this three-part congregation of karnawalkuna, there is no obvious practical reason why they have to be organized in this way, and it is worth noting that on their return at the end of the day, the karnawalkuna separate not into three groups according to zona but into two groups according to the "upper" and "lower" division that will organize the community for most of the rest of the fiesta.

When all three groups had gathered, they set off as a single group of karniwalkuna, the women waving their flags, the flautists playing. In San Lucas the group proceeded down the main road until they reached the house of doña Lia, the only refiner of cane alcohol in town. Here they stopped in the street and played and danced in a circle. Doña Lia quickly came out, and began serving trago to everyone. After a few minutes of playing and drinking, we set off again, this time to the town's main square; the group danced a brief circle at each of the plaza's corners, then went to the house of the *alcalde*, or mayor,[10] of San Lucas, Macedonio Valverde, who also happened to be the schoolmaster in Quirpini and owner of the largest store in San Lucas.

When I asked Quirpinis who they visit in town, their responses varied widely, and it is possible that different people are visited on different years. The people most consistently mentioned, who were clearly visited by many pantillas from around the region, were doña Lia, the mayor, the corregidor, the priest, and the police station. In addition, the karnawalkuna would visit any Quirpinis who had houses in the town; normally one of them served as a host for the delegation in case they spent the night.[11] These visits follow a loose ideal pattern or script: when the pantilla arrive, announced by the sound of their flute music, the people they are visiting greet them warmly, either inviting them indoors or joining them in the street, and always offer them an alcoholic drink (normally chicha). It is traditional for the host to sprinkle the visitors with confetti, toss hard candy at them (which the visitors scramble to pick it up), and smear their faces with white flour. The visitors, in turn, play music and dance at each house they visit. The visits are extremely festive; generally everyone is drunk, including the San Luqueño hosts, who, at this point, have already been celebrating Carnival for three days.

The day's visiting ends at the marketplace behind the mayor's office, where the mayor throws a huge party attended by groups of singers and dancers from all over the region. Each plays its own music, while comparsas of youths perform line dances accompanied by accordions, and people from the town and rural communities stand around drinking and talking. My overall impression of the gathering in the market was of a joyful cacophony that I can only call carnivalesque. As the evening draws near people begin to drift away, and the visiting groups from the communities withdraw to their borrowed houses either to return home the next morning or leave right away.

The authorities' visit to Quirpini involves another crescendo, when hundreds of campesinos converge on the town as Carnival concludes in San Lucas. This ritual convergence, repeated on a smaller scale several times over the year, is a key part of what makes San Lucas the regional center; it is able to draw people from the surrounding communities not only as individual economic actors who come to the town's shops but as manifestations of their communities. It was with dismay that members of the town elite told me that fewer groups came to town for Carnival in recent years, one result of the erosion of the town's regional hegemony.

This visit by the authorities and their entourage anchors the communal geography they have just enacted in a larger hierarchical geography, and subordinates Quirpini to San Lucas, even while expressing Quirpini's equivalence to Querquehuisi, Yapusiri, and other communities. Because dancers come to San Lucas only from whole communities and never from zonas, for newer communities like Avichuca, sending people to San Lucas today can be a way to assert their autonomy among the campesino communities.

In the course of Carnival, people focus much of their movement on places of convergence: the authorities' houses, San Lucas, and, at the end of the celebration, the school. In most convergences, such as gathering at the school during Carnival or going to San Lucas for a major fiesta, people speak of their movement as if they are going from the "outside" (hawa) to the "inside" (ukhu). Their movement is centripetal, as if they are going farther "into" the social entity in relation to which they are moving. Regular convergence on places like the school, the chapel, or wasis can articulate major elements of the internal spatial and social structure of Quirpini. At the same time, by gathering in a certain place people give that place significance, even as it is the significance of the place that leads them to converge there. Convergence on a center is an instance of people creating the terrain through which they are moving; gathering at the school or at the corregidor's house or at the chapel makes a social group real and at the same time embeds that group in a terrain with specific characteristics and a particular structure. Yet a place does not take its nature from a single incident; a house does not become the center of Quirpini just because Quirpinis gather there once. Instead, centers take on a certain character as people gather there repeatedly, for various purposes. Permanence comes from repetition.

In each of these events, the action culminates when many people collectively make some space a center by converging on it. The people who gather are different in each case, the center they gather at is distinct, and the nature of the center varies significantly, but the broad pattern employed to create the center remains the same. When people take part in a convergence, the place where they converge becomes a center of some kind.

For instance, Quirpinis gather in the school at different times in different combinations throughout the year. Consequently the school as a place takes on a depth, a multiplicity of ways in which it centers Quirpini, whereas the cemetery, visited only in the course of three fiestas and during funerals, does not.

Those who do not go into town on Wednesday may simply stay home to take care of domestic matters, but when people spoke about what to do at home during Carnival, they always mentioned ch'alla-ing one's house and major possessions[12] or livestock. This ch'alla is no simple libation but a significant ritual in itself. Fairly close friends and kin are invited to the household and served chicha and trago. Any goods to be ch'alla-d are brought out to the wirkhi in the center of the patio and decorated with paper streamers; then the hosts invite the guests to libate them, perhaps while murmuring a short prayer. Livestock are ch'alla-d in their pens. After the libation and prayers, everyone settles in to drinking, which can last for the rest of the day. Like the wirkhi itself, and the q'uwara, this is an offering to the Pachamama, intended to invoke her blessing.

In contrast to the pattern of ascending convergences played out in the karniwalkuna visits of Tuesday and Wednesday, a ch'alla is an enactment of household networks. This seemed to make some people anxious; because so many people were offering ch'allas in such a short amount of time, everyone had to decide, sometimes awkwardly, about which ch'allas to attend. Carnival was the occasion when I was most often reproached for failing to attend people's social events. Like corn-planting mink'a, these celebrations invoke a space that is ideally balanced through reciprocal visits. Also like mink'as, they are focused on the Pachamama.

On Thursday morning the musicians and dancers who had gone to town the day before divide into an "upper" (*patakuna*) and "lower" (*urakuna*) group; the first starts out from the extreme "upstream" point in Zona Quirpini, and the second begins at the "lowest" part of Sakapampa. At each house the *carnavalkuna* enter and must be greeted, served chicha and trago, and strewn with confetti while they dance; flour might be smeared on their faces. They stay from a few minutes to half an hour and then proceed on. The procession of visitors grows as the day goes on because people often join in once the group arrives at their house. Every Catholic household is visited in this way, and each one has prepared corn beer and bought cane alcohol. The community and school authorities must, in addition to serving everyone who comes, arrange for someone to climb up on the roof and throw hard candies and peaches down on the visitors, all of whom grab as much as they can amid great merriment. The two groups have made plans in advance to be fed at certain houses, and usually know which house they will spend the night in. Both years that I was at Carnival in Quirpini, the two groups met at the top of Villcasana close to Miguel Paco's house, which was near the spot where the dancers from Quirpini crossed the river into Villcasana (see Figure 4.3). To be more precise, both years they met at my house, just below Miguel's.[13] They normally met somewhere in this area, I was told.

By the second year I realized that I would be expected to entertain at least one pantilla, and my comadres Anisa Ibarra and Carminsa Santos agreed to

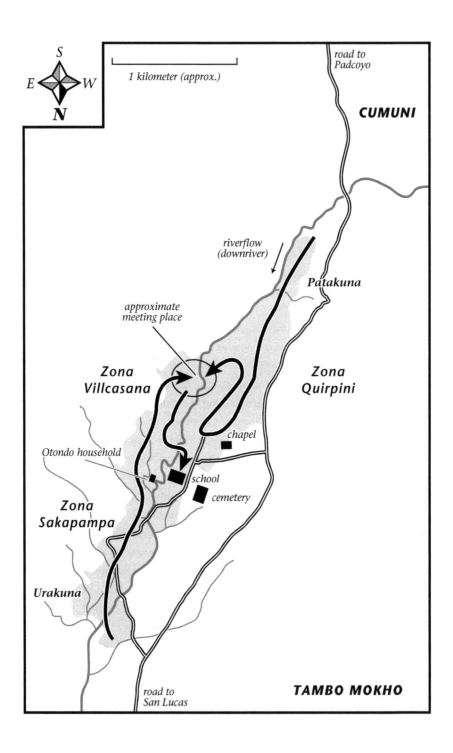

S E W N

1 kilometer (approx.)

road to
Padcoyo

CUMUNI

riverflow
(downriver)

Patakuna

approximate
meeting place

Zona
Villcasana

Zona
Quirpini

chapel

Otondo household

school

Zona
Sakapampa

cemetery

Urakuna

road to
San Lucas

TAMBO MOKHO

help me. It turned out that in order to welcome the pantilla properly, it was necessary to have a good supply of chicha and trago, as well as a separate bottle of trago for the musicians to drink as they danced around the pot of chicha in the center of the patio. There had to be a special place for the tata kurajkuna to sit together. Once the pantilla arrived, there would be more things going on at once than one or even two people could keep track of, so normally friends or kin were needed to help with the serving. The hosts started serving as soon as people arrived in the patio—a glass of chicha followed by a cup of trago for everyone, and they had to hurry up and drink so that the next person could be served. Any kurajkuna who came by were seated in their places and anointed with confetti and flour.

There is tremendous leeway in the amount of effort to exert in welcoming people. Those who are doing full-scale ch'allas that year will have arches of greens put up in their patios and are likely to have prepared more expensive drinks such as *coctel* (soft drinks mixed with alcohol). A host might ask a few friends to stay after the pantilla has left, and then ch'alla the house. The kurajkuna are expected to put on a bigger spread, serving food to their guests, and they often invite people to come directly to their celebrations before the pantilla, joining the larger group only when it arrives at their houses.

The most obvious peculiarity of the visits of the last two days of Carnival is their division into two halves. It is well known among Andeanists that indigenous communities are typically made up of two moieties, usually called the "upper" and "lower" parts (see, for instance, Platt 1978; see also chapter 1 of this volume). This pattern of social strcture is consistent with a widespread Andean notion that wholes are ideally made up of two complementary halves. Although Quirpinis share this view, an attitude that finds expression in kin terminology, rituals, drinking habits, and sundry routine activities, there was for the most part no hint that Quirpini itself was made up of two halves. On the contrary, the visits on Thursday and Friday of Carnival are the only times when Quirpini is treated as an entity having

Figure 4.3. Approximate route of the "urakuna" and "patakuna" pantillas on Thursday and Friday of Carnival. Based on Instituto Geográfico Militar maps: Hoja 6533I (Serie H731) and Hoja 6533II (Serie H731) as well as Instituto Geográfico Militar aerial photos.

an upper and lower half. Even during Carnival, the community cannot be said to be divided into two geographically distinguished halves as Andean communities are wont to be, since the meeting point where the "uppers" and "lowers" meet can shift slightly from year to year. Thus, although someone who lives in Sakapampa (far below the middle of the community) will never be visited at home by the patakuna, and someone in upper Zona Quirpini will never see the urakuna in his house, I never heard anyone say that his house was in the "upper " or "lower" part of Quirpini. The identification of the core dancers in the two pantillas is arbitrary as well: since most of the community's flautists live in Sakapampa, and a pantilla must have flute music, both the "upper" and the "lower" groups are dominated by people from the lower part of Quirpini. For two days of the year Quirpinis act as if their community is made up of something like moieties, but they do not act that way at any other time.

When the two groups of dancers and revelers came together, the music and dancing reached an even more intense pitch, as the flautists competed to be heard and the two groups of dancers merged. By now most people were quite drunk and boisterously enjoying themselves. After a short time dancing in the house where they met, the now united group continued visiting houses downriver in Villcasana, until the group arrived at Potrero, the home of Adolfo Otondo. There Adolfo gave everyone food and drink, entertaining them somewhat in the manner that the town notables had done on Wednesday. From there, the group crossed the river and arrived at the school in the late afternoon or early evening. Some people skipped some or all of the visits and went directly to the school, so the group reached the largest numbers it had had all day, even outstripping the number of people at the corregidor's house on Tuesday.

One aspect of the San Lucas Carnival celebration seemed to influence the Quirpini celebration while I was there. Entirely apart from pantillas and their visits, many youths of the community had begun forming comparsas. Dancing in a comparsa required no "traditional" clothes; boys wore sandals, trousers, and shirts, and girls dressed in *polleras*, pleated skirts with petticoats, which, though ethnically marked, were viewed as modern rather than traditional. The music was popular *huayños* and *cuecas* played on a boom box carried by one of the youths, music one might hear at a truck stop or a party in a mestizo town. The youths organized their comparsas by zona, and each one had an *alferéz*, or an adult sponsor, as well as various sponsors, or *padrinos*, who paid for aspects of the revelry.[14] The comparsas held a series of "practices" before and during Carnival, at which young men and women danced and drank together; their public manifestation came on the last two days of Carnival when they visited the houses of their padrinos (who were expected to entertain them in the usual Carnival fashion) and were given a party by their alferéz; they then turned up at the school at about the same time as the combined pantilla did, usually not quite as drunk as the adults. It was impossible to tell whether the comparsas would replace the pantillas as the youth grew up, or whether they represented an addition to the more traditional kind of visits, or whether they were a passing fancy.

The one time I made it to the school, everyone was exhausted after four days of intense celebration, too drunk and worn out even to dance very convincingly, and many people either never made it there or left right after they arrived. Only the youths of the comparsa had the energy to dash about in a kind of snake dance, trying to be as disruptive as possible. By the time it was getting dark, the dancers and flautists had fallen asleep or gone home, and few people remained in the schoolyard.

The culmination of Carnival is an echo, in Quirpini, of the visits to the town notables. Sometimes these visits are followed by a gathering at the local center of official power. Tuesday culminates with a dance at the mayor's office, and Friday's final dance takes place in the school, which, as discussed in the next two chapters, is the main site through which outside authority is exerted on Quirpini.

As on Tuesday, Thursday's and Friday's activities were made up of visits spanning the "whole" of Quirpini. But these later visits were anything but a repetition of Tuesday's visits; their spatial organization, and the sociality they evoked, was strikingly different from the earlier visits. Most obviously, while the visits on Tuesday were organized to be homologous with the community's authority structure, the only large-scale structure apparent in the course of the later visits was the upper-lower division and the bringing together of the entire community in the school. Although the kurajkuna were honored during these visits, only some aspects of the day's action were organized around them. Whereas the repeated pattern of visits on Tuesday was a convergence, the dominant spatial pattern on Thursday and Friday was a series of sequential visits, which ultimately take in "every" household in Quirpini.[15] The only significant convergence was centered on the school, at the end of the day. That there was no host at the school I take to be evocative of the community's self-constitution; at the pinnacle of its own space, Quirpini hosts itself.

Where convergence is a way of creating/invoking hierarchy through movement, sequential visits have the converse effect, spatializing a relationship between the traveler (or the traveler's household, community, and so on) and a group of people, households, or places treated as broadly similar to one another. An effect of such visits is to constitute, for each household, a social field, or totality, characterized by the (situational) equivalence of all its members. For instance, in the course of Thursday and Friday, Nicanor Huarachi normally visited Agustín Villcasana, not out of friendship, nor in light of any history of cooperation and visits existing between their households, but because the pantilla that started at the bottom of the community passed through Pumakuna (where Nicanor lives) before it reached the main part of Villcasana (where Agustín lives). By the same token, once Nicanor joined the pantilla, he could not avoid visiting Agustín, even if they did not get along, and Agustín could not refuse to offer him chicha. Nicanor would also visit Pablo Puma, and although he was much more intimate with Pablo than with Agustín, his visit to each household would not reflect strongly the different social relationships. During the two days of visits within Quirpini, most interpersonal and inter-wasi relationships are trumped by infra-communal relationships.[16] People's interactions during these visits are mediated by their common membership in the totality of Quirpini.

At the same time these visits inscribe relationships onto the terrain of Quirpini—they have a strict spatial order to them, dividing the community into upper and lower parts, which are united at Otondo's house and the school, and in the course of the visits Quirpinis traverse large sections of the community's inhabited area.[17] On these days, as people avoid the mountains out of fear of the mallkus, and travel from house to house stealing stalks of corn from the growing fields, they occupy a terrain that is collapsed into the irrigated parts of the valley where people live, and entirely filled with Quirpinis and fields. In these serial visits, Quirpinis physically traverse the land that contains their social relations; their travels do not just embody aspects of their social structure but put them in place, as well, enacting a social field as part of a terrain.

These outward-oriented series of visits are a spatial and structural complement to the inward convergences. Convergence, going toward a center, decenters the travelers in relation to some place, which is rendered a center by those who are traveling to it. Those gathering there are rendered in some sense equivalent (they are all Quirpinis, all subject to the authority of the corregidor, or to the preeminence of San Lucas; in other situations, they might be all Christians, subject to the Church and Jesus, all Bolivian citizens exercising their vote, and so on). In contrast, serial visits center the traveling subject in relation to a field of equivalent people, groups, or places. This sort of visit emphasizes the equivalence of those visited in relation to the visitor. The field so constituted is not inherently hierarchical.

Sequential visits enact equal social and geographical fields in many other situations. For instance, funeral processions always stop at a series of *samas*, or resting places,[18] on the road to the cemetery. Every procession that takes a given route stops at the same samas; they are permanent parts of the terrain for those familiar with them. Another ascending sequential movement comes during cleaning of the irrigation canals. The process starts with a convergence, as men from each household with land on the canal gather at a spot near the bottom of the canal, and then they move upstream, digging silt out of the bottom and sides of the canal. Each person present is given a section of canal to dig, about two meters long, measured out by a rod (vara) carried by someone designated by the water judge. When everyone has completed his section, and a stretch of the canal is cleaned, each climbs out of the canal and walks to his next section and begins digging again. In this way, a work group can clear several kilometers of canal in a day, each person working on a sequence of sections; together the group traces the entire course of the canal.

In both convergence and serial visits, travelers encompass wholes through their movement but in different ways. In serial visits, the subject is centered in relation to some whole, made up of parts. In convergence, subjects act out a structural/spatial hierarchy, in which a larger place made up of moving parts is manifested in a smaller, central place. Convergence tends inherently to constitute hierarchical spaces, although the places (and hierarchies) created may have different levels of permanence.

For the next few days, through Sunday, which is the day of Tentación, people are mainly occupied ch'alla-ing their households and goods, and drinking leftover beer and trago. Some people visit back and forth during these days, depending on whether anyone close to them plans to ch'alla and how much more drinking they want to do. Many people still have chicha even after all their domestic ch'allas and spend the weekend drinking, not out of ritual propriety but just enjoyment. Visits on these closing days are entirely domestic; people invite and visit their friends and kin, and all rituals are held in people's homes. Everyone who takes part in Carnival goes about in something of an exhausted torpor.

During the entire Carnival period of about six days, one must be careful to avoid going into the mountains, as the mallkus are particularly active and dangerous, much as they are in August. The danger is greater than in the winter, however, because of the *paquma*, the mallku who looks, I was told, "just like a Carnival dancer" and roams among the paths and houses, trying to lure people into the mountains. Anyone who joins the *paquma* runs the risk of being driven mad or just disappearing into the mountains, never to be seen again. Although I never saw anyone express doubts about joining dancers because of the *paquma*, I knew people who had nearly been fooled by them in the past. After Tentación, which marks the end of Carnival for Quirpinis, a few people begin observing Lent, while the others go back to normal life.

Celebrations like Carnival have no social exterior in that, unlike border rituals, they make no reference to any human space that is not part of the activity going on (Rockefeller 1998). In fact, the one inside/outside distinction made—avoiding the mountains and fear of the paquma, who invades the cultivated valley bottom—does not even define a place but rather marks a categorical contrast between the social world, where all is inclusion, and the world of wild animals and mallkus, which must be kept out.[19] The place people enact in Carnival visits is characterized by houses and paths, communal and regional authorities, reciprocal ties between households; borders command no deference during these days. The places of Carnival are not marked by gestures of separation (such as not talking with women) or fixture (such as placing rocks on a mujun) but by patterns of connection and inclusion— mainly by the visits which make up so much of the fiesta's activities. In Carnival, there are no social spaces beyond those that people visit.

People's movements during the fiesta cluster around certain social groups (households, communities, the region), both in that people go to places associated with those groups (patios, the school, the San Lucas plaza) and that people move about in groups which reference those groups (e.g., the household visits on days 3 and 4 or the dancing groups that go to San Lucas on day 2). Yet at no point do the festivities make any special gesture to the borders of any of these things; the borders of Quirpini and San Lucas go completely unmarked when they are crossed. So consistent is the lack of emphasis on borders that when the dancers arrive at someone's house on the first, third, and fourth days, they do not call out, wait to be invited in, or in any way acknowledge the domestic space of the house; instead, they barge directly into the patio.[20] When the pantilla goes down to San Lucas, it passes right by the resting spots observed by funerals and most other processions.

Several important articulations come to the fore in this dance of encompassment. First of all, Quirpini is one of the key moments in which households and the networked sociality they engage in are enacted as constituent elements of the community. This is done to a great extent through the kurajkuna, which, as I discuss further in the next chapter and in the conclusion, is a prime institution by which Quirpinis (particularly men) realize the full social possibilities of their personhood: to serve in the full hierarchy of kurajkuna positions, with the considerable costs and sacrifices entailed, is the ideal goal for a man and his family.

The other main articulation is between Quirpini and San Lucas. At the first moment that "all" of Quirpini comes together at the house of the corregidor, enacting the community and its authority structure, the authorities set off for San Lucas to visit the people who have the most direct authority over them. At the moment that Quirpini represents itself to itself, it subordinates itself to the criollos of the town and incorporates itself into the ethnic hierarchy of the region. At the end of Carnival, when the "uppers" and the "lowers" meet at the school, their celebration is modeled on the regional dance sponsored by the mayor two days earlier. And as we will see in the next two chapters, the school, though in many ways the most important locus and instantiation of communal unity, is also the most important locus of Quirpini's inclusion in, and subordination to, various institutions of the dominant criollo society. It would be a mistake, then, to place much emphasis at all on Quirpini as a place with any but the most momentary capacity to define its own terms of existence. It exists as an ethnically subordinated place, home to a subordinated people.

Getting to Quirpini

Insofar as Quirpini persists, and insistently impresses itself on Quirpinis and others, it is because of its polymorphous quality, the way it manifests itself as a border, a center, a system of authority, a set of rights to grazing lands, a collection of households bound by mutual obligations, three zonas, a school, and so on. Quirpini is such a complex and rich schema, or schema of schemata, because of the many appearances it has according to the various things people do in it and in relation to it.

All these are enacted through movement, which is always located but only provisionally contained. Just as houses exist in connection to other houses, to fields, and to the water flowing by, Quirpini only exists in its connections, its subordination, and its inclusions. This is why looking at multiple scales is indispensable. In trying to understand the order of the place, my main approach has been to look at what we could think of as "rhymes" in action. The pattern of visits in Carnival, for instance, is a kind of rhyme—the repetition of key features (of travel, rather than speech) of an action in different situations, with different frequency, which creates, as Jakobson (1960, 1970) points out for all sorts of formal repetition in poetry, a sense of order. As in Jakobson's poetics, the main element that makes it possible to sense that something is significant is that it is repeated as part of a structured pattern. So the definition of a visit that I gave at the start of my discussion of Carnival, and the further generalizations I made about visits, are abstractions from the dozens of visits I witnessed and the conversations I had with Quirpinis about Carnival. Similarly, placing stones when entering and leaving certain parts of Quirpini is a kind of formal repetition whose result is a border, or an indexical reference to a border.

These movement-rhymes tell us a great deal about the space in which Quirpinis live. Internally Quirpini is, on the one hand, a space of egalitarian networks, as seen in the many kinds of balanced mutual visits of Carnival, corn planting, and the many occasions of daily life. It is also somewhat like a nation-state, an undifferentiated class of households, all equally part of the community; this aspect of the community's social space is acted out in the serial visits on the last two days of Carnival, as well as at moments like the house-to-house invitations that precede the monthly community meetings. This nation-like space centers on the school. Third, Quirpini is a hierarchically organized space articulated entirely through the communal authorities. The last two kinds of space—the uniform group and the hierarchical structure—culminated outside of Quirpini, linking it inextricably to multiple aspects of the dominant criollo world.

PART 3 ～ FROM QUIRPINI

5 · Ethnic Politics and the Control of Movement

Not long before I came to Quirpini, the major political role of its kurajkuna, apart from ritual duties, was performing menial services for officials in San Lucas. Most of the kurajkuna had to go to town weekly for tasks like sweeping the mayor's patio, taking eggs to town authorities, or gathering their firewood.

A commonplace in the political anthropology of the Andes is that it is central to the roles of communal authorities to represent the community to outsiders, particularly neighboring communities and elements of the dominant Hispanic society and government (Abercrombie 1998; Rasnake 1988). Seen in this way, the services the kurajkuna provided to San Lucas officials were much more than perquisites enjoyed by the central town's Spanish-speaking elite. They represented Quirpini's subordination to San Lucas. By performing menial tasks and giving minor tribute, authorities repeatedly enacted Quirpini's submission to the regional center. By traveling to town, as did the kurajkuna of other communities, they underlined the key spatial element in regional political hierarchies: Quirpini is peripheral; San Lucas is central. This was the politico-spatial import of authority visits to town during Carnival, Christmas, Easter, and other fiestas.

That is how things stood until a new priest, Juan Miranda, was assigned to San Lucas in the early 1980s. He began a program aimed at reducing campesino communities' subservience, and key to this was putting an end to the kurajkunas' services to town authorities. In Quirpini this change took place through an attack on the kurajkuna itself as it then existed. According to the then head of the communal peasant union, Justiniano Cruz (my main source about these events), the official leader of the community (at the time called the cacique) was ineffective. With Miranda's support, the union got the community to remove the kurajkuna, including the cacique, and to institute a number of changes in their functioning. Each new official would be chosen by popular vote at a meeting, rather than by his predecessor, as in the past. Whereas each authority used to change on a different date, according to the cycle of fiestas, now all the kurajkuna would be chosen together, and take office together.[1] And, finally, the community unilaterally declared that the kurajkuna would no longer perform services for town authorities.

These reforms radically altered the way the kurajkuna represented Quirpini. Up to the 1980s Quirpini authorities mostly represented their community to others by embodying its subservience to San Lucas. When this relationship ended, the kurajkuna's political role became unclear.

The reader might be suspicious by now of what looks like a familiar trope: indigenous people trapped within a changeless situation until a white cosmopolitan instigates historically transformative, liberating action. This is the basic theme of stories such as the classic tale of cold-war developmentalism, *The Ugly American* (Lederer and Burdick 1958), not to mention a major rhetorical justification of colonialism.[2] Although better than Whitman's consignment of "aborigines" to a receding past, this certainly was no endorsement of indigenous people's capacity for action. I argue that, in fact, these events, including how they happened and their aftermath, are emblematic of the political reality prevailing in the San Lucas valley at the time. If it seems at times that Quirpini campesinos were without historical agency, it is because the ethnic-political order of the region was devoted to achieving precisely that condition. If "aborigines" are outside history, it is because they are kept out.

By looking at the various political structures purporting to govern Quirpini and by interpreting several actions Quirpinis were able to take together, this chapter reveals the severe, although nearly invisible, constraints on historical action under which Quirpinis operated, both individually and collectively. Many of these constraints depended on the elite's control of space—how people, goods, and even information could move, and particularly how people could come together to extend their own actions across the terrain.

Quirpini was full of political institutions and authorities that appeared to do something but in practice did very little. The kurajkuna were the most glaring example: universally invoked as the "political authorities" of the community, they were notable for being unable to take or initiate collective action on their own that might transform the community's situation in the long term. Taking them as the first of several examples, I show how the conditions under which they were able to act consistently left them dependent on some faction or other of the Spanish-speaking elite of San Lucas. The very basis on which the kurajkuna acted gives the terms of their disempowerment.

My central concern in this chapter, then, is how it was that institutions whose apparent raison d'être was to bring people together for transformative action failed in practice to provide a basis for this sort of action. I demonstrate how this failure followed in the way they were situated in regional political conditions: their place in the regional political terrain. This issue is particularly apt for a place like Quirpini because of the combination of clear ethnic divisions between the town's elite and the campesinos, and the extremely subtle and indirect way that the elite maintained power, even amid their insistent talk of equality and cooperation. Though it was rare to see a townsperson in Quirpini, and there was little sign that the elite maintained direct coercive relations with community members, the village was clearly dominated by the town.

This is evident in how regularly Quirpinis had to go into town, for example, to buy dry goods, baptize infants, get the priest's blessing, acquire government documents, take part in legal proceedings, find local wage labor, or attend regional fiestas. Regional power relations can be traced by observing people's patterns of movement. Most Quirpinis maintained asymmetrical fictive kinship relations with townspeople; regional political posts were dominated by townspeople; and when campesinos and members of the town's elite encountered one another, the deference of the first and expansiveness of the second clearly indicated their relative status.

The basis of elite dominance eluded me at first. It was not maintained through the regular use of force or even the threat of it. There was usually only one regional policeman, and though he was generally considered abusive and corrupt, as noted in chapter 2, he rarely impinged on life outside town. The San Lucas elite did not own all the land, as many regional elites did in rural Bolivia until the 1950s. They owned the best land and generally had the largest plots, but nearly everyone in the valley was part of a household with at least some land. Quirpinis often spoke as if they were largely independent of the town, and in many respects they were. They alone made everyday decisions about their personal and social lives. Indeed, my sense was that most members of the town elite felt more ill-at-ease in the countryside than campesinos did in town. Members of the elite rarely ventured outside the town's immediate environs without a specific reason, and the town's young people occupied a practical geography comprising the town, its immediate environs, the main road, and some nearby cities. The surrounding countryside seemed hardly to exist for them as a space in which they could move.

Yet the elite reproduced their power by maintaining certain positions in an overall scheme of regional movement, and especially by mediating relationships between others. I show here how the elite held power by arbitrating—and thus limiting—the ability of campesinos to act. I also demonstrate how this mediation depended on the ability to influence the movement of things, forms of value such as money and goods, and, most notably, people. I begin with the complex structure and positions of the town elite, and then examine a series of institutions in Quirpini which one might suppose to be loci of collective agency, showing how they are neutralized by the capacity of the town elite to insert themselves into campesino projects at crucial junctures.

The San Lucas Elite—Mediation and Power

The San Lucas elite were in no way monolithic or united. Heterogeneous, riven by divisions, they were joined only by a shared position in regional politics. This internal fracturing turns out to have been central to their way of maintaining power. Quirpinis did not have any single generic term for members of the town elite. They were variously called *caballeros* (gentlefolk), *refinados* (refined people), *gente del pueblo* (townspeople), and occasionally *wiraqhuchas* (an archaic name for a pre-conquest Andean god, widely used as a term of respect for non-indigenous people).[3] They called themselves *gente decente* (decent folk) or *San Luqueños*. Rather than arbitrarily generalizing any one of these labels, in calling them an "elite" I have coined my own descriptive term. Occasionally I refer to them as "refinados," a term I heard often in Quirpini.[4]

This landed group generally supplied the mayor and corregidor, as well as certain lesser government functionaries such as the notary public and administrative staff of the court. Most stores and trucks were owned by members of this group; until shortly before my fieldwork, all of them were. Unusual for a small rural town, almost all the teachers in the town's two schools were from the local elite. San Lucas has long been famous for its teachers, who work in schools throughout the department. Teachers in the countryside, too, were drawn overwhelmingly from the town.

Some movement between the campesino and elite identities was possible, although this scandalized members of the elite. I was sometimes told, as though it were a dark secret, that so-and-so was *really* a campesino, having grown up in a village, or speaking Quechua, or extremely poor. Although they strove to maintain the distinction between the two groups, the elite of course had constant relations with campesinos, sometimes intimate but generally hierarchical. Most common, providing the dominant metaphor for campesino-elite relations globally, was the relation between a padrino/madrina (godfather and godmother) and their *ahijados* and compadres. A padrino fictive kin who assists his ahijado (godchild) at a major Catholic sacrament such as baptism, confirmation, or marriage customarily accepts some responsibility to help the child materially and personally. Campesinos looking for a padrino for their child's baptism would balance the desire for someone most able to bring benefit with the need for someone with whom they had the sort of ties that could insure that they would fulfill their obligations. Many parents asked members of the town elite to be padrinos, thus involving their children, and themselves, in long-term exchanges of unequal favors. Padrinos might have their ahijados work for them or offer to train them so they could assist in the padrino's enterprises. These relations could be advantageous for children but also highly exploitative and even abusive, in which case there was little recourse. Ahijados were expected to support padrinos in public matters, work for them when asked to do so, and perhaps sell them produce at special prices. They could ask for loans and other monetary favors, as well as intercession with other powerful people. The parents of the ahijado referred to the padrinos as compadre and comadre, or "co-father" and "co-mother," and also enjoyed relations of mutual obligation with the padrinos. Ostensibly equal, in practice these relationships often involved the same asymmetries as those between padrino and ahijado.

Members of the elite lived overwhelmingly in the center of town, within about three blocks of the plaza, in large enclosed houses with multiple patios and tile roofs. Most houses had a spigot in the patio and electric light for the two hours a night when the town ran its generator. As with campesinos, livestock owners kept them in their compounds, and some had cornfields within the town grid. A few owned no land, living off government salaries. They invariably had kin and friendship ties extending to cities, often through close kin who moved there. In fact, many had lived in cities like Sucre or Potosí at some point, and some maintained dual residence. They often sent their children to the cities for secondary school, and most elite children went on to college or professional school. Many prominent members of the older generation of the elite had only a rudimentary education, and I knew one woman, generally accepted as *refinada,* who spoke only Quechua and could neither read nor write. For reasons I discuss later, the traditional elite were abandoning the town and had been reduced to a shadow of their former numbers and power.

Many of these refinados could trace local lineages back to the nineteenth century or even to colonial times. Many were descended from owners of haciendas in the highlands outside the valley, but none appeared to identify with these hacendados. Others had arrived in recent memory, mostly enterprising Spanish-speakers, not of the privileged class, who had worked their way to positions of local prominence. Andrés Burgoa had arrived nearly fifty years before I knew him, buying land and settling in town after working as a transportista and merchant throughout southern Bolivia. Adolfo Otondo's father, Rodolfo, had been a horse trader in the early twentieth century, running horses north from Argentina into Bolivia. He bought land in Quirpini as an intermediate point in which to keep some horses and later settled there, taking up commercial agriculture. I heard of no such outsiders settling permanently in San Lucas during the previous three decades, a period of economic stagnation in the southern Bolivian countryside.

Although the difference between campesino and elite was routinely treated as a matter of race, the San Lucas elite was not easily distinguished by appearance. Some campesinos claimed kinship with undisputedly elite people, although all such ties dated back at least a few generations. My impression was that, until the Land Reform, boundaries between the two identities were more fluid than I found them to be, particularly because, until the 1960s, the elite was much more geographically scattered—they held land throughout the valley and in many instances lived in campesino communities. In the seventies, after large highland landowners were expropriated and the peasant sindicato increased its power, members of the town elite began to concentrate their holdings and move to town. Although no one said so, I sensed that they did this in response to the elimination of the previously dominant highland hacendado class of the region. The elite I encountered appeared to be descended from a mix of the remnants of the hacendado class and those who had occupied an intermediate position between hacendado and campesino (in Bolivia, people in this position were often called mestizos). Their power came indirectly from elsewhere: from the relationship between the San Lucas region and the national government as well as distant markets. They controlled the distribution of goods to external markets, as well as access to most goods coming into the area.

Alongside the traditional elite was a 'rotating elite,' whose members resided in the town temporarily and occupied positions whose power came directly from an outside source. The rotating elite included, for example, the priest and government functionaries such as the policeman, the judge, and most employees of the local government development agency. The judge and priest were necessarily educated, and thus generally of relatively prosperous origins. The policeman was usually of humble background, thrust into distinguished company by the authority of his position. These people could expect to be in town for only a few years and, except for the priest, were generally thought to be corrupt and abusive, intent on profiting from their positions while they could.[5] They mostly hoped to move (back) to a city soon and regarded their time in San Lucas as a step toward that goal. In most Bolivian towns similar to San Lucas, the teachers at the regional schools would also have been members of the rotating elite.

Members of the landed elite continually engaged in factional disputes with one another, some dating back for generations. They tried to recruit members of the rotating elite to their side in the bitter factional rivalries that characterized town politics. Party politics often became a vehicle for these rivalries, which at times made it impossible for certain people or groups to work together. At stake was the control of various local power bases. The *junta civil*, or civic club, is a common Bolivian institution that frequently lays strong claims to being an extra-political body that speaks for all. While I was there, the San Lucas junta civil was controlled by one faction of the landed elite but still maintained a certain prestige. The mayor controlled government funds and some patronage jobs; although the position was popularly elected, the winner always represented some faction of the landed elite.[6] The corregidor, an appointed position, was officially the agent of the provincial prefect and controlled much of the flow of information to and from the government; as a result, the corregidor could influence the distribution of government monies. The corregidor is named by the party in control of the department which helps to ensure that local factions and national parties reinforce each other. This factional infighting (unlike personal and political divisions in Quirpini, which tended not to generate strong factions) gave rise to an amazing level of backbiting and vicious rumor mongering.

All these positions of power were based on larger regional, national, and international sets of relations. The development agency was a governmental entity organized at a departmental level to funnel money from international granting bodies. Ostensibly one of its main goals was to promote agricultural import-substitution (CORDECH, n.d.), but its most effective work was in improving and expanding the region's road system. The priest had money and considerable power to assemble people, thanks to his role as local representative of an organization with long traditions of power at all levels of Bolivian society. This enabled him to control significant monies for educational projects and gave him the legitimacy to convoke people both for church and secular projects such as a network of "mothers' clubs." The judge and the police officer, as well as most of the lesser officials, were local instantiations of theoretically omnipresent national bureaucracies, meant to regulate the relationships among Bolivians, and between Bolivians and the government.

Clearly the elite were not a unified body working together to hold power. But the interests of all its elements were served by a situation where San Lucas dominated regional campesino communities, and certain classes dominated San Lucas. They shared a political position in which power arose from the capacity to articulate relationships between local people and external sources of value and agency. This "brokerage" role gave the whole elite a common interest in maintaining the political centrality of San Lucas in one way or another. Simply put, they made up a dominant social class.

Historically an important tool of regional domination for the San Lucas elite has been control of movement. Like most of rural Bolivia the region had few roads, and the few vehicles in the area were owned by townsfolk or large landowners in the countryside. One manifestation of the town's regional pre-eminence was the large fairs it held three times a year. People came, I was told, from hundreds of kilometers around. Controlling long-distance travel, as well as the terms on which people could gain access to forms of value from elsewhere, San Luqueños used their control of mobility to heighten the town's importance as a place, thus strengthening their control of regional space.

Members of the elite controlled the most important productive resources in the area. They held the most productive land in the valley, and more land than most campesinos, as well as the most productive assets—trucks, a still, a bakery. These assets, although individually owned, came to benefit the whole elite through a combination of kin ties, racist attitudes, and cultural preferences that tended to reinforce bonds among its members. These bonds allowed the class to function even in the face of internal enmities and ideological differences. Yet control of resources is a means to power, not power itself. Most interesting to me is how such control was made into actual local power, and in this regard control of movement was crucial.

During my fieldwork, most vehicles in town were owned by the elite. People traveled between San Lucas and any place outside the area mostly by truck or by "taxi": the latter simply a car or truck that spent each day driving back and forth between San Lucas and Padcoyo, where people caught trucks or buses. Three men in San Lucas devoted themselves mainly to ferrying people back and forth on this route. This put these elite elements in a privileged position to profit (mainly from campesinos), and also to develop prestige and patron-client relations by giving free rides. The concentration of vehicles in elite hands was one way elite solidarity was made into actual class power.

Similarly, until only a few years before I arrived, no campesinos owned stores in town. Store ownership was not unrelated to vehicle ownership: San Lucas stores dealt exclusively in non-local products made, packaged, and distributed in cities. Things in stores came from far away and were brought on trucks. Some store owners also had trucks but most did not, instead making regular trips to Potosí in whatever transport was available, arranging return passage for themselves and for their many bundles of goods. The two or three largest store owners were important figures in town, and were accorded great respect and deference by campesinos.

The largest store belonged to Macedonio Valverde, a man in his late fifties whose family had lived in the area for generations, although now his grown children lived in various Bolivian cities and only visited from time to time. Consisting of a single room in the front of his large, painted adobe house on the main street of town, a half block below the plaza, it boasted a display-case counter and shelves stuffed with canned food, bags of rice and noodles, soap, iodized salt, medicines, cheap plastic toys, small packets of ground red pepper and other spices, flashlights, propane lamps, locks, wire, glass and other hardware, a selection of agricultural implements, pens, notebooks, batteries, and more. Behind the counter were bolts of factory-made cloth, as well as women's blouses and polleras, a crucial wardrobe item for campesina women of the area. From the ceiling hung a single light bulb that was lit when the town generator was running, but for most of the evening on any given day the store was lit by a propane gas lamp. The store had relatively irregular hours but was open for much of each day; inside one could usually find Macedonio himself, his wife Trifonia, or one of his children or grandchildren. Most often there were a few other people there as well, perhaps some refinados sitting about gossiping or a campesino from one of the surrounding communities discussing a purchase. The store was a site for the expression of ethnic hierarchies, and campesinos always showed respect to any townspeople there. Many campesinos were hesitant to enter the store, instead murmuring a request from the door or waiting there until they were urged to enter. Macedonio maintained a kindly condescension with campesino customers, just subtly different from the understated way he interacted with everyone else; the more expressive Trifonia was likely to greet her elite customers affectionately, while often becoming impatient and testy with campesinos. Campesinos invariably called Valverde "don Macedonio," and his wife "doña Trifonia" unless they were linked by fictive kin relations, in which case they called them "compadre" and "comadre." The two of them usually referred to campesinos by their first names or by the more familiar honorific *tatáy* and *mamáy* (particularly because Macedonio had great difficulty remembering names).

Quirpinis constantly used goods from cities and distant rural areas. Many could be bartered, like salt carried by llameros from the highlands near the Uyuni salt flats and hot peppers from the Pilcomayo valley, but households depended increasingly on goods that could be had only for money. Families no longer made most of their clothes but bought cheap manufactured items instead. Any festive meal had to include rice or noodles, and *pikanti*, the dish that was de rigueur for corn-planting parties, required a powdered red pepper only available in town. Those with available cash might eat rice and noodles to vary an otherwise monotonous diet of corn, fava beans, and potatoes. Vegetable oil was used for frying, and people were urged by health officials to use commercial iodized salt. In late summer, as stocks of food from the fall harvest ran low, more and more households supplemented their diet with bought food. All the supplies that children needed for school—pens, notebooks, paper—came from stores. Crucial agricultural tools such as picks, shovels and plough blades were only available from stores.

All these things, which Quirpinis needed from elsewhere and which passed through the cities, could be acquired most readily from stores in town. Until the late 1980s, all the stores had been owned by members of the elite, and during my fieldwork the few stores owned by campesinos were small, with a limited range of inexpensive goods. The main alternatives to buying from elite stores were to travel to cities directly, which meant going there in trucks mostly owned by other members of the elite or buying from regional fairs. Three major fairs were held in San Lucas, reinforcing the town's centrality. To the extent that they controlled the movement of goods from cities into the region, the elite were enriched, and their power enhanced, by campesinos' routine life activities, which could be realized only through some arrangement with members of the elite.

The landed elite generally had much stronger ties with Bolivian cities than campesinos did, and they were able to maintain those ties more effectively. Many had close relatives in cities, and some maintained dual residence. These ties had become stronger as refinados began to abandon San Lucas. With urban ties came influence—a friend at a government office, familiarity with markets and employment, and so on. In practical terms, this meant that one of the most effective ways for Quirpinis to act in cities was through elite connections. Many went to cities to work for refinados from San Lucas or settled in cities with the help of refinados' contacts. Here again, members of the elite could maintain control over campesinos' access to cities and could turn that to their benefit.

Another key to the landed elite's ability to control movement was their domination of government positions. The alcalde and the corregidor influenced how state money was distributed. The alcalde was also the final arbiter of disputes over irrigation water, and in the past he could enforce San Lucas's privileged access to water during a scarcity. Both offices were centers of convergence, as people went there for funds or favors, for mediation, and generally to establish productive relations with these figures. The notary public, who registered all births, marriages, and deaths, was a necessary destination for anyone who sought the state's recognition of a life transition. This role is an example of how the state can turn social transformations (the birth of a child or the event of a marriage) into spatial movements: in order for their social status to be recognized, people had to make the trip to San Lucas, pay a small fee, and fill out a form. Though this position brought little profit or power to its holder, it was another manifestation of the town elite's control of the state's entry into the area, and of other people's contact with the state.

Outsiders such as the judge and policeman were also co-opted by the landed elite, as they were included in most social events and treated as equals. Both were invited to drink with elite men, and their presence was generally requested at weddings and birthday parties. As such, they were able to mingle with elite society, naturally forming alliances there. The San Lucas elite did not so much control access to the courts and law enforcement as incorporate the judge and police into a coalition of interests whereby they supported them in their corrupt practices, and the two authorities generally served the interests of the elite. It also helped that the small court staff was drawn from the local elite. The latter thus held influence over the judge and was in a better position to know what he did. Finally, superior access to state institutions in cities meant that members of the elite were better able to resist abusive behavior by officials and could threaten their positions if the tacit alliance collapsed.

Church and priest also underlay San Lucas's ritual centrality to the region. Many campesinos converged there for five Catholic celebrations: Carnival, Good Friday, Easter, the Patron Saint's Day, and Navidad, or Christmas, when the owners of hilltop crosses brought them to town for blessing. The Patron Saint's Day is a major regional fair, and two other fairs are held on saints' days. Until Quirpini obtained permission to establish a cemetery, people also had to go to town for Todos Santos (All Saints' Day), San Andrés, and San Pedro, the three days when people visit recently deceased kin. In addition to these days, the priest always urged attendance at Mass each Sunday, and sacraments such as baptism, confirmation, confession, and marriage usually took place in church after Mass.[7] In other words, throughout the year Quirpinis and other campesinos had to go to the Church—or to town under Church auspices—to realize key rituals and take part in region-wide gatherings. As during Carnival, constant and repeated convergence reinforced the town's centrality. Ritual convergences also brought people to stores in town, gave them opportunities to visit state officials or the priest, and generally reinforced San Lucas's role as the regional center.

While I was in the area, the San Lucas Church was run by Vicmar Miranda, the brother of his predecessor, Juan. Also a progressive, he shared his brother's program to undermine the town's hegemony. He was consequently subject to a rain of criticism from the town elite. There was even talk of driving him out of town.[8] Disappointment with the Mirandas was particularly intense because, historically, the Church had allied with landed elites; indeed, this was a key part of colonial Spanish strategy to control indigenous people.

Although the position of the town elite was steadily weakening, they still occupied the center of a regional system geared toward reproducing their control. Campesinos, especially those of the valley, had little choice, in living their lives, but to play to elite strength, allowing the elite to enrich themselves while entrenching their position. The rest of the chapter examines how institutions that one might expect would be effective vehicles for Quirpinis' autonomous action on the part of Quirpinis instead reproduced elite positions, either because of inherent limitations or because they were co-opted. I begin with what is ostensibly the main locus of Quirpini's political agency: the kurajkuna.

Structures of Disempowerment

THE KURAJKUNA—MEDIATION AND AUTHORITY

Whenever I asked about communal authorities, Quirpinis referred me to the kurajkuna, never mentioning, for example, the school committee or peasant union leader. It was difficult, however, to establish exactly what kurajkuna had authority over, and what each did. As mentioned in the previous chapter, the ideal was that all Quirpini men[9] hold each position for a one-year term, in a set order as described in the previous chapter: caminero, alcalde segunda, alcalde mayór, kuraka, cacique, and culminating (as of a few years before my fieldwork) in corregidor.

A good part of the action of Carnival consisted of visits made and received by authorities. This is just a part of the structured pattern of movement they enact. They gather weekly for meetings at school, attend a series of rituals in their year of service, and go to people's houses to resolve disputes and report community meetings. Yet they are strictly localized. They are supposed to stay in the area while in office and refrain from long trips. This is not something they always manage (Felix Villcasana spent half his year as alcalde mayór in Argentina), but if they leave for a lengthy period they must name substitutes.

When I finally sat someone down and asked him to list the roles of the various kurajkuna, it became clear why I had such trouble. Apart from the caminero, charged with keeping the community's main paths in good repair, and the corregidor, who authorized certain decisions at weekly meetings, and coordinated activities of other kurajkuna, the only specific role my interlocutor could list for each post was to mediate land disputes. He said, as a group, the kurajkuna could charge fines, but I never heard of this happening while I was there. Except at fiestas and weekly meetings, I only saw authorities acting in their official capacities when they were called upon to mediate disagreements.

This mediating role helps explain the curious distribution of kurajkuna positions. In its simplicity, Quirpini's authority structure is anomalous among Andean communities. Quirpini is one part of what was once a large and complex polity (Abercrombie 1998; Langer 1989) controlling what is now the San Lucas region. Sometimes called Kellaja (Zulawski 1995), this group, itself originally an offshoot of a larger federation of pre-Inka polities based at the southern end of Lake Poopó in Oruro (Abercrombie 1998), comprised three large ayllus—each of which had its own kurajkuna and controlled widely scattered territories interspersed with lands and peoples belonging to unrelated groups. Each ayllu had a hereditary lord, called *kuraka,* and apparently subsidiary groups had lesser authorities in the classic Andean pattern (the difference being that there is no sign the whole was ever divided into halves, but rather into three parts). In the twentieth century the overall integration of the region both weakened and was restructured, with the sub-ayllus of each large ayllu becoming autonomous.

In the 1990s Quirpini was not part of any inclusive "ethnic" whole, although it was integrated into both the greater sindicato structure and the governmental structure whose regional center is the town of San Lucas. Its internal structure was tripartite, yet the zonas had no directly associated authorities. One Quirpini told me that if zonas had authorities of their own, they would separate. The upshot of these changes was that Quirpini appeared to have a complete authority structure with no segmental element at all. But, in a way, the kurajkuna did reflect the community's tripartite structure. In order to choose new officials at community meetings, three individuals, one from each zona, had to be nominated for each position. There was usually little or no discussion of voting, but at the end, each zona nonetheless counted two authorities among its residents. I was told that the positions should rotate among the zonas. If the kurajkuna are understood as representatives of the community, there is no obvious reason for this pattern. But its sense becomes clear if the kurajkuna are understood as mediators of relations within the community. Then, in the case of conflict between zonas, or between people or families from different zonas, each side of the conflict is guaranteed that a mediator will be available.[10] So Quirpini maintained some segmentary elements in its formal political structure, with zonas (ayllus) acting as the constituting element of the whole.

But what did this mean in practice? What actions could the kurajkuna take or motivate? Some examples might help clarify the subtle and indirect action open to them. The fiesta of Santa Wila Cruz (Holy Cross) was most prominently celebrated in Zona Sakapampa. During the 1993 fiesta a youth from Zona Villcasana left his bicycle in the courtyard of a house near the Sakapampa chapel. Late that night when he went to retrieve it, the house owner woke to hear somebody in his patio. Thinking it was a thief he grabbed a large stick and attacked the boy, injuring him quite badly. Over the next few days this became an issue between the two families, and then between the two zonas (which have a history of conflict). The problem was resolved only when the senior kurajkuna from both zonas brought the families together to talk and eventually negotiate an agreement whereby the older man paid for the youth's medical care.

A teenage neighbor of mine in Zona Villcasana, Esteban Ibarra, married a girl from a fairly distant highland community. They never got on well, and he even beat her on their wedding day. After the wedding they fought often, and she repeatedly threatened to go back to her father. Finally, in a particularly bad fight, she beat both her husband and his mother and left for home. The young husband went to corregidor Justo Cruz, the highest authority in Quirpini (and a relative), and together they traveled to the girl's father's house and persuaded her to come back. She returned, and they went back to fighting as before. In this case, once she had returned to her father, who was distant from her in-laws both geographically and in terms of kinship, the best way to mediate was to treat the conflict as an intercommunal problem, sending the community's highest authority. This strategy worked, in part, because he was a relative of the husband.

As a general rule in Quirpini, when people become embroiled in open conflicts—whether husband and wife, siblings, neighbors, the users of different irrigation canals, or members of different zonas—the first step is to find one or a pair of mediators who can take a neutral position because they are not party to the relations dividing the antagonists. Ideally this mediator is at the "lowest" possible level, meaning the person least removed from the relationship without being part of it. The closest such people are relatives or fictive kin. When Adrián Paco drunkenly attacked his wife Eugenia, their neighbor Constantino—friend of the couple, kin to Adrián, and padrino of one of their children—intervened and cajoled them to make up. As I have mentioned, Miguel Paco and Emiliana Puma fought often. Several times the madrina of their marriage, Anisa Ibarra, came to mediate, and once their daughter came to me to make peace. Where no close person can take a neutral stance, an uninvolved party represents each side. In marital disputes there is normally no need to go to the corregidor unless, like Esteban and his wife, the couple represents a broader social divide than usual. Part of the problem in that case was that no one could reasonably take her part or claim to stand in a neutral position between them. Everyone was his relative or neighbor and had not yet developed any strong relations with her.[11]

These incidents also demonstrate how the kurajkuna could shift between different social levels in their mediation. Although the corregidor might represent a Quirpini in his dispute with his wife from another community, he might also represent his own zona in a conflict between two zonas, or take a neutral stance between two households in his zona. Here the seeming vagueness of their role becomes comprehensible. Their position was defined not by a requirement to orchestrate actions but rather by a responsibility to mediate relations. This they could do best when able to reposition themselves freely in relation to factions involved in conflicts—and they were most free when their roles were most undefined. Nonetheless, this vagueness also disguised the extent to which they were incapable of initiating major historical action or mediating relationships beyond a limited range.

If the padrino/ahijado relationship is the ruling metaphor for relations between campesinos and refinados, unity through the mediation of conflict between equals was the metaphor for relations between campesinos. The kurajkuna thus embodied Quirpini as political entity, being the primary mediators of differences between members. Their political centrality can also be seen from their failings in this area. At least a few people felt that the limits of Quirpini's autonomy arose from the limits of the kurajkuna's mediating ability. Hilarión Condori once lamented to me that Quirpini was unable to manage its own affairs. He explained that if two people had a dispute over land, today they would resort to the policeman in town, who would decide in someone's favor and charge fines all around. Had the two gone to the kurajkuna instead, explained Hilarión, they could have worked out a compromise that would prevent the dispute from recurring. And no one would pay a fine.

When Quirpinis spoke about the political vulnerability of the community, one of their most common reference points was internal conflict resolution. That serious disputes went to the police, the judge, the corregidor, or even the priest revealed for them their own lack of power. One reason for this was simply these external authorities' presence and their willingness to intervene when asked. Anyone sufficiently displeased with the kurajkuna's mediation of a problem could simply continue appealing to higher authorities until they reached one with power to enforce a decision—a power no Quirpini authority held.

Even though mediation was the major task of the kurajkuna, then, they were notable for the limits on their ability to mediate. Mediation and alliance-making are essential to any collective action. Where conflicts are successfully resolved, new conditions for parties' interactions are brought about, enabling ongoing peaceful relations. And because they play a major role in creating conditions for further social action, mediators' identities or positions are crucial. The mediator, in effect, creates a social space in which people come together either to interact normally or to act to a common end. Mediators are therefore the condition of the relations they help to regulate.[12] Considerable power is conferred when this role becomes habitual or institutionalized, for mediators can then either enable or block collective action and, in so doing, can easily come to be understood as representations of the relations they effect. The latter was the case in Quirpini, where the kurajkuna were universally treated as the "leaders" of the community, and together were the clearest ritual expression of Quirpini as a political and spatial entity.

These examples of the kurajkuna's (in)ability to mediate relations in Quirpini reveal a key to the regional domination of San Lucas elite. In many crucial areas, one or another elite faction could insert itself in relationships between campesinos. In this way they could either obviate unity among campesinos or, even more powerful, make their own participation into a requisite of that unity, so whatever was achieved through it would have to take elite interests into account. Insofar as the interests of campesinos and elite conflicted, campesinos would have difficulty acting.

To return to the abolition of services to San Lucas officials, with which this chapter began, the reforms were clearly conceived of as being liberatory for Quirpini, being designed to give the community some autonomy. But they also had other results. Ridding communal authorities of their role as, in effect, representatives of Quirpini's submission to San Lucas, the changes deprived those authorities of much of their role as external representatives of the community. This role might have been taken up by the peasant union, but this has not happened, for reasons discussed below.

The change created a new political reality, but not one that allowed institutions in Quirpini independence from the town elite. By undermining the role of the kurajkuna, the reforms further dispersed power in Quirpini, leaving actions still dependent on alliances with external powers, most likely in San Lucas. The reforms probably changed the way further action could be taken by Quirpinis, by attenuating San Lucas authorities' domination and showing the priest to be capable of alliances against some sectors of the town's elite. What they did not do was alter a situation in which Quirpinis could only take historical action on a matter of collective interest if they were in alliance with some elements of the San Lucas elite. The only factor that changed was which element of the elite they could go to.

THE REPRODUCTION OF ELITE PRESENCE—
REUNIONES GENERALES

So far I have described two key actors that govern Quirpini: the kurajkuna and the diverse San Lucas elite. The rest of the chapter considers the variety of political institutions in Quirpini, showing how they work and how their functioning limits the range of what they can do. I start with the periodic "general meetings" in Quirpini, and with the conflict, described in chapter 4, over the new border between Quirpini and the breakaway Zona Cumuni. After the mujun were put up and then torn down, a meeting was called between the two communities. Each group was accompanied by teachers, who were townspeople, from their respective community school. The latter brought along the community record books, in which resolutions and agreements are recorded and signed. They opened the proceedings, described the agenda, periodically summarized the issues, and freely suggested resolutions to problems, shifting between advocating for their communities and taking a neutral position. The teachers' handling of this meeting is indicative of the way that teachers, in general, and the rest of the Spanish-speaking elite in San Lucas, in particular, maintained their political position. They received no direct benefit except that they held onto and expanded the role they had already established in running the school and community meetings.

Quirpini's highest decision-making body is the reunión general, the periodic general meeting held at the school. This is the only situation in which most Quirpini households come together to deliberate, which means that if, say, development officials want to address a message directly to "Quirpini," they must come to a reunión or ask that one be called. From a political perspective, the reunión is the only time Quirpini is enacted by its members en masse as an entity with political agency, just as Carnival is a ritual enactment, or performance, of Quirpini's internal order, and marking a border is an enactment of Quirpini as a territory.

The kurajkuna and the junta would call a reunión at their weekly meetings, according to need, and in practice reuniones were held roughly once a month. Word of an upcoming meeting spread in advance, but authorities visited households early on the day of the meeting to give official notice. Normally the meetings were held at ten in the morning. Theoretically every family was obliged to send at least one adult. In reality, however, there were problems of chronic attendance and lateness; in fact, the start of some meetings had to be delayed sometimes more than an hour, until the quorum of 50 percent of households was present. People invariably drifted in throughout the first half of the meeting.

In reuniones Quirpini seemed at times reduced to its school, the reasons for this leading back to the problem of the paralysis of Quirpini institutions. First of all, reuniones were held in the school auditorium, the only suitable meeting space, and the school was the only institution run at the community level.

As with the kurajkuna, one can see in the reunión general the possibility of an autonomous source of power, by means of which the community could express itself. That this possibility was not realized can be attributed in large part to the way meetings were run. The school auditorium was an adobe room about fifteen meters by five meters. For reuniones, the two long walls were lined with rough plank benches; a table and chair sat at the front. Men mostly sat on the benches; the women (fewer in number) sat near the door in the rear on the floor or on concrete bleachers at the back.[13] The kurajkuna and members of the junta escolar, the school committee, sat on benches toward the front, although if a woman represented an authority family, she sat on the floor with the others. At the front end of the benches sat the teachers in attendance, as well as respected visitors. The school director sat at the table and faced the room to run the meeting.

Positioning people by their gender, political status, and ethnicity created unbalanced power relations. Campesina women hesitated to talk, and when they did, they spoke only briefly and in a low voice. Teachers (male and female) spoke up easily and freely exhorted campesinos to adopt what they regarded as the right decisions, even though they were not part of the community and could not vote. The school director decided the agenda, how much time to allow for points, when to call for a vote, and so on. One time he spent twenty minutes alternately haranguing and cajoling the assembly when he disagreed with their evident will to reject an offer of free breakfast for the schoolchildren. No one was swayed, but only the director or another teacher could have done this.

Effectively, then, when Quirpinis converged on the school to deliberate, they found their meetings run by members of the elite. Most events that happened at school, in fact, were mediated by teachers. The school, one of Quirpini's central spaces, and the reunión, one of its central institutions, were conduits for elite influence over the community. This made meetings more effective: there was always communication between Quirpini and some faction in town, as well as between Quirpini and the teachers, who could influence the distribution of school funds and were better positioned to bring requests to others in the elite if so inclined. Exercising direct, public authority over one's peers was embarrassing for most Quirpinis. It violated a strong egalitarian ethos, particularly among men. The leeway teachers felt directing meetings could make for a more efficient decision-making process. It also, of course, gave teachers subtle power over the subject taken up, how it was addressed, and what actions were mandated. Still, the presence of teachers at meetings was not solely oppressive, nor did Quirpinis treat it as such.

The reunión general, one of the key events whereby Quirpini displayed itself to itself, then, was not only run by someone from the dominant outside element, and physically structured such that its enactment inscribed relations of power furthest from its supposed function. Quirpini's very political being was here represented as mediated by inclusion in a larger whole, dominated by the San Lucas elite via the educational system. When people gathered to make decisions collectively for Quirpini, the teachers were always already there, making themselves—by virtue of their authority at the school and their insistence on running the meetings—one of the conditions for people's gatherings.

SCHOOL AUTHORITIES

To an extent not widely recorded elsewhere in Andeanist literature, the entity most able to represent Quirpini in dealings with outsiders was the junta escolar. Returning to the border conflict between Quirpini and Cumuni, it is significant that during the meeting on the road, the authorities on both sides were school officials. When Quirpini unilaterally put up *mojones*, each group was led by a school official—the president and vice president, respectively—carrying a Bolivian flag.

Throughout the San Lucas region, having a school seems to be the primary requisite of being a community. One of Cumuni's first acts in separating was to build its own school; indeed, some Quirpinis felt that the split was caused by the regional school system's practice of sending Cumuni children to a different high school. When Avichuca separated from Quirpini, building its own school seemed virtually identical to establishing its own community; some Avichucas told me that they wanted their own community largely because the school in Quirpini was too far away. Communities were fragmenting throughout the region, and yet none was without a school to define it.

Quirpini's junta escolar was an institution of six officials elected annually. Much like the graded offices of the kurajkuna, men and their families were expected to progress through the hierarchy of junta positions, from *auxiliar* through *presidente*. Apart from the treasurer's job of handling school money, the roles of the junta's members were mostly interchangeable. They had to attend community meetings and the weekly meetings of community authorities, and the men maintained the school while the women prepared meals for the children. All junta family members planted and harvested the school field.

Not only was the school the one institution explicitly devoted to social reproduction, and thus a crucial place for a community to maintain control. It was also, as mentioned, the only institution that routinely handled money, administered property, and initiated work projects.[14] The junta also officiated at the relatively new local fiesta of Easter, assuming the role enacted by the kurajkuna at other celebrations.

All this might suggest that the school was capable of initiating independent action. Yet the original schools and juntas were created by the San Lucas elite, acting as agents of a national project to create better Bolivian citizens; it is the one area in Quirpini where the elite can intervene in communal affairs and act like authorities in a completely legitimate way. Even in a matter such as the conflict with Quirpini over borders, teachers from both communities' schools took an active, vocal role in discussions. The upshot is that the community's most agentive institution was the point at which elite authority also had the clearest, most legitimate role.

The town of San Lucas, as a kind of regional center (*ukhu,* or interior), was also the point from which the state exercises authority, and from which San Lucas whites exercise control over campesinos in outlying (*hawa*) areas. It is common for places imagined as centers to represent connections with transcendent, overarching power or value (God, the law, a colonizing nation). It is helpful, then, to examine the value or power found at the center, and how it organizes that for which it is a center. In the case of San Lucas, the regional center is occupied by agents of the Bolivian state, the Catholic Church, and the landed elite and their commercial interests. Quirpini's school, similarly, enables acquiring skills regarded as necessary for functioning in the larger society, but it also represents the imposition of state power via the San Lucas elite. Thus it is one of the main places in which all Quirpinis gather to celebrate the wholeness of their community, and yet it is also the place most thoroughly under the control of the San Lucas elite, who run the school in concert with the Church, as agents of the Bolivian state.

The discussion above demonstrates how a complex of influence held by the town elite worked to reproduce elite power by making Quirpinis' potential centers of agency into elite power centers. To show more concretely how this complex of influence worked, here I elaborate on the situation of Macedonio Valverde, the person who, of all the San Luqueños I knew, most effectively combined the possibilities inherent in the elite position. I have already described his store, the largest in Quirpini. He owned relatively large amounts of prime land in San Lucas, on which he mainly grew corn for sale in Potosí. He normally planted and harvested by hiring local San Lucas campesinos, paying them either through *jornal,* a set wage for a day's labor, or through a form of mink'a in which there was no expectation that he would return the labor.[15] He delivered this corn to the market, and supplied his store, with an ancient truck he kept running by constant tinkering. He was also director of Quirpini's school until late 1993, so he normally ran the reuniones. This he did with a somewhat overbearing if apparently well-intentioned air of authority. Ironically one of his favorite refrains was that campesinos should unify and learn to act in concert. He would periodically harangue the assembled Quirpinis for being passive and disorganized, for waiting for people from town to do things for them instead of taking action on their own. As long as he was the one making this speech, he had little reason to worry that they would do so. Macedonio took an active interest in the school's well-being, offering free transport in his truck for school supplies, intervening with town or development officials for the community, and taking time on weekends and vacations to help with school projects. This put him in a somewhat patronal relationship with the entire community, augmenting his already extensive network of compadres and ahijados throughout the area.

Shortly after Macedonio retired from the school, he was chosen as one political party's mayoral candidate. When I saw him in town at this time, particularly if we were in the company of Quirpinis, he would often say that the Quirpinis were his "favorite children."[16] He had done them many favors and expected them to turn up in numbers to vote for him. This overtly paternalistic language revealed more about the actual relation he was building with Quirpini than did his speeches on the need for collective action. He won the election, although the role played by the Quirpinis' broad but grudging support is unclear. Valverde managed to turn his advantageous position into a central site for the circulation of goods and money (through his store and truck), as well as exert great influence over gatherings of campesinos (through the reunión general and the school overall). By the same token, he could influence any collective actions Quirpini took as a result. As a landowner who often hired labor, Valverde became a significant node in the circulations of people, goods, and money in San Lucas. Finally, he managed to parlay these advantages into a key position in governing the town. By establishing patronage relations with Quirpini's school, thus turning one of the community's means of collective action to his own purposes, he was able to claim a power position within the town elite.

THE CAMPESINO UNION AND SPATIAL POLITICS

The CSUTCB, or Sindicato Campensino, described in chapter 1, is one institution that seems to respond to exactly the sort of diffusion of campesino power described here. Oriented to taking significant political action, the union had the advantage of being a national segmentary structure, enabling it to coordinate decisions and actions on many levels and scales. In the San Lucas highlands the sindicato had an activist history, and most non-valley communities were substantially run by the union—a common situation in rural Bolivia (Izkó 1992; Rivera Cusicanqui 1990). Early in my fieldwork I spoke with a development worker who had spent several years visiting a highland community, working so exclusively with the union that he was not even aware that the community had kurajkuna.

The union's *centrál,* or regional command, was dedicated to ending the region's domination by the San Lucas elite. In response to the latter's centrality to inter-campesino relations, the union set up structures of meeting and action excluding the town. The valley sub-*central* rotated meetings between communities but never met in San Lucas, and men who lived in town were not allowed to be members.

The sindicato's struggle was a virtual "cold war" against San Lucas. One aspect of town preeminence was the three commercial fairs held there annually, as well as town authorities' control of revenues from fairs throughout the region. These were part of a large system of annual fairs that brought together local agricultural producers and itinerant urban salespeople, salt vendors from Uyuni and hot pepper growers from the Pilcomayo valley.

The union took control over highland fair revenues in the 1980s, and then took the battle to town, as it were, by trying to undermine fairs in the valley. The raison d'être for the fairs was the trade in peppers from Pilcomayo. Because San Lucas was close to the end of the main road toward the Pilcomayo valley, Pilcomayo traders and producers brought their harvest by donkey to fairs from which other traders shipped them out to sell elsewhere. Between the town and these valleys, however, lay the main highland regions. When an improved road was built to this area in the early 1990s, the local union branches set up a series of fairs on the same days as the fairs in and near San Lucas, hoping to divert the pepper trade to their own towns. Initially they even blocked the roads so that pepper carriers would have to stop in the highlands, and though they were forced to abandon such strong-arm tactics, their overall strategy was effective, and the fairs in town were shrinking every year.

Since the reform of the kurajkuna, in which the sindicato had played a major role, Quirpini's union local had fallen largely into inactivity. The position of general secretary had become just one more public obligation adult men had to fulfill—normally young men with little political standing. For much of my time in Quirpini the community union representative was personally opposed to the union's activities, seeing its leaders as arrogant and undemocratic.

This loss of influence largely came about because the sindicato's struggle against San Lucas had turned into a highland valley conflict. Valley communities like Quirpini were more tied to the town than were highlanders. They used town-based transportation, and campesinos sold their surplus either to San Luqueños or with their help. Valley campesinos depended on valley fairs for consumer goods, not to mention peppers, and for selling their produce easily. When the union turned against the economic and political centrality of the whole valley, Quirpini lay on the town's side of that struggle. One instance of the division of interests came when the union organized protests demanding that the local development agency improve the old mining road connecting the bulk of the region's highland communities to the main highway. The agency had widened and graded the valley road from the highway to San Lucas but ignored the smaller road that went to the highlands. The decisive moment came when dozens of highlanders, organized by the sindicato, rolled rocks onto the road and largely isolated the town and the valley. Inasmuch as Quirpinis depended on regional commerce passing through San Lucas, geography put their interests squarely in line with those of the town elite.

Holding meetings everywhere *except* the valley's center, struggling over the placement of roads, and using tactics like roadblocks, the peasant sindicato practiced a spatial brand of politics. It is not happenstance that my problems with the union began when I walked uninvited into one of their meetings. Much like the town elite, the sindicato maintained its power by controlling people's movement, and it was locked in a deadly struggle with the town over that control. But in spatial politics location is everything, and Quirpini was in the same geographical position as San Lucas.

By offering alternative alliances that bypassed the town elite, the union tried to alter the terms on which history is made in the region. Its segmentary organization allowed for alliances of varying breadth, and thus for bringing considerable resources to bear in any given place or time. Since Quirpini opposed the union on one of the most important regional issues, the local by itself could not mobilize Quirpinis to engage in this system of alliances, and the main place Quirpini could turn for strategic allies was some element of the San Lucas elite. This is precisely what happened in the kurajkuna reform, when the union was energized through an alliance with the priest. Here again geography ruled or, rather, the town ruled through geography: A faction of the elite was able to assert its centrality to any change, even one that undermined the town's geographical power.

INFRA-COMMUNAL ORGANIZATION—ZONAS AND CANALS

But perhaps I am looking in the wrong place for the capacity for autonomous action. Maybe such action simply was not organized communally but by smaller-scale entities instead. Here I look at the two most significant of these entities, the zonas and the irrigation canals, or larqhas. Organizationally they are closely tied up with one another and often carry the same name, so I examine them together.

The zonas were the constitutive parts of Quirpini, as ayllus are in much of the rural Andes. All the community's territory and all "Quirpinis" were part of one of the three zonas (see chapter 1). People of a zona did not necessarily think that they were relatives and held no ideals of exogamy. Zonas were to some extent associated with one or two extended kin groups, referred to by surname. The main part of Sakapampa was dominated by Huarachis, and two smaller areas were mainly inhabited, respectively, by Pumas and Huallpas. Villcasana was named for its main family, who predominated in the lower part, while the upper part, Ibarra, was home to more Ibarras than any other family. Zona Quirpini, the largest, was less clearly associated with any single family, but people spoke of it as the home of the Pacos.

Lands watered by a single canal were in some ways like sub-ayllus, although no one ever referred to them in terms comparable to zonas. Named subdivisions with the clearest identities were usually based on canals—everyone knew Villcasana had two parts, and that Sakapampa had one main and two smaller areas—whereas areas not associated with canals were less widely mentioned. With the exception of the very extensive canal in Quirpini, canals were more clearly identified with kin groups than were zonas. And only canals, not zonas, could make decisions or mobilize collective action. On the other hand, connection with a canal was only a minor part of identity. Evaluating character or talking about social position, everyone placed much more emotional emphasis on people's connections to zonas.

Of the three zonas, Quirpini had the simplest irrigation system. In effect, it had one canal that watered virtually all its fields. A second canal, drawing water from the Castillo Mayu, a small tributary of the San Lucas River, served a few fields until its waters were taken for the benefit of San Lucas residents in 1993, but this canal had little political significance to begin with and, by 1994, had none. The main canal, called Quirpini Larqha, started above the zona, in neighboring Cumuni, with an immense stone water-intake, or *toma*. Above the point where a bridge took the canal across the Castillo Mayu, there was an outlet that allowed water to run back into the river for the lower canals of Villcasana and Sakapampa. Below this outlet the canal divided in two.

The only official whose purview took in all of Zona Quirpini was the water judge of Quirpini Larqha, who directed semiannual cleanings and ensured that someone was available for repairs and to open the outlet at allotted times. Most crucial, the judge allocated water to zona fields. The judge was chosen at an annual meeting of all landholders receiving canal water— the only political activity assembling residents of Zona Quirpini as such. While I was in the area I saw no indication that Zona Quirpini could act as a whole except through irrigation structures. The zona also restricted collective action to issues directly related to the canal, such as donations and work obligations. As an entity capable of action, Zona Quirpini had no existence apart from its canal.

Two canals watered Zona Villcasana, across the river. The larger, Villcasana Larqha, irrigated the lower two-thirds, lands belonging to some twenty households. The smaller, Ibarra Larqha, watered lands of about eleven households including Cancha Loma, where I lived. Like Quirpini Larqha these were administered by water judges, chosen at a meeting every year, and Zona Villcasana's political structures were entirely related to canals. But since there were two separate canals, no single political entity could act for the zona. In fact, as an entity that could act in its own right, Zona Villcasana had no existence. I never heard of Villcasana acting as a zona. Householders on each canal were able to act together (although they only did so in relation to the canal), but Villcasana as such never did. When I offered to give a gift to the zona, it quickly became clear that Zona Villcasana had no way to decide what gift "it" wanted, nor any way to accept it. I was forced to talk to people as "members" of a canal, on which basis they could say they wanted cement for canal improvements. When I actually produced the cement for each canal, they had no difficulty organizing work parties or gathering contributions for a celebration after the improvements were completed.

In Sakapampa, zona and canal were more complexly intertwined. Sakapampa had four canals. Three were quite small, serving only four or five families, and the largest, Sakapampa Larqha, served most of the zona households. In the last fifteen years or so, the political functioning of the lesser canals had been largely integrated into that of the larger one. A chapel and a meeting room built by members of Sakapampa Larqha served as a meeting place for the entire zona.

Apart from these varying internal functions, the three main canals—Quirpini, Villcasana, and Sakapampa—had ongoing relations mediated by shared access to a single source:[17] the waters flowing into the San Lucas River from a spring high up on Antahawa, one of the two mountains at the head of the valley that I had seen on my early visit. Sharing a single source was fraught with conflict and required careful planning. The Cumuni canal, which also shared Anatahawa's waters, had a toma that took only a part of the flow. The three in Quirpini used a complex time-sharing scheme: Quirpini Larqha received all the flow at night, and Sakapampa Larqha and Villcasana Larqha divided the day. Since the huge tomas could not be opened or closed, division occurred through *desagües,* or outlets, which returned water into the river. The desagüe of Villcasana Larqha was in a tiny locked adobe house to which only the Villcasana and Sakapampa water judges had a key. Sharing led to continual tension, recurrent confrontations, and negotiations. Part of the bitterness around Cumuni's separation arose from the (later refuted) claim that Cumunis could take all the Antahawa water to irrigate heretofore un-irrigated highland fields in Mishkamayu. But as discordant as it was, this ongoing negotiation over water seemed to underpin part of Quirpini's sense of unity.

Each canal[18] also used to have a cross to protect its fields from hail.[19] These belonged to particular individuals and had names as well canal designations: Ibarra Cruz or Quirpini Cruz. At least one appeared as a person in its owner's divinatory dreams. Normally they were stored in their owners' houses, but on Christmas Eve, regarded the start of hail season, the water judge carried his canal's cross to a Mass in town to be blessed. Each was then placed in a shrine, or *calvario,* on a specific hilltop. There they stood until May 2, when the fiesta of Santa Wila Cruz (Holy Cross) marked the end of the hail season, when each cross's owner had to take it down and throw a small celebration.

On Quirpini Larqha and Ibarra Larqha this had not been observed for several years when I began my work, although it was revived while I was there. Sakapampa saw more elaborate changes. There used to be at least three canal-related crosses in the zona. The cross for the main canal was for years located on top of a high peak outside the zona, but more than a decade before I came to the area, I was told, people decided it was too dangerous to hold a fiesta up there, because people fell off the mountain while walking home drunk. The cross was moved to a lower hill, and then again, in the 1980s, to the zona's new chapel. The zona's minor canals retired their crosses at about that time, and the main cross became the zona's ritual focus. Whereas Santa Wila Cruz on other canals is modest, attended only by those with land on the canal, in Sakapampa it has become a large celebration, drawing people from neighboring communities. It is the only Quirpini fiesta attended by traveling vendors from San Lucas.

Because they were subsumed into Sakapampa Larqha's ritual, the lesser canals were also included partially in its political structure. Even people without land on the main canal joined its work parties. The Producers' Group (Grupo de Productores), set up by the development agency CORDECH to facilitate cooperation with Sakapampa, also helped the zona act together. All this left it, by far, the zona most able to act collectively, primarily because the "whole" zona periodically gathered to deliberate—the Grupo and larqha administrations providing foci of intentionality. For instance, Sakapampa built its chapel without outside influence—the priest was not even aware of it until I mentioned it to him. Shortly before my arrival many households that obtain their water from Sakapampa Larqha descended on the house of Villcasana Larqha's water judge because he had been cutting short their hours, and forced a resolution with no outside interference.

The Grupo also made Sakapampa more able to work with CORDECH, however, because it made the zona a better client. To a great extent, CORD-

ECH was looking not for groups that acted for themselves but ones that could form dependent ties with CORDECH. The Producers' Group existed mainly to bring requests to CORDECH and to execute its plans. It was also effective partly because it doubled as the local campaign headquarters for a national political party with control of local development efforts.

Viewed "from inside," the three zonas were hardly comparable. Villcasana had in effect no internal structure, no means of combining actions or bringing people together. Members never gathered, and there was no occasion for anyone even to visit all the other zona members. It was hardly more than a place with a name and a recognized population and character. It could confer identity and be referred to, but it could not act. Across the river, Zona Quirpini had its single canal with the consequent authority and decision-making apparatus. Should someone want to address the zona in some way, it could be done through the canal and all the zona's people could act together. Politically Quirpini existed through its canal. In Sakapampa one canal had subsumed the others, and the zona had established its own patron fiesta on Wila Cruz. It was able to focus and mobilize activities in such a way that residents could, for instance, work collectively with CORDECH—something other zonas, and the community as a whole, were unable to do consistently.

In relation to the whole community, the zonas displayed some of the recursive structure found in traditional Andean ayllus (see chapter 1), such as their own authorities, yet even such features were semi-covert, and, as noted earlier, people even denied that zonas had their own authorities. Zonas are best seen, then, as vestigial sub-ayllus stripped of most recursive features, probably precisely because such segmentary systems are inclined not only to expansion (Sahlins 1967) but also to fragmentation.

Keeping History in Town

A great deal of politics in San Lucas happens through place and movement: Who controls how people and things move, and who controls the places (literal and figurative) through which collective action moves? Over and over, one or another element of the town elite managed to situate itself where campesinos came together, and make itself a condition of the latter's collective actions.

What appeared to be power structures operating in Quirpini were, in effect, extensions of elite power because of San Luqueños' insertion into their functioning, mostly through the school and the Church. The power of Quirpini's political structures was evanescent; they appeared to almost everyone to be means by which Quirpinis acted in concert, but in practice they were means of disempowerment. Although Quirpinis were indeed engaged in making their own history, the various factions of the San Lucas elite just as busily worked for control over the conditions, and the places, in which they did so.

This chapter addresses a problem implicit, then, in part 1 of this book. If places are created by movement, how is it they so often seem static? The apparent stasis of "local communities" leads many globalization theorists to think that with the generalized circulation of people, goods, money, and information, such "places" must disappear, or at least their representations stand revealed as frauds. If locality is dynamic, why do peasant communities so often appear resistant to change? The answer lies in Lefebvre's approach to how places are produced. Things in the San Lucas region were kept the same by those who actually ruled and who were themselves resistant to change.

But this rule was not direct control or coercion by force. One of its major tools was the artful capacity to control the terms on which campesinos acted. This exemplifies the "structuring interpretation" mentioned in chapter 2. Running meetings, controlling stores, and holding government positions, the elite had a powerful impact on what campesinos could do and how they could do it. In many cases, this meant enhancing campesinos' abilities to act. Decades before my fieldwork there were scarcely any cars in the region, nor many passable roads; by all accounts, since nearly all travel was on foot or horse, no one could monopolize the means of transportation. The introduction of trucks and cars dramatically increased everyone's ability to travel, but it also made control of transport a key element of elite control. This kind of power was premised on the understanding that campesinos' social worlds were made real only through their own actions. The trick was thus to create conditions for action that would reproduce campesinos' subordination.

European elites have long tried to exercise control over peasant mobility (Williams 1973:85), and a key element of colonial Spanish policy relied, only partially successfully, on efforts to keep indigenous people from moving off officially sanctioned paths. The San Lucas elite used their privileged position to maintain control of contacts between the "locality" and the relatively "global" realm of commercial markets, government power, and development money. It was the terms on which Quirpinis could engage distant and inclusive realms of value that rendered the community historically passive.

Nevertheless, the elite found that the conditions under which they made history were changing. Improved transportation infrastructure weakened their position as geographical brokers, as the region became more integrated into national and international economic circuits. Numbers of people migrating, mainly to Buenos Aires, had increased dramatically in recent decades, and by the 1990s some campesinos were returning not just with new consumer goods but also with capital. A few had set up stores in town, and one returnee from Argentina bought himself a large new truck: the first to be owned by a Quirpini. These changes in campesinos' abilities to move on their own were rapidly undermining elite capacities to act as brokers and mediators.

Another factor is that in many ways the urban elite and the central government have been becoming increasingly antagonistic to local elites for several decades, viewing their power not only as often unjust and repressive but also as a regional threat to national integration. This conflict is behind the antagonism of the last two priests to the town elite. Dramatic examples came with the reorganization of local government called Participación Popular—in the name of decentralization it bypassed traditional regional power brokers—and reforms now being promoted by the Movimiento al Socialismo (MAS), giving considerable power to popular organizations at the expense of traditional brokers.

In response to these changes the town elite were on the move in several senses. First, the dominant national classes were taking more power, squeezing out regionally dominant groups. Bolivia's rural ruling classes responded by trying to make themselves part of the national elite, moving from places like San Lucas into the cities and sending their children to universities. They were giving up their city/country mediating position and moving directly to cities themselves. The position of "rural elite" was far more precarious than it had been decades before when people like Andrés Burgoa and Rodolfo Otondo settled in San Lucas. The number of old significant landholding families in San Lucas was dramatically reduced,[20] but whereas few of the elderly elite had even secondary schooling, the norm for their children was to go to college or technical school, and many have advanced degrees as well. Most of this younger generation had moved to or were born in cities, and one lived in Germany. Some relatively wealthy campesinos were also moving into town, where they were on their way to joining a newly constituted dominant group, occupying the mediating space abandoned by old town families.

In sum, both elite and campesinos were becoming less strictly localized in their possibilities for movement, although their spatial practices were changing in different ways. Campesinos bypassed much traditional elite control by working in the cities of Bolivia and in Buenos Aires, opening possibilities to move into the traditional center of regional power. The center was also opening up because the elite were abandoning it. Finding the exploitation of campesinos no longer profitable, they were joining the cosmopolitan society of urban Bolivia.

The foregoing can be taken as a treatment of the limits on action in "normal" times and of how such times are kept normal. Dandler (1984) and especially Lagos (1994) show what happens when alliances cease to limit campesinos' abilities to change the conditions of their own actions. In Dandler's work, Cochabamba campesinos found they could ally with the radical new national government against local landowners, forcing serious land reform. Lagos, in her study of "autonomy" in a rural Bolivian town, demonstrates how the web of alliances that normally constrains transformative action can, under certain conditions, generate it. Though divisions among the San Lucas elite have not become so severe that any faction would enter an alliance that truly threatened the town's centrality, any number of contingencies could facilitate change. If highland unions "won" their struggle against the town, or valley campesinos switched their allegiances in this struggle, the old San Lucas elite would be rapidly marginalized. A slightly more radical Church, or populist central government, could ally with campesinos in ways that put them in an entirely new position. One of the aims of the Movimiento al Socialismo government is precisely to seize historical agency for Bolivia's indigenous campesinado. Only time will tell how their policies will influence the ways that Quirpinis can act.

6 · *Placing Bolivia in Quirpini: Civic Ritual and the Power of Context*

On the cement stage of Quirpini's school auditorium stood a throne: a rough wooden chair, set on top of a wooden table, both covered with colorful factory-made textiles of "indigenous" design. Adorning a stage with textiles of this sort, the carrying-cloths that many Bolivian women use every day, is a technique I had seen at public performances in the cities, signaling that the event under way was of an indigenous nature. This particular native throne was prepared for the crowning of the "Queen of Quirpini," the key figure in the Día del Estudiante (Day of the Student), a pageant celebrated on September 21 in Quirpini, and at schools throughout Bolivia.[1] In Quirpini, the Day of the Student is one of a series of civic rituals celebrated at the school in the course of the year, including Mother's Day, the Day of the Campesino, the great national celebration on August 6, and the *hora cívica* ("civic hour") held before class begins each day.

As well as being one of the main sites through which the town elite of San Lucas reproduce their power in Quirpini, as discussed in the previous chapter, the school is a key stage in which the Bolivian state makes itself present. Although the regional elite and the state had increasingly conflicting programs by the 1990s, a good part of elite power derived from mediating relations between the communities and the state, and the state still relied on the elite to make it present in the San Lucas area. The school, then, was a crucial place in which many of the terms on which Quirpini was integrated into larger, inclusive wholes were established. Included in this role was the school's centrality to the state's efforts to represent itself in ways that would move those who are legally its citizens to experience themselves as such, to encounter themselves and their fellows as members of the Bolivian nation, and as subjects of the Bolivian state. The literature on the nation-building project in Bolivia and Peru is extensive (see, for instance, Abercrombie 1991; Canessa 2005; and García 2005; and for valuable accounts of the role of rural schools in this process, see Luykx 1999 and Arnold 2006). The main tool I use to illuminate the role of the Quirpini school in the production of Bolivian citizens, however, is a modification of Appadurai's argument that nation-states domesticate what he calls "neighborhoods" through the manipulation of contexts for action and interpretation (Appadurai 1996d). This manipulation of context has a powerful yet elusive impact on the way people perform themselves (Butler 1998, 2006). Taken in a geographical sense, Appadurai's point can suggest new ways for thinking about the multi-scalar nature of the social reality people live in nowadays.

This nation-making project had not been without success in Quirpini. While I was working there, I found that people routinely incorporated references to the Bolivian nation and state into their spatial and political practice. The flags that the school authorities waved during the attempt to fix a new Quirpini-Cumuni border were intended to validate the making of a new border by appealing to an inclusive, authoritative political realm. Many people took part in national election campaigns, mostly by benefiting from various parties' patronage systems. All official documents drawn up by Quirpinis included references to Bolivia as the ultimate location of the actions being recorded. Although Quirpinis were by no means the sort of total citizens states yearn for, being Bolivian was a significant part of their identity, their political reality, and their sense of place. Arnold (2006) gives a brilliant discussion of ways that schools and state imagery, including flags, have been incorporated into local Andean realms of meaning. To put it in Weberian terms, a significant portion of campesinos' practice in Quirpini and elsewhere is "oriented to" Bolivia.

Any would-be embracing whole, such as a nation-state, must distribute traces of itself to the places it would claim as its parts. At some point, a hegemonic context must place itself *inside* what it would contain.[2] In this chapter I argue that civic rituals such as the Day of the Student are one part of how

Bolivia is made into a context that contains Quirpini and lends meaning to Quirpinis' actions. Treating such rituals as context-creators is one element of a multi-scalar approach to understanding Quirpini, given that a major aspect of the significance of inclusive political and spatial wholes to a small community is the ways in which they impose themselves as the context for action and its interpretations.

Day of the Student

The date of the event, and the broad outline of its format, is set nationally; the celebration is interpreted in each school, under the direction of the teachers, with assistance from the women of the junta escolar. I attended the pageant in 1993.

The first event was the usual Monday morning hora civica and seemed not to be significantly different from the civic hour held every week.[3] At about eight in the morning the students assembled outside the school, in the dusty semicircular parade area in front of the school gates. The teachers lined them up in rows by gender and grade, facing the flagpole. A pair of students was designated to put up the Bolivian national flag, whereupon everyone put hands over hearts and sang the national anthem. Then the teachers had the students perform some marching drills, and one of the teachers made a short speech on an uplifting subject having to do with comportment or the Bolivian nation.

On most Mondays, once the hora civica was over, the students marched into the school and entered their classrooms. But today was different. Some adults arrived at the school before and during the hora civica, and for a short while after the ceremony the students and most of the adults were left to their own devices—the children, to play in the front and back courtyards of the school, and the adults, to chat and help with the preparations for the rest of the day. In one of the school's back rooms the women of the junta escolar prepared *leche*—powdered milk and chocolate—which they soon served to all the students. The children lined up to receive their hot breakfast, and then went off to play again. A number of adults began wandering into the auditorium where the main events were to take place and then leaving again. Meanwhile, in the back room, the men of the junta and others were putting the finishing touches on the stage decorations in the school's auditorium, as well as on the costume and banner of the *Reina*, or Queen—whose throne we saw at the start of this chapter—a role that would be filled by a student who had been chosen as the most beautiful/talented /nice member of the school. The coronation of the Queen is the central event of the day, and in the town of San Lucas many people refer to the entire celebration as the "*coronación.*"

The year I attended the Day of the Student, it began in earnest at about eleven in the morning. A student was sent to ring a bell, and all the children, as well as the adults who had been drifting into the school all morning, filed into the auditorium and sat down. As always, at events held in the school auditorium, the men removed their hats and sat on rough-hewn benches toward the front of the room, and the women sat nearer the door at the back, especially on the cement risers at the very rear of the room. The teachers sat at the front of the room when they were not directing the proceedings. Macedonio Valverde played music on a battery-run boom box. At the end of the song he called a student up to the front of the room to read a patriotic poem. The boy, no more than ten, dressed in nice pants and a jacket, mounted the stage and recited the poem in a determined monotone, complete with stiff and stylized hand gestures. When he was done, one of the teachers came out and requested that we applaud, which we did, as the boy returned to his seat.

Then the procession began. We were here to celebrate not just a single Queen, but an entire aristocracy. Announced over the boom box by one of the teachers, the children entered in pairs: a princess accompanied by her prince. First the Princess of Goodness entered, then of Poetry, then Beauty, then Studies, accompanied by the Count of Sakapampa, the Prince of Shadows, and two others whose names I do not recall. As each couple entered—the girls in long frilly dresses with plastic tiaras, the boys in suits, some carrying fake swords—they proceeded together to the front of the room, mounted the stage, and took their positions beside the throne. When all the princesses and princes were in place, the *predilectos*, or "favorites," of each class entered—a boy and a girl for each grade. These students, who had been elected by their peers, also went to the stage, where they stood to the outside of the princes and princesses. Finally the Queen entered, accompanied by her King, with two students in the lead carrying her scepter and crown. She was resplendent in a long gown and a sash. The Queen was about ten years old, her consort two years younger. The two proceeded to the stage, where the King helped her ascend the throne, placed a crown on her head, and stood beside her while we were encouraged to applaud heartily.

The coronation over, the school *promotora,* Lucía Huallpa, lined up all the students in the middle of the auditorium, put on a tape of old-fashioned criollo dance music, and cajoled the students into doing a courtly line dance. As the adults began to drift away, Lucía repeatedly urged the uninterested children to continue the dance. Eventually the students went home to eat with their families, and the teachers invited me to a lunch of spicy chicken prepared by the women of the junta escolar.

One striking aspect of the event was the reaction of audience members (mainly parents of schoolchildren). Throughout they were quiet and atten-tive, but rather impassive, applauding when called on to do so but otherwise giving little overt response to the performance. I take this quiet response not as disapproval or even disinterest but rather to be something like parishio-ners' mode of orientation to a Mass: reserved attention. This reaction, entirely expected in a Catholic Church, was much more distinctive in the face of an event which, to my eyes, was meant to be both comically grave and adorable. It seemed to me that the implied script of the event, were it presented to the kind of audience accustomed to this sort of occasion, would have included both af-fection and merriment at the sight of the miniature aristocrats, and frequent exclamations at the utter cuteness of the children in their costumes.

The implied audience of the event, however, was not a group of largely Quechua-speaking campesinos but Spanish-speaking, school-educated Bo-livians. The pageant for the Day of the Student, along with the other civil celebration held at the school, operate by locating themselves and those who participate in them in a context that is national and criollo, rather than local and Quechua or campesino.

In the previous chapter I showed how the regional elite maintained their power by inserting themselves in most of the significant political relations among campesinos, making themselves a condition of campesinos' coming together. This is apt for our current discussion, as it implies that when people join together for some purpose, the circumstances or conditions under which they do so have a great deal to do with what they can accomplish together. What I refer to as "circumstances" are better known in performance and lin-guistic literature as "context," a rather ineffable category denoting that which surrounds some performance but is not part of it.

Ineffability

In an article about how locality is produced in an age of globalization, Arjun Appadurai (1996d:184) pointed out that the production of what he calls "neighborhoods" (which I treat as functionally equivalent to "places") requires the construction of a context in relation to which the neighborhood is understood. Further, by the actions of production and reproduction, people "contribute, generally unwittingly, to the creation of contexts" (185). Nation-states, Appadurai argues, like other encompassing social forms, strive to make themselves into the defining contexts of neighborhoods (187) so as to turn them into the sites of the production not of "local subjects" but of national citizens (190). In other words, a key element of the nation-building process is to incorporate communities and other local social forms into a uniform national context; for this to happen, people's context-creating activities must be bent to creating that national context. Key to understanding how a community like Quirpini is being fit into the "Bolivian nation" or other inclusive wholes has to involve looking at how people are engaged in the production of those realms as a context for their own actions.

By invoking "context" as a way to understand the terms on which people generate and interpret meanings, Appadurai draws on an anthropological approach most often applied in studies of folkloric performance (e.g., Guss 2000; Handler 1984, 1986, 1988; Herzfeld 1982; Kurin 1991) and linguistics, particularly the analysis of texts (Bateson and Reusch 1951; Bauman and Briggs 1990; Briggs and Bauman 1992; Dilley 1999; Hanks 1990, 2000; Howard-Malverde 1981, 1997; Silverstein and Urban 1996). All this work constitutes an effort to develop a methodology from the rather obvious point that the meaning of a text or an action arises in part from that which surrounds and informs it, that in relation to which it is performed, composed or read; that against which "local practices and projects are imagined to take place" (Appadurai 1996d:184).

But actually doing contextual analysis has proven difficult, and there has been a lively debate, mostly among anthropological linguists, about how to incorporate context into the analysis of texts. As Bauman and Briggs (1990) point out, just about anything that is connected to a performance but is not part of it can potentially be treated as part of its context; context is endlessly rich, and does not lend itself to clear delimitation.

Some scholars find the ineffable nature of context frustrating, view its very openness as an impediment to a clear understanding of how it affects the text that it surrounds. Here I take up a particularly extreme version of this critique: Sandor Hervey's claim that trying to incorporate context in any systematic way into an interpretation of linguistic data is indefensible, and nothing but "explaining the unexplained by the inexplicable" (Hervey 1999:67). His argument is that incorporating context in an interpretation forces the investigator into one of two untenable positions: either to include a potentially infinite amount of material in the analysis or to arbitrarily exclude elements of context, thus reducing the problem in an ad hoc fashion that is methodologically opaque. Both these solutions to the problem of including context in interpretation require researchers to make use of material which they cannot account for in terms of their theoretical approach.

For Hervey, this problem is a wrench gleefully tossed into the wheels of contextual analysis, sufficient to bring the whole contraption to a shuddering halt. I contend that, contrary to his own understanding of his argument, Hervey has actually explained why contextual analysis is interesting and useful, and why context matters in the first place.

Hervey never suggests that there is any alternative to contextual analysis or that context does not play a crucial role in determining the meaning of utterances. He only says that *we* cannot employ context in any orderly way to understand statements, although speakers do so all the time. Hervey assumes that what a speaker does in making or interpreting an utterance bears no similarity at all to what linguists do in interpreting the same utterance. But if we imagine that an important similarity exists between what we are up to and what our subjects are doing, then things look quite different. In order to illuminate this difference, let us take a detour to another public performance celebrated in the San Lucas region.

In an earlier article, I examined a folklore festival held every year in the town of San Lucas (Rockefeller 1998). The festival was organized by San Lucas's Catholic Church, in order, as the priest told me, to help revive local indigenous culture by showing the campesinos that it was valuable enough to be presented on stage. In the festival, campesinos from the communities of the region competed in performing traditional songs and dances before an audience of townspeople and campesinos from all over the region. The festival is unusual among such events in that it is put on neither for tourists nor for people held to be estranged from the customs on display, but to an audience made up mostly of people who could just as well be on stage themselves.

Given the audience, it seems unlikely that the dances themselves would be the key communicative element of the festival—they were already too familiar. Rather, the festival was novel, distinct from the fiestas from which the dances were drawn (and the Quirpinis I talked to certainly saw it as something very different), because of the way the dances were framed. They were transposed from a fiesta to a church-sponsored but secular celebration, from the courtyard of a rural house to an assembly hall, from merely accompanying days of general revelry to being the focus of brief but undivided attention from a mass of silent audience members, from a devotional act honoring a religious figure to competition oriented toward winning a prize. In other words, the stage performances were different from fiesta dances because they appeared in a different context.

The effect of the contextual changes wrought by the festival was to detach the dances from their focus on specific localities and divine figures (for example, saints and mountain spirits) and focus them instead on the audience as an invisible presence whose gaze validated the customs on display. This audience and its gaze, I argue, stand in for an encompassing, unstructured, open-ended whole, much like the Bolivian nation. Although the form of the dances may have remained largely unaltered, their telos changed dramatically from being a way to relate to a locality and a variety of divine figures to a means of self-presentation to a validating whole through the medium of "culture." In the folklore festival, culture was implicitly construed as a form of display, a spectacle.

Thus a change of context had the capacity to alter the potential meaning of the dances. Performed in the church assembly hall, the dances no longer connected people to saints or to mountains, no longer insured good rainfall or articulated people within a nested series of encompassing wholes as Carnival dances do. Instead, the dancers were articulating themselves and the audience with the Bolivian nation as spectator to the display of her own citizens.

The change of context was enough to transform the potential meanings of the dances—the new venue established a new range of possible meanings for them, while erasing the ones with which they were originally associated. Context was a source of the performances' value. It is important to note, however, that the campesinos who took part in the event and those who attended as audience members thought it was simply wonderful. They said that the dances were done properly—perhaps more correctly than in actual fiestas—and they were delighted to see them treated as sufficiently important to other people that they could be performed for an audience and occasionally even broadcast over the radio.

No one remarked on the absence of saints or geographical references. People happily took part in the festival, clearly enthusiastic about the intervening speeches on the significance of "Quechua culture" and undisturbed by the way the dances were cut off after only ten minutes and the dancers ushered off stage. In fact, no one even mentioned this aspect of the festival; their attention was focused solely on the dances.

Apparently unconcerned about the shifts of meaning brought about by the different venue and the ancillary changes in context, the people seemed, in fact, to have difficulty addressing the nature of the contextual changes that had created this realm. And this is where Hervey comes in. He demonstrates that contextual analysis always involves incorporating information for which we cannot fully account. If we imagine that the campesinos of Quirpini are themselves always trying to evaluate the import of their own activities and those of others, but that like us they are unable to draw clear conclusions from the endless context in which all actions take place, the power of context to establish values becomes apparent.

By manipulating the surroundings of some performance, a person or institution can potentially alter the field of value in which it takes place, taking control of its potential meanings without making any overt alteration in the performance itself. Yet the ineffable nature of context, its tendency to escape understanding, creates the possibility that the precise nature of this change will go unremarked or resist clear understanding.

This ineffable quality is why context is a source of power and why it lends itself to contestation: context can never be final.

The power of this kind of recontextualization can be seen in another change in ritual context. After years of opposition from San Lucas, the community of Quirpini succeeded in obtaining permission to build its own cemetery instead of bringing those who died to the main cemetery in San Lucas. This meant that the Quirpinis could bury and venerate their deceased without subordinating themselves to the town's Spanish-speaking elite. Both symbolically, because they no longer had to incorporate the town in their care for their ancestors, and practically, because they did not have to deal with their social and political superiors during All Souls Day and other days commemorating the dead, the new cemetery helped to free Quirpinis from the town's dominance. In fact, the struggle I described in the previous chapter about where rituals would be held was played out largely in the idiom of spatial context. The underlying argument was based on the understanding, shared by Quirpinis and the San Lucas elite, that where people carried out certain significant acts was, to a considerable extent, constitutive of the significance of those acts.

By the same token, it is difficult for anyone who would recontextualize a performance to fully know what they are doing; they are little more able than the audience, performers, or anthropologists to know how each aspect of context affects the performance. Thus some Quirpinis were able to take advantage of the new emphasis on culture-based identity favored by the folklore festival to draw away from the Catholic Church and adopt many of the beliefs and attitudes of the growing minority of evangelical Christians in the area, but without rupturing their social bonds the way evangelicals must. They could enter into and operate within the realm of values set up by the folkloric recontextualization of traditional dances while improvising on those values in ways that the Catholic Church, which had organized the festival, would never have supported.

There are two ways in which context can become the site of struggle: people can differ over the way it will be changed (as in the conflict over the cemetery), and, once it is changed, they can struggle over which of the new potential meanings that have been created will become the real meanings of the activity.

Ineffability—the quality of there being no obvious or immediate way to decide what aspects of the conditions surrounding an event are relevant to it—is at the heart of the power of context and its ability to shape the significance of actions. Any person, institution, or even tradition that can establish which aspects of the surroundings are directly relevant to the matter at hand is able to constrain what the event can be "about." This can be done through contextual references in the text of the event or through ad-libs or ancillary commentary. Were the relation of an event or textualized action to its context unambiguous or easily read, it would not be "in play" and would not be available for negotiation. The trick for approaching rituals and other sorts of textualized action, then, is to work out how the actions themselves define their relationship to their context, which in turn establishes what the significance of the actions can be. In other words, such events, if they communicate successfully, will contain "clues," some explicit, some implicit, but comprehensible to their audience, that establish certain aspects of the vast realms of surrounding conditions, as the meaningful "context" in which the action takes place, and from which it draws its potential significance.

The context for a performance or a place—those exterior elements that would govern an action's possible meanings—must insert itself within that which it would contextualize, it must make itself context. This process of becoming the context for an action or place I call "encontextualization": just as a rite, a story, an object can be "entextualized," or made into a text that can be shifted between contexts, contexts must be made within that which they would contain. If the Bolivian state seeks to convince Quirpinis that they are in Bolivia, it must place Bolivia in Quirpini.

Context in the Day of the Student

What is at stake in the Day of the Student is quite different from what is going on in the San Lucas folklore festival. First of all, in the school pageant, there is no appropriation, verbal or enacted, of local cultural forms. Even the textiles adorning the throne evoke the most generic sort of Andean indigeneity, rather than the particularistic focus on regional practices that is so central to the spirit of the folklore festival. A ruling value of the folklore festival, for both organizers and participants is authenticity; it is crucial that the performances be as "real" as possible. In contrast, questions of cultural fidelity play no role in the school ritual. The pageant makes no claims to represent some more "real" pageant; the aristocracy and royalty are clearly metaphorical inventions, not intended to depict actual lords or rulers. While the event does incorporate a number of important representations, they do not open themselves to evaluation in terms of authenticity.

For this reason, the school pageant does not really engage the issues of decontextualization and recontextualization so central to most discussions of context and representation (see Briggs 1996; Briggs and Bauman 1992; Handler 1986; and Kurin 1991). Yet the pageant carries a heavy representational load, and it does so mainly through the ways it acts on context. It is not so much representing Quirpinis as it is a broader world that is identified with the Bolivian nation. It largely does this indexically, through a series of contrasts and plays on cultural distinctions comprehensible to Quirpinis.

The pageant emphasized the contexts that connect to the Spanish-speaking world generally, and Bolivia specifically, rather than to Quirpini or to international sites. At the outset, this orientation was marked by the fact that it was organized and run by the schoolteachers, representatives of both the regional elite and national, criollo values, and by how it was presented. Valverde emphasized that the event was being held simultaneously in schools throughout Bolivia, that it was national. But of course this sort of explicit, verbal contextualization hardly has the power of ineffability.

These contexts are signaled more subtly in the clothing of the children who participate. Normally girls in Quirpini would dress, like adult women, in polleras, topped by blouses and cardigans. Boys would normally wear sandals, simple pants, and T-shirts, perhaps with a sweater. The girls who took part in the pageant, however, wore long dresses, clearly drawn from the criollo culture of the cities. The boys wore fine pants, shoes, jackets, and ties. Wearing and talking about clothes is, of course, a key way that people establish and negotiate ethnic distinctions in the Andes (Tolen 1995; Stephenson 1999; Weismantel 2001). One of the terms by which Quirpinis designate the San Lucas elite is *gente de corbata*, or "people with ties." Wearing a pollera instead of a skirt is a strong marker of ethnic identity. Shoes also delineate boundaries of identity and therefore social norms; when Demetrio Condori once wore shoes to a fiesta, people there openly criticized him for putting on airs. The clothes worn by the princes and princesses invoke an ethnic distinction that is palpable to Quirpinis.

This contextualization of the Day of the Student in urban criollo culture also appeared in the line dance the children performed at the end of the pageant; it resembled dances that members of the town elite enjoy at their fiestas and that, though seen as a bit old-fashioned, were also popular in the cities. The Spanish titles of all the nobility, though more-or-less comprehensible to Spanish-speaking Quirpinis, clearly marked the event as having a Eurocentric formality. It seems unlikely that many of the parents or children at the event would have appreciated the whimsical archaism of the titles, the throne, the swords, and so on, but they doubtless realized that these elements were drawn from urban high culture. The Spanish poems read throughout the beginning of the program, not to mention the Spanish anthem the students sang during the hora civica and the very practice of dressing children in costumes and showing them before an audience, were all characteristic of the civic rituals performed at the school, and Quirpinis were unlikely to encounter them elsewhere.

The entire pageant, a distinctly criollo and Euro-centric fantasy, is a kind of pantomime, quite different from the folklore festival in the way that it deploys representation. Rather than enacting their own culture in a new context which changes some of the potential meanings of their performance, the children who take the central roles are all playacting what urban Bolivians often call *civilización* or, tellingly, *educación*. They do this by acting out not an actual vision of Bolivia but rather a vision of how "civilized" Bolivians would put on a pageant. The children are called on to act out the imagination of their betters.

The Queen and her Prince are elected by the students, under the supervision of the teachers, according to a vague criterion of "niceness." In 1993 the members of the royal couple were brother and sister, the young children of Hermogenes Villcasana, the man who had recently returned to Quirpini after years living in Argentina with his family (see the conclusion). He was probably the wealthiest Quirpini, and his family was also the most versed in the "civilized" criollo norms of Argentina. It made perfect sense, then, that his children, with their criollo style and their weak command of Quechua, would be chosen as the most perfect expressions of the values implicit in the event.

Although all the schools of the San Lucas region theoretically teach both Spanish and Quechua, Bolivian criollo culture reigns in the school in Quirpini and Quirpini parents expect nothing else. Much of the school's value comes from the ability parents expect it to convey to their children so they can move freely within the worlds of cities, commerce, wage labor, and international travel. In a word, school is expected to teach sophistication and be a means to more possibilities in life. Like Carminsa Santos, who insisted on using her very limited Spanish when talking to her baby, Lino, because that was the language he would need to succeed in life, most parents in Quirpini wanted the school to enable their children to move without restraint and function effectively in a wider world. In practice, that world is one where people speak Spanish, regularly communicate by writing, are required to be able to make various monetary calculations with some ease, and have mastered the discipline of performing tasks set by others for fixed periods of time, and following orders. The San Lucas school district was one of the first in Bolivia to introduce bilingual Spanish and Quechua education in schools, but the teachers told me that, initially, parents resisted the idea of having their children learn to read Quechua, on the grounds that it would not help their prospects.

Not only does the Day of the Student allude to criollo cultural norms, it also makes various references to the Bolivian state. One effect of this is to identify the regional elite based in the town with national political and moral authority, both of which represent the elite's capacity to mediate the gathering of campesinos and the elite's privileged access to the encompassing moral space of Bolivia. In the school performance held on August 6, the major Bolivian national holiday, the children perform "folkloric" dances drawn from other ethnic groups throughout the national territory: here the elite-controlled school and the national school system become the mediator for the circulation of interethnic communication or, rather, its simulacrum.

Although the pageant works differently than a folklore festival does, the two kinds of events have important features that contrast similarly with norms of public events in Quirpini. In taking the form of a performance directed at an audience, both invoke a social space quite distinct from any fiestas not organized by members of the elite. Carnival, for example, relates multiple scales of social places—households, communities, and the region—through a complex sequence of visits to places which, in various ways, are emblematic of those places as geographical and political wholes. The spatial context enacted in Carnival is quite consistent with the segmentary logic of ayllu structure, although the spatial-political hierarchy is capped by the town elite, which necessarily stands outside any ayllu. The places that Quirpinis enact in Carnival are treated as if they have no social exteriors—the pattern of visits constitutes a series of inclusive spaces, defined by what they contain (households, in the case of Quirpini; dependant indigenous communities, in the case of San Lucas) rather than what lies outside them. One way to understand this is to note that no actions performed as part of Carnival implicate any social space "outside" the events going on. During the Carnival celebration of 1994, this caused some awkwardness for two young nonresident elite women who only rarely came to San Lucas. They invited a group of Carnival dancers into their house because, as they told me, they wanted to "see the culture"; they were somewhat nonplussed to realize that having dancers in their patio required a specific series of actions from them—as if they were expected to be as much a part of the "culture" as the campesinos they were watching.

Participants in civic pageants such as the Day of the Student or the San Lucas folklore festival invoke a very different space. The basic organization of the performances, in which the people on stage (the folkloric dancers or the students, as well as the elite emcees) are the focus of the attention of an audience that sits quietly, with little overt attention paid to them, is based on a spatial schema in which most of those present are "outside" of what is presented as the main action. Although all sorts of performances include an audience, whose role can vary greatly, this kind of audience is a curious sort of absent presence. It is a group of people who are present at an event, to whom the event is oriented, and, indeed, whose presence is normally the justification for the event, but to whom very little direct reference is made at all. In most forms of what I call "spectacles" (Rockefeller 1998:8), the main action involves only subtle indexical references to the audience's presence: the way the setting and the action are oriented, how voices are projected, the timing of an event to accommodate the comfort and convenience of audience members, and so on. All the overt action appears to deny the audience's presence, with the exception of patter (usually confined to transitional moments) by mediating figures such as emcees or ringmasters who are not seen as fully part of the action. Yet no spectacle would be much of anything without people to spectate; the presence and attention of the audience are just as crucial to the success of the event as are the performers.[4]

One effect of this absent presence, this anonymous quality, is that audiences tend to be undefined and lack internal structure. At the Day of the Student, for instance, the only people who came to watch the day's events seemed to be connected in some way to the school—either parents of students or members of the junta escolar. Yet anyone from Quirpini could have attended without provoking surprise. The folklore festival audience could include anyone who turned up, with no apparent effect on the performance. Although the groups of dancers were carefully identified by community of origin, the audience was treated as a uniform mass of people. One effect this achieves is that an audience can stand in for a large number of absent people. In the folklore festival, part of the point of transposing traditional dances to a festival context is that the audience implicitly stands for Bolivia, and being part of the audience gives campesinos the experience of being part of Bolivia. This happens even more clearly with the school pageant. The stage activities of the Day of the Student are addressed to the Bolivian nation, which is made clear in the teachers' invocations of Bolivia and their emphasis on the celebration's simultaneous occurrence at schools throughout the country. The audience, then, stands not only for all of Quirpini but for the people of Bolivia.

The internally undifferentiated absent presence that is an audience is an apt image for a uniform citizenry; training people to be part of an audience fits easily into a nationalizing project. This sort of uniform citizenry is the demographic equivalent of the internally undifferentiated national territory that is so crucial to the idea of the nation-state, as Appadurai (1996d) points out. It also has similarities to the reading public whose rise, Anderson (1991) argues, was a crucial moment in the development of nationalism.

The Day of the Student is a particular encapsulation of the ideals of a rural Bolivian school; it is, in effect, a display of criollo cultural values to the Bolivian nation, with most of the central roles pantomimed by Quirpinis. The children are seen as the embodiment of criollo values, while the parents' watchful eyes take on the role of the Bolivian nation. This wider world, as mediated by the school, is the context that gives the celebration its value.

The Bolivia that appears in the Day of the Student is not a "real" Bolivia or anything that could actually exist as a nation or state. Bolivia has no king or aristocracy or even any royalists to speak of. Playful courtly fantasies do not comprise any significant part of the functioning or representation of the Bolivian state. The state, however, has long identified citizenship in terms of criollo culture values and norms of comportment. The whimsical nostalgia of the Day of the Student, the clothing of the personifications of the community's highest values in long dresses and ties, the habit of representing oneself to oneself through spectacle: these are the traits of civilized citizens, those who comport themselves as subjects of Bolivia. The students and parents of Quirpini inhabit that imagination for a day.

Where Is the School?

In his discussion of "locality," Appadurai (1996d:178) explicitly calls it "contextual" but not "spatial." This stance is consistent with his broad program of de-emphasizing the spatial aspect of social life in light of globalization, but I differ with the distinction he makes, and find Ferguson and Gupta's (2005) emphasis on the "spatialized" state more to the point. I have found, indeed, that any contextualization opens itself to spatialization. Much of what is at stake in establishing the context of an event can be expressed as a question of where it occurs, taken in a broad sense, meaning in what framework of signification the actions are performed. This is why the question "Where was I?"—discussed in the introduction—is not easy to answer and yet is very important. Any action or site of action has a huge number of potential localizations, each of which offers different potential meaning for the action it situates. The encontextualization of Bolivia in relationship to Quirpini, for instance, is a highly spatialized process. Civic celebrations like the Day of the Student and the *hora civica*, along with the way that national authorities address the community through the school, have the effect of placing Bolivia to a great extent "in" the school by invoking the nation as a context. In the next chapter we will see that when Quirpinis migrate to Argentina, their most intense experience of the Bolivian nation and state comes at the international border. At home, Quirpinis encounter Bolivia largely in San Lucas and in the school.

What, for instance, are the places that could be invoked to locate the Quirpini school? It could be variously said to be in Quirpini, near Lucía Huallpa's house, on the San Lucas River (or on the Jatun Mayu, the same body of water seen from Quirpini rather than from the perspective of San Lucas and the nation), in the ayllu Jatun Kellaja, within the San Lucas school district, in the Department of Chuquisaca, in Bolivia, in the Andean highlands, in South America, on Earth, in *kay pacha*,[5] and so on. Each of these localizations suggests certain perspectives and concerns, and implicitly privileges certain potential significances to whatever is done there.

Some potential localizations have no significance for Quirpinis (the school is not located in "the Southern Cone" in any way that interests them, for instance). Others have only the most fleeting significance (that the school *promotora*, Lucía Huallpa, lived nearby was rarely of importance to anyone but her). However, the school has three crucial localizations: it is at the center of Quirpini; it is near San Lucas; and it is in Bolivia. These locations are invoked in various ways at various times: the culminating dance of Carnival, for instance, places the school at the heart of Quirpini but does not invoke Bolivia in any way. Civic rituals like the Day of the Student and the *hora civica*, however, are powerful enactments of all three of these localizations, and thus are central to the school's multiplex situatedness.

The school is a flexible space for Quirpinis, subject to multiple contextualizations. As noted in chapter 3, during corn planting the school is treated much as if it were just another household. At the culmination of Carnival, it is the spatial instantiation of "all" of Quirpini. During the reuniones generales it is simultaneously the instantiation of Quirpini as a political whole and the site of domination by the San Lucas elite. It is also, as mentioned in the previous chapter, the main place where representatives of national institutions come to communicate with the community; these visits are a recurrent contextualization of the school in the Bolivian national space, and the social relations and values it represents. On a daily basis it represents the government's ability to compel people to send their children there, and it is also the locus of parents' aspirations for their children to be literate in Spanish, and generally master the skills necessary to operate in the urban, Spanish-speaking world which is universally accepted to be the best source of money and advancement available to them. As migration to Buenos Aires has become a more routine part of people's lives, this aspiration increasingly contextualized the school, not just in Bolivia but in relation to Argentina and Buenos Aires.

The school is the most immediate context invoked in the pageant, and is made present as an environment throughout the event. From the hora civica at the start of the day, to the physical presence of the pageant in the school *salon,* to the central role of the teachers and frequent invocations of the school, clearly the action is overtly situated in the school and the school system. But there is a larger context evoked in and through the school. The pageant places the school within Quirpini, but also, through the emcee's pronouncements, it places the school in Bolivia, by placing Bolivia in the school.

But again, contextualization not only resists knowing, it resists control. For instance, the invocation of national sentiment through criollo values has a way of undermining itself. In the pageant that I saw, this happened through a re-spatialization of the relatively abstract and weakly spatialized criollo values and fantasies at play. The two children elected as Prince and Princess, the Villcasana siblings, were certainly exemplary criollos among the children in the school: they barely spoke Quechua, were unfamiliar with local customs and mores, and had grown up in a capitalist world in which food was grown to be sold and commerce was the dominant mode of exchange. Surely they were seen as the most appropriate main players in the criollo fantasy the children were called on to inhabit. Yet they were also the least "Bolivian" of children in the community, having grown up in Argentina, speaking with marked Argentine accents, and having had little experience of Bolivia before they moved to Quirpini. Here, because of the migratory context in which Quirpinis deploy the criollo values and skills that they master in the school, the local quintessence of those values was not even Bolivian, but Argentine. The weak spatialization of the values that have historically represented "Bolivia" as a fitting aspiration for campesinos have left an opening for their redeployment in a non-national spatial and cultural context. That year, the pageant claimed not just Bolivia, but also Argentina, as a significant locating context.

Context is an often spatialized possibility that creates and limits the potential meanings of actions, or places of action. The choice of location is made through gestures included in the performance or immediately surrounding it in space or time. Put differently, a textualized activity takes much of its meaning from the way it evokes a context—that is, a field of values—but the context of that activity itself exists largely by being invoked in various ways and for various purposes. An activity and its surroundings mutually constitute each other.

People cannot help but be creative—in their actions, their movement, and their imaginations. But they do not always control, or understand, what it is they are creating. One of the central tools of power is to take control of what people create, and one important way to do this is to control the context in which actions take place. The "circumstances" under which people operate are constantly conjured and invoked, so gaining control of those circumstances is a key means of achieving power. In creating Quirpini through the school, and the school as a key communal institution (partly through rituals such as the Day of the Student and the hora civica), Quirpinis are complicit in creating their community as a subordinate part of the region, and as a place on the margins of the Bolivian nation-state. Yet, by employing the open-ended and uncontrollable techniques of encontextualization in the campaign to create a national sentiment in rural Bolivians, the state runs the risk that as the script it has created is realized in people's actions, it will be rewritten.

7 · *Where Do You Go When You Go to Buenos Aires?*

On any given day, during my time in Quirpini, a good number of the community's inhabitants were elsewhere. Nearly one-fifth of them actively maintained households in other communities of the region and spent a good deal of their time there; others would be on short trips to nearby communities or to San Lucas. But, generally, people's sojourns outside Quirpini for more than a few days were travels for work. Many households had one or more members absent at any given time, although absence was highest during the times between planting and harvest. Some people traveled every year, some went for years at a time, and others migrated for work only a few times in their lives. A considerable number of Quirpinis had left permanently and sold their land. In the early 1990s migration was a central fact of life for nearly all families in Quirpini, and for the community as a whole. The money that men brought back from their travels was necessary for many families to have enough food through the year; a substantial minority of the families in Quirpini farmed plots that were too small to feed a household. For others, wages provided the means to sponsor fiestas, to send children to school, to acquire store-bought food such as noodles and rice, agricultural and other tools, cooking pots, medicine, alcohol, and many other necessities of life in Quirpini.

The entire community was implicated in, and partly constituted by, people's travels for wage labor. As I will detail presently, the local labor market was largely generated by migration, and the community as a whole depended on a constant influx of cash. The earnings of those who brought in the most cash were distributed throughout the community, either as their wives hired other men to work their fields in the migrants' absence or as they entertained more lavishly than otherwise, particularly in corn planting. The social relations of Quirpini happened partly in distant towns and cities, as young people abroad met and married partners from far away or as conflicts occurring abroad divided the kin of the antagonists back home.

In the main part of this chapter, I describe the trip a Quirpini companion named Nicanor Huarachi and I made from San Lucas to the immigrant neighborhood in La Salada. The trip is just one aspect of the transnational circuit (Rouse 1991) connecting San Lucas to Buenos Aires. Other circuits connect San Lucas with various cities of Bolivia. The substance of these circuits is the movement of people (and money, goods, and news, but primarily people) as well as the relative immobility of people who do not travel the circuit.

We will see how, on the one hand, Buenos Aires and the national spaces of Argentina and Bolivia have been produced in part by people in motion, and are constantly being re-created by the movement of people, money, and goods. The migrants I knew from Quirpini and other parts of the San Lucas area are part of this ongoing process of re-creation. At the same time the repertoire of spatial practices with which they navigate and create the world they come from are challenged as they move through worlds that have been created under different cultural, economic, and social circumstances.

A recent series of events had a dramatic impact on migratory strategies for southern Bolivians. In December 2001 Argentina's economy collapsed into the worst depression the country had ever experienced, the result of years of financial policies that undermined Argentine industry and all sorts of exports (for an account of the crisis and its causes, see Blustein 2005). In response to the crisis, the government put severe restrictions on bank withdrawals and defaulted on international loans, which temporarily cut the Argentine economy off from external credit; the currency lost more than half its value. Unemployment and poverty soared. All these shocks directly disrupted Bolivians' ability to successfully seek work in Argentina. Without credit, there was no construction and no factory activity, so Bolivian men's preferred jobs disappeared; Bolivians tended to work informally and get paid in cash, which was suddenly in short supply; should they get work, Bolivians (as well as other foreign immigrants) found that their wages were worth half of what they were a year before. Finally, rural Bolivians typically entered the labor market at the bottom, taking jobs that most Argentines found too poorly paid or too demanding; with so many people out of work, competition for available jobs intensified. All the evidence suggests that although Bolivians resident in Argentina did not return home in large numbers, migration to Argentina essentially stopped. It has since recovered, along with the economy, but the crisis has had profound effects on the Argentine economy and the situation of working people there.[1]

Who Goes Where?

For Quirpinis who migrated, the overwhelmingly favorite destination was Buenos Aires, followed by Santa Cruz and Tarija. I conducted a survey of fifty of the approximately one hundred households in Quirpini, and the resultant data provide a sketch of the overall patterns of movement. More than four-fifths of the men surveyed[2] had migrated at some point; close to three-quarters had worked somewhere in Argentina, and nearly two-thirds had been to Buenos Aires.[3] Just over a quarter of the men had gone to the booming lowland Bolivian Department of Santa Cruz and a similar number to the small city of Tarija, near the Argentine border; nearly all these men had also been to Argentina.[4] Men also traveled to Cochabamba, to the nearby vegetable-producing region of Camargo, and to various other cities. Most men start migrating when they are young, in part because it is the most practical way for them to acquire land of their own back home so as to gain a measure of independence from their parents before marrying and having children. Broadly speaking, migration follows one of three patterns in men's lives. Some migrate until they have saved enough to buy land and sustain themselves from the land and local work; they might never migrate again, or do so rarely. Others continue migrating frequently, every year or close to it, acquiring more land with time, or simply supplementing their subsistence with income from migration. Many eventually move elsewhere permanently.

Just over two-fifths of the women I surveyed had migrated at least once, and only about one in seven had been to Argentina, one in twenty to Buenos Aires.[5] Women made fewer trips than men, did not travel as far (they were as likely to go to Santa Cruz as to Argentina, for instance, whereas twice as many men went to Argentina as to Santa Cruz).[6] The most common pattern for women who migrate was to go to a Bolivian city when still single, work for a few months or a couple of years as a domestic servant, and then move elsewhere permanently to join a husband who has been traveling back and forth for some time. In fact, the only women in my survey who had been to Buenos Aires included one woman who had lived there for five years with her husband (they both returned to Quirpini) and three sisters who were living in Buenos Aires, having first gone there because their father made the trip often and bought a house there. The households of two of those sisters formed the core of the small concentration of Quirpinis in La Salada.

Overall women traveled much less than men. They were more likely to travel as young girls and stay home once they established a household, or else leave permanently, usually with a husband. Most of the actual traveling was done by men, and, as a result, many of the spaces I describe—those affected by the transit of migrants—were mainly the product of men's actions and experiences. In other words, migration from San Lucas was primarily a male phenomenon, and this chapter is largely (although not entirely) an ethnographic treatment of men's migration.

Starting

I went from Quirpini to Buenos Aires in December 1993, accompanying Nicanor Huarachi on his trip during the small exodus after corn planting in November. While there I stayed in La Salada, an immigrant neighborhood outside the city of Buenos Aires. It had been difficult to plan my departure, as everyone I talked to was tremendously vague about when he might leave. Some seemed puzzled that I even expected them to set an exact date for their trip, and others changed plans frequently.

Nicanor was an affable and thoughtful man, if a bit insecure. He lived with his wife and three daughters at the lowest extreme of Quirpini, across the river from Pumakuna, and he farmed several parcels of land in different parts of Sakapampa. For the last two decades Nicanor had supported his family by farming and occasional work repairing radios. He had visited Argentina once in the 1970s, but in 1992 found it necessary to leave Quirpini again for work; now, in 1993, he was planning to return to Argentina.

Figure 7.1. Map of the Bolivian part of the route Nicanor and I took to Buenos Aires, showing the main Potosí–Tarija road, the circuitous route we traveled to reach Yacuiba, and the more common crossing at Bermejo. Based on *Oxford Atlas of the World* 2001:173.

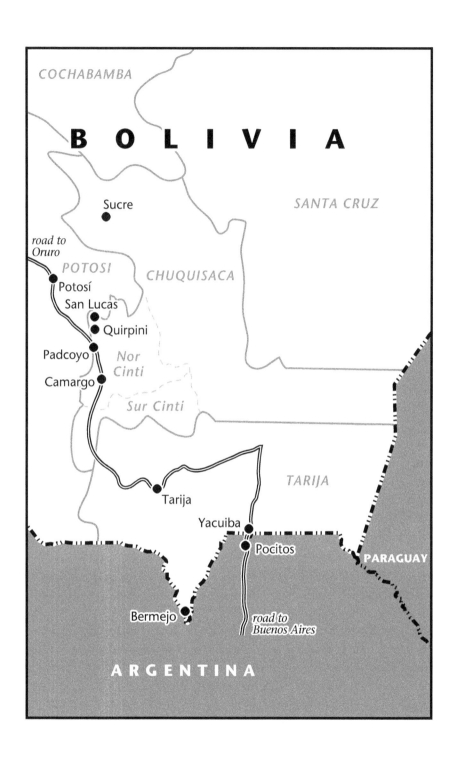

COCHABAMBA

B O L I V I A

SANTA CRUZ

Sucre

road to
Oruro

POTOSI

CHUQUISACA

Potosí

San Lucas

Quirpini

Padcoyo

Nor
Cinti

Camargo

Sur Cinti

Tarija

TARIJA

Yacuiba

Pocitos

PARAGUAY

Bermejo

road to
Buenos Aires

ARGENTINA

The plan Nicanor and I had for the trip was to set out early in the morning for the road from Quirpini to Padcoyo, the town at the junction with the main Potosí–Tarija road. If we caught a ride early enough, we could arrive at the main road while the southbound buses were still passing by. Failing that, we would take a truck, which is cheaper but slower, probably delaying our arrival in Buenos Aires by a full day. Normally people took the bus. The first bus would take us to Tarija. From there we would catch an overnight bus to Yacuiba, on the border with Argentina. We would cross the border on foot, and then catch another bus on the other side of the border. The trip from the border to Buenos Aires would take an additional twenty-four hours, but we would travel in the lap of luxury (see Figure 7.1).

There was one curious aspect about the route we planned. Normally people going from Quirpini to Buenos Aires traveled by way of Bermejo, a large border city on a more direct route to Buenos Aires. To get to Yacuiba we had to follow a route that detoured far to the east after we passed through Tarija. Nicanor initially explained that he wanted to visit his son who lived in Yacuiba, but eventually he admitted that the real reason was that there was less police control in Yacuiba, and he was worried about his ability to cross the border. The problem was not with his Argentine documents; on the contrary, he was technically an Argentine citizen, having acquired papers on the trip some twenty years before, when control of the border was more relaxed. Nicanor first entered Argentina illegally on his way to the northern cane fields, discovering to his surprise that it was very easy. When he presented himself at a government office he was immediately given citizenship papers. His problem was that several years ago he had lost his Bolivian documents, which are required for Bolivians who travel, and he risked a large fine at the border. He felt that in Yacuiba it would be easier to make the crossing without any interference from Bolivian officials.

On the Road

After a bout of miscommunication and bad luck that delayed us for a few days, we set off, first taking a taxi to Padcoyo and then catching a passing bus (we had arrived late in the morning, after the buses had all departed). There were about twenty of us in the truck. Trucks like this one are the most common form by which people get their goods and themselves across long distances in rural highland Bolivia; they are small- to medium-sized trucks like those that carry cargo in many parts of the world. The back, where the cargo and people go, is invariably a wooden structure built on the chassis: it has a wood floor and high wooden walls, and large doors open at the back to allow goods to be loaded and removed. Many of these trucks have a small ladder going up one side to help people get in and out; the larger ones have a small door cut into one side of the cargo area. Passengers on these trucks sit wherever they can on the cargo; a truck with no cargo in it can be uncomfortable indeed. Each truck normally followed a regular route, for instance from Potosí to Tarija, stopping for passengers along the way whenever the driver wanted to.

The ride took us through dry and rugged valleys; no one spoke much, and we were sitting too low in the back of the truck to see out much without standing. As we neared Camargo we descended; the terrain turned from the rocky slopes of the highlands to red and sandy cliffs. It became hotter and hotter, and by the time we reached Camargo, a major center of vineyards, we were trying as best we could to shelter ourselves from the harsh sun.

In Camargo we joined forces with an acquaintance of Nicanor's from a community near Quirpini. The three of us ate lunch at the main truck stop, then found a truck that was going to Tarija immediately. The land south of Camargo was dominated by vineyards; by evening we began to ascend a line of mountains that lay between us and the plains of Tarija; it grew cold as we gained altitude, and as we neared the pass we had to bundle up as well as we could. Our descent was rapid, and we arrived in Tarija, the largest city in southern Bolivia, near midnight.

In Tarija it became clear that we had at some point crossed a border into what could be called "officialdom." This is made up of the areas on the main roads and in cities where the government is able to regulate people's movements with some degree of effectiveness. Nicanor was worried that as an undoubtedly Bolivian person who had only Argentine documents, he might not be able to get into a hotel (it turns out that this was the reason he had wanted to travel by bus rather than by truck—we would have spent all our nights on the road, in effect passing over officialdom until we got to the international border). We went to a dormitory by the town market, and in fact he had no trouble getting in.

As Rouse (1991) points out, borders need not be lines. In traveling to Argentina, the truck or bus in which people travel becomes something like a border or a border crossing. From a truck or bus, one's connection to the external environment becomes attenuated and tangential. The vehicle itself becomes an environment—in fact, it is a place with its own boundaries.[7] In one respect, a bus is a more perfect realization of at least one key aspect of borders than are lines marked on the ground: when you enter it you are in one place, and when you leave you are indisputably in another. This unambiguous shift of location is one effect that traditional boundaries are meant to achieve but can generally effect only with the help of a considerable ideological and enforcement apparatus. A moving border has some peculiar effects: Nicanor's hope to travel by bus and avoid having to sleep in Tarija can be seen as an attempt to extend the border between Quirpini and officialdom nearly all the way through the latter, so he could pass to the other side unnoticed. He wanted to turn the buses into a border between Quirpini and Argentina, bypassing "Bolivia" almost entirely.

By now we had left behind the familiar topography of San Lucas. Padcoyo was really the last place we passed through that worked like places do in the area; it was recognizable as a point of convergence for weekly fairs and a Carnival celebration, and was also incorporated into local systems of visits and the circulation of goods. Tarija, in contrast, does not bring together any meaningful collection of people from the point of view of someone from Quirpini. Nearly everyone there is a stranger, identifiable more by social identity (campesino, cholo, refinado) than through any direct relationship. It is largely patterns of travel and circulation that made Tarija what it is, but these are not patterns that anyone from San Lucas has any special role in or knowledge of. Insofar as a town like Tarija is meaningful in the terms by which Quirpinis enact their space, it is similar to a *sama,* a resting point in a familiar path; people did sometimes say that they would *sama* ("rest" or "stop") in a city along their route.

Borderlands

In the morning we went to the bus station, where we ran into a young man who, on hearing we were from San Lucas, said that he had been born there. He offered to help us get bus tickets from the border to Buenos Aires, as well as a place to stay in Yacuiba. From all accounts the border area is full of such people who work for Argentine bus companies directing migrants to them. He was employed by the bus line on which Nicanor wanted to travel, so we happily accepted his help. This man was an accomplished salesman, who seemed to have a relationship with a certain hotel in Yacuiba as well as with the bus line. He told us we would stay in the hotel, and gave us the impression that the bus line would cover the cost. When we left the hotel we learned that there was no such arrangement, much to the dismay of Nicanor and his friend, as the hotel was considerably more expensive than any they normally would have considered. In the end, I doubted that the man had any real connection to San Lucas at all.

From Tarija we followed winding, mainly unpaved mountain roads further downward, through increasingly damp and green terrain. Our destination, Yacuiba, was set in what appeared to be rain forest and surrounded by low hills. Not as hot as Camargo, it was far more humid and filled with a tremendous bustle of people and construction. Many of the sidewalks seemed to be taken up with market vendors, and buses and hotels were everywhere. Nicanor explained that in Yacuiba there was a tremendous trade in contraband clothes; like most consumer goods, clothes were much less expensive in Bolivia than in Argentina, and many Argentines came to buy as much clothing as they could take across the border and then sell the clothes back home.

We were going via Yacuiba in part because it was not as well controlled by the police. We soon discovered the downside of this situation, as the trip began to go wrong. We had an afternoon and a night to stay in Yacuiba before we caught a bus the next morning, so on my insistence Nicanor and I went on a stroll around town. Nicanor had been warned that the town was dangerous and not to go out, but there was no way I was going to pass up a chance to see it. We walked about, looking at the street market that took up much of the center of town, at the construction going on, and took in the general sense of large numbers of people coming and going. As we returned to our hotel we were approached by a large man who identified himself as a policeman. He said he was investigating a fight the night before in which a gringo was involved. He showed us some identification and told us to come with him. The man got us into a taxi, which drove slowly around the outskirts of the city while he physically intimidated us, and then insisted on examining my money and possessions "to see if there was any blood on them." I handed over my things, although by now we felt that he was probably not a policeman. He examined them, handed them back, and quickly demanded that we get out of the car and wait on the street for him to return. It was only when we got back to the hotel that we discovered he had switched my money for bits of paper in an envelope and never returned my video camera.

This incident was, for me, an announcement that we had entered yet another realm. Now we were in the borderlands, an area where it is impossible to control or keep track of representations. At the place where the self-representations of Argentina and Bolivia meet, where people are constantly moving back and forth and changing their status by doing so, it is relatively easy for people to create the representation they want. In Quirpini no one misrepresents himself as thoroughly as this thief had; it simply would not work for long. The irony is that it was precisely in this realm of doubt and illusion where Nicanor feared that the Bolivian state would see through his masquerade and find that it had not managed to put its stamp on him. The realm of doubt is also one of the places where the state applies its controls most anxiously and intrusively, yet erratically. One way to understand this irony is to realize that, in Quirpini, Nicanor was not misrepresenting his nationality. As long as he did not try to vote, the question of whether he was legally Bolivian never came up. Only on the border, where questions of nationality are crucial, was he forced to "pretend" to be Bolivian.[8] For his purposes, then, the borderland was the heart of "Bolivia," encountered as a threatening and controlling state.

The National Border

The next day we set out for the bridge that crosses the small river dividing the two countries. On the far side, in the town of Los Pocitos, we would be able to board our bus and set off for Buenos Aires. Argentine border control was in the middle of the bridge, presumably at the very point where Argentine territory legally began. Although the bridge had been built for vehicle traffic, everyone was required to cross on foot. We took a taxi from the center of town to the bridge, then set out for the border control. At the actual crossing there were two lines: one for Argentines, another for foreigners. We had not anticipated it, but of course Nicanor and his friend had to go through the line for Argentines, while I went through the much longer and slower line for foreigners. Nicanor and his friend went through their line and waited for me nervously as the foreigners' line crept along. Eventually we realized that I would not get through the line before our bus left. Other buses were leaving that day, but it was not at all clear that any would have enough seats available for the three of us. Our "friend" from the Tarija bus station had reappeared, and he managed to establish that there was one seat open on the next bus, so we decided that Nicanor and his friend should go ahead and I would follow. We would meet the next day at the Buenos Aires bus terminal.

With that, I was on my own. I finally reached the head of the line, where it turned out that my visa would require special permission, but the officer who was able to grant it was having lunch. There followed several hours of anxious waiting as I tramped between offices full of soldiers who were not excessively interested in my problem or how to solve it. I ran into some Bolivians who were having similar visa problems, and we commiserated. At what seemed like the last possible minute my official returned and gave me the permission I needed, and I raced to catch my bus.

Now we had crossed *the* border, the real border—the dividing line between Bolivia and Argentina. Not only did it divide two countries, it divided us into two categories, administratively speaking: Argentines (Nicanor and his friend), and foreigners (me).[9] It also separated us for the next day, leaving me to proceed on my own and Nicanor a nervous wreck lest he lose me. Clearly this is a border with some power.[10] Nevertheless, like the borders of Quirpini, the Bolivian–Argentine border exists by being crossed, and it has grown more important as many Argentines apparently view it as under assault by the masses of immigrants from neighboring countries.

In a strange and ill-tempered book, a former employee of the Argentine Dirección de Migraciones, Miguel Angel Cornaglia, details the long and frustrated history of the Argentine state's efforts to establish a controllable border (Cornaglia 1994). Six amnesties, repeated reorganizations of immigration laws, and an interminable national debate about how migration policy should be run all played their part in forming and transforming the national border. What most exercises Cornaglia is that various congresses and presidents had established rules for the control of entry into Argentina, and each one had gone unenforced. Cornaglia says that, immediately after World War II, transit across Argentina's borders with other countries was virtually uncontrolled; this corresponds to what people told me in Quirpini. Those who traveled in the 1950s say that they encountered no border to speak of and experienced no need for documentation. By the 1970s, as the number of migrants increased,[11] people told me that it was still possible to cross the border without documents but that some subterfuge was necessary; the most common ploy was apparently to enter clandestinely and then ask for Argentine papers at the next government office one encountered. In Quirpini, in the 1990s, entering

Argentina or obtaining work without papers was regarded as relatively easy. Today there is a considerable apparatus of border control, both at the national boundaries and throughout the country.

Cornaglia makes frequent impassioned calls for a firmer and more consistent policy for Argentina's borders, claiming that the lack of control over borders has become a national crisis. De Marco and Sassone (1983) had earlier made the same claim in a more temperate fashion, although they went so far as to endorse the idea that any nation that was not protective of its borders was "psychopathic" (Paz 1978:185, cited in De Marco and Sassone 1983:77); like Cornaglia, they put some of the blame for the sorry state of Argentina's borders on the uncontrolled movement of immigrants. In taking this nationalist, anti-immigrant position, Cornaglia anticipated a stance that became pronounced among political leaders, the media, and much of the Argentine populace in the late 1990s (see Grimson and Kessler 2005; and Grimson 2006.)

Indeed, it could be argued that only in the last few decades has Argentina as a nation started to discover its own boundaries. Escudé (1988) argues that although Argentines have long been convinced that they undervalue their own national territory, this worry has increased noticeably since World War II. Historically, there have been few moments when the control of the country's outer geographical limits has concerned members of the ruling elite to the extent that it appears to worry them today, at least from the perspective of Buenos Aires. For most of Argentine history, a far more pressing issue than protecting its borders has been how to fill the vast spaces of the pampa with citizens (Luna 1993; Castro 1991). The spatial narrative of the country, from the 1870s until recently, had been one of outward expansion from Buenos Aires, rather than defense of the outer margins of a fixed territory.

There is an ironic dilemma implicit in Argentines' sometimes xenophobic focus on the nation's borders. Argentina's national consciousness, even more than in the United States and perhaps more than in any other country today, is informed by the idea that theirs is a nation of immigration. From 1870 to 1950 many millions of people, most of them Spaniards or Italians, came to Argentina to supply the ever expanding need for industrial and agricultural labor, and to populate the vast expanse of the pampas with citizens to replace the native population which, by the end of the nineteenth century, had largely been exterminated or displaced.

Although in recent years a relatively small part of Argentina's population was born overseas (only 5%, according to the 1991 census, as cited in Programa 1997:124), more than half the population can trace their ancestry to postcolonial immigrants—usually parents or grandparents. But what was in certain respects a remarkably open and nondiscriminatory immigration policy had a contradiction built into it from the start. This contradiction can be glimpsed in the wording of the 1860 constitution. The preamble, in language preserved in all subsequent Argentine constitutions, says that "the federal government will promote European immigration and may not restrict, limit or tax the entry into Argentine national territory of foreigners whose object is to work the land, improve industry and introduce and teach the arts and sciences" (cited in Oteiza et al. 1997:17).[12] In short, the constitution indicates that European immigration is to be encouraged, but all immigration is allowed. Around the turn of the last century, the only large mass of mobile population likely to come to Argentina was in Europe, so an open immigration policy and a dynamic economy had the effect of making the Argentine population, and especially the population of Buenos Aires, predominately of European extraction. For Argentines, being a "country of immigration" meant being a European country, a notion that excluded both Argentina's oppressed and increasingly exterminated indigenous population, as well as the indigenous, African, and mixed-race populations of neighboring South American countries, and even of the Argentine provinces (Oteiza et al. 1997:16–17).

The Europeans stopped coming decades ago, but in the 1990s cross-border immigrants were as numerous as they ever were and had come to comprise more than half the foreign-born population (Programa 1997:124) and a much higher proportion of current immigrants. As a result, two elements of the Argentines' way of thinking about themselves and about immigration conflicted for the first time: Is Argentina a country of immigration or a country of Europeans? Whereas immigration had once made Argentina European, it now seemed likely that it was making the country multicultural and South American. Alejandro Grimson points out that this dilemma has continued, and, if anything, has intensified since the economic crisis of 2001–2002 (Grimson 2006; Grimson and Kessler 2005).

Another significant difference between the immigrants of the past and those of recent decades is that European immigrants arrived overwhelmingly by boat, never crossing an international land boundary. As a result, their influx was relatively easily controlled, and they arrived not in an ambiguous and difficult-to-define region such as the border but in the very heart of Buenos Aires, the economic, social, and political center of the nation.

The movement of immigrants to Argentina in the 1980s and 1990s, then, was problematic in two ways: in terms of the racial/cultural identities of the immigrants and because of how they entered the country. Argentine responses to their continuing entry have been conflicted and ambiguous. In the late 1990s there were factions that advocated a major change in the country's policy toward immigrants: increased border controls, more policing of the documentation of immigrants currently in the country, and a general effort to slow or stop what they saw as disturbing social changes. These factions included President Menem and other national political leaders, segments of the press, many labor unions, and the military.

In early 1999 the government ordered a crackdown on undocumented immigrants, claiming that they were a source of crime and disease (Clarín 1999a, 1999b). Much of the concern focuses on the border and the need to strengthen the state's control over it. Thus the minister of the interior announced, shortly after the crackdowns began, that a digital system of immigration control would soon be in place at all border crossings (ibid., January 23, 1999), even though hardly anyone was turned back at the borders. This was because, to obtain a tourist visa, a citizen of a neighboring country only needed a valid national identity document.

The relative rise of cross-border migration is not the only factor in Argentines' growing concern with national borders. A near border war with Chile, growing regional trade, and the fact that the national territory has been successfully occupied and made productive all signified that the country's relative isolation from South America, and its sense that it could expand, as it were, without limits, had come to an end. In the 1990s, more than at any time since independence, the nature of Argentina's boundaries was being defined, and the movement of migrants played a major role in determining what those borders would become.

Since the economic collapse in Argentina, signs are that the xenophobic reaction has crested (Grimson 2006). This appears to be just one aspect of the increasing integration of Argentina into the region (Grimson and Kessler 2005). At the same time, as the extent of the country's economic problems became clear, cross-border immigrants lost their power as a scapegoat, and politicians largely ceased making appeals to xenophobia, presumably because these appeals stopped yielding results.

In Buenos Aires

Having more or less successfully crossed this changing border, now by myself, I found my bus. It was indeed a sight to see—a double-decker, with a toilet and a machine at the back that dispensed sugary soda and coffee. The seat next to me was occupied by a man from Yura, a Quechua region just over one hundred kilometers to the west of San Lucas. On the Argentine side of the border the road was straight, the terrain a treeless plain covered with vast farms. We sped along the paved road at a tremendous clip, pausing only to stop at a series of roadside restaurants several hours late for each mealtime, where we were served generous helpings of grilled beef. We stopped briefly in a few cities on the way, where I indulged in the pleasure of textual overload and bought myself a pile of newspapers and magazines,[13] but essentially the bus was an express from the border to the capital. In the late afternoon, a full day after the bus departed Los Pocitos, we pulled into the Buenos Aires bus station, and to my relief I found Nicanor there waiting for me in a state of high nervousness.

We immediately set off to find a city bus, which took us to a large terminal in Plaza Once, from which we took another bus. I stared eagerly out the window, overcome to again find myself in a huge and bustling metropolis after nearly two years in Bolivia. Nicanor, though slightly nervous about just where we would spend the night, was showing off his casual familiarity with the city. In fact, his expertise applied mostly to a few bus lines in the central neighborhoods from which we set off, since he, like most unskilled immigrants, he rarely had reason to go to the central parts of the city.

For the Quirpinis I knew in Buenos Aires, the city effectively had the shape of a half-doughnut: Most of them lived near the outskirts of the city, especially in the south and southwest, and worked digging ditches or doing construction near the city's northern outskirts, primarily in the partidos of Vicente López and General San Martín (see Figure 7.2). Most travel takes place in the outer margins of the city, or along the Avenida General Paz, the road that follows the perimeter of the city proper. The main exceptions to this pattern were those who worked in the brick factories in the rural areas well outside the city; they lived at their work sites and traveled little once they found work, except to visit their friends and kin living elsewhere in the urban area.

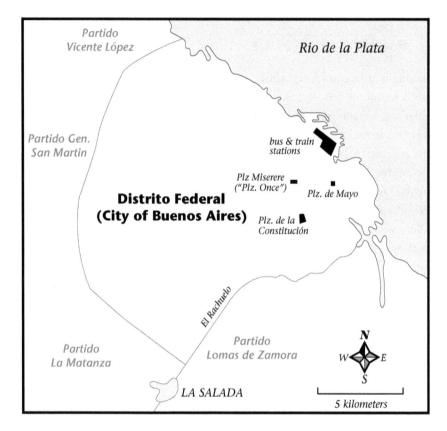

Figure 7.2. Map of Buenos Aires, showing the location
of La Salada and the center of the city. Glew is about
twenty-five kilometers south of La Salada. Based
on *Oxford Atlas of the World* 2001: Map 7.

Our second bus took us south, passing, as I later discovered, through
the working-class neighborhoods of Villa Soldati, across some parks, then
alongside the unregulated garbage dumps just across the Riachuelo, a pol-
luted stream that defines the city's southwestern border. We passed the city's
southern tip at the Puente de la Noria and rode further south through an area
of less dense population. A few kilometers outside the city, we descended
from the bus into a commercial district made up of relatively new one- and
two-storey buildings, some painted and others of unfinished brick or cinder-
blocks. From here we walked a further kilometer down a dusty road, across a
stream and some railroad tracks, and past a few weedy fields; we then turned

into a neighborhood of low, flat-roofed houses, all different, laid out in large plots on rectangular blocks.

This was when we tried to stay the night with Nicanor's cousin Santiago, only to be turned away. We finally spent the night in the only bed in the nearby shack of Paulino, who lived in squalor and had just been abandoned by his wife, a cousin to both Nicanor and Santiago. We had arrived in La Salada.

But where, and what, is La Salada?

In the mid-1990s, Quirpinis arriving in Buenos Aires had two general options for where to go. Many had already established a relationship with one employer or another, and went directly to a factory or construction company office. Since migrants usually got jobs through kin and friends from back home, migrants from one area tended to cluster in certain work sites. As a result, a Quirpini returning to an old work site could usually count on finding people he knows there. That usually meant that he was assured of finding a place to spend the night as well as having first call on any available jobs.

Employers preferred hiring laborers through such informal networks, feeling that the laborers worked better in teams and that they themselves had in the network a ready source of information on any prospective employee. In visiting a number of ditch-digging gangs in the city, I found that working in teams based on affinity (common nationality, acquaintance) was the norm. At one point I was trying to find the work site of someone from Quirpini (because he was digging ditches, he only had known that he would be in a certain area), and I had to walk about a suburban neighborhood looking for diggers. As it turned out, teams of workers were out digging ditches all over the place. I asked a foreman of one team if he could help me, and he went through a verbal checklist of the work crews in the area, saying, "the Peruvians are a block over that way; the Brazilians are by the park; the Argentines are down the street," but he could not locate a Bolivian crew. Another time I went to visit Constantino Paco, who was also digging ditches. When I arrived at the street where workers were digging ditches for sewage pipes, I found that about half the team of twenty workers was made up of San Luqueños—almost all the others were Bolivians.

Those who go directly to a job site usually go to the brickworks in the rural outer parts of the Province of Buenos Aires or to construction and excavation companies in the inner suburbs. The brick factories tend to be near one another, presumably close to a source of suitable clay. At the cluster of brickworks I visited, in the town of Glew, several factories were clustered along a rural road, surrounded by scrub woods and agricultural land. All the workers there were foreign or from other provinces of Argentina; they lived in dormitories or small apartments provided by the factory owners, who were all Argentines.

But there are various reasons why someone might not go directly to a work site. First-time immigrants have no relations with employers, nor do those who have not been to Buenos Aires for several years. Others might not want to return to an old job, perhaps because they were dissatisfied with the employer; the most common complaint I heard from Quirpinis in Buenos Aires was that employers simply did not pay their workers. Or they might not return because they are unsure of obtaining a job there. Others may have heard of a better job opportunity or simply prefer to start out staying with a relative.

Other immigrants stay with friends or kin in various places on the outer fringe of Buenos Aires proper or in the *villas miseria,* dense squatter settlements in various parts of the city (Rojo 1976; Torres 2001). Most neighborhoods where immigrants live are on the margins of the city or outside it, in the most central partidos, or counties, of the Province of Buenos Aires. This pattern is a result of years of effort exerted by the city's elite to push immigrants out of the central parts of the city.

Only recently have migrants from San Lucas begun to congregate in a single area—a recently settled section of La Salada. The town lies in the partidos of Lomas de Zamora and La Matanza, just south of the southern corner of the city proper, in what is known as the Province of Buenos Aires, or Gran Buenos Aires.[14] La Salada is a few kilometers outside the city, straddling the border with the partido of La Matanza. These two partidos are home to some of the largest concentrations of international immigrants in the entire urban area (Programa 1997). The central streets of La Salada have been built up relatively recently and are lined with low buildings, some of which house groceries, general stores, and a few restaurants. The earliest reference to such a town that I was able to find was on a map from 1975, and Laumonier et al. (1983) claim that the area has been a center of immigrants since the 1970s.

A few blocks northwest of this "downtown" was a new neighborhood, established, people told me, in the late 1980s.[15] This neighborhood was laid out on a wide, flat area in large rectangular blocks divided by dusty unpaved streets. The blocks had been divvied up into deep, narrow lots, about ten by twenty-five or thirty meters. Nearly every lot had a house or two built on it. The provincial government, I was told, had sold these lots cheaply to anyone who wanted to build on them. The province was gradually putting in infrastructure such as electricity and running water (available only in public spigots while I was there) and was also formalizing residents' title to their lots. Everyone living in this area was from elsewhere; during my time there I encountered roughly equal numbers of Bolivians and Paraguayans, with a small number of Argentines from the northwest of the country.

In a six-block area of this neighborhood there were five households from Quirpini; at least twenty households from the San Lucas area were spread throughout the new neighborhood. These are small numbers compared to the size of the neighborhood, but if we consider that at the time there were about one hundred households in Quirpini, we can see that La Salada represented a significant outpost.

After my initial days of orientation, described in the introduction, I went back to the activity that had brought me to the area: following Quirpinis. Nicanor had disappeared to the site of a job and a free bed (an employer who had not paid him the year before agreed to put him up in a warehouse in lieu of his debt), and each morning most of the male Quirpinis I knew, and some of the women, went to the city for work. Finding them, and the many other Quirpinis that I knew were in the area, meant asking around about people's jobs or living sites, collecting careful bus and walking instructions, and hoping for the best. Sometimes I was unable to find people because they had changed jobs or because I could not find a roving work crew; there were some Quirpinis of whose whereabouts no one was certain.

The Quirpinis resident in La Salada came from a fairly small group of kin centered on two sisters. I rented my room from one of them, Elena Puma, and her husband, Adalberto Paco; they lived with their three children in a small house from whose front room Elena ran a vegetable stand patronized by local residents. Adalberto normally worked in construction, but he was recovering from a work injury; they rented out the tarpaper room and the cinderblock room for extra cash, usually to new immigrants not from San Lucas. Elena's sister, Alicia, lived about a block away, and ran a larger vegetable store than her sister's. She was married to a Cochabambino who she had met in Buenos Aires and who appeared to be chronically unemployed. Benencia, the eldest sister of Elena and Alicia, lived in the city proper and was married to a Bolivian who ran his own metalworking shop. He once told me that he had tried to claim a lot in La Salada on the strength of his wife's kin ties, but the neighbors pressured him to give it up, on the grounds that the land was intended for those who had no financial alternatives; he was too prosperous. The sisters were the daughters of the wealthy (by Quirpini standards) and ambitious Pablo Puma, who seemed to be on his way to becoming the leading elder of the Pumas in Sakapampa. He bought the house that Alicia lived in and had encouraged his daughters to take the very unusual step of migrating as single women. Pablo stayed with Alicia on his frequent trips to Buenos Aires. Their brother, Agústo, also lived in Buenos Aires, and I was told that he had fled Quirpini after murdering someone; on his frequent visits to his sisters, he made feckless efforts to convert his fellow immigrants to his new evangelical faith. Santiago Gómez, who also worked in construction, was married to Sabina Puma, a niece of Pablo's and cousin of the three sisters; they had three children.

Adalbert's sister, Josefina Paco, had lived in the area until she abandoned her non–San Luqueño husband, Paulino Flores, and their three children shortly before our arrival. I never met her, and even her brother agreed that she had acted scandalously. He and Paulino were eagerly awaiting the arrival of a senior relative from Quirpini who they hoped could sort things out and reunite the family.

A couple blocks from the Puma sisters lived Grover Paco, who was, without doubt, the most successful Quirpini in La Salada. He ran his own small construction business; it was a mark of great success that he was not only a highly skilled laborer but was able to hire others to work for him on jobs. His wife, Viviana Colque, ran a dry goods store at the front of their large house, which Grover was constantly expanding, and raised their four children with the help of her mother-in-law, Juana. Juana spoke no Spanish, but when her husband died Grover brought her to La Salada, where she cut her long campesina hair into a bob, doffed her pollera in favor of skirts and blouses, and miserably took care of the children. She complained bitterly to me that she had nothing to do now; in the multicultural neighborhood she could not even run the small store without knowing Spanish. Grover was a kind of moral center of the small group of Quirpinis, frequently called on to mediate disputes or to help people out because of his intelligence, calm demeanor, and financial resources. In spite of his success, he, like Adalberto, expressed great ambivalence about living in Argentina and frequently talked about returning to Bolivia, perhaps to a city.

The San Lucas region and the San Luqueños in the neighborhoods of Buenos Aires, particularly La Salada, were tied together by visits and exchanges of goods, money, and information. The five Quirpini households in La Salada were beginning to become a center of San Luqueño networks in the urban area by virtue of the fact that it was quite safe and the one place where people knew they would be able to find kin. While I was there, a constant trickle of people passed through the Quirpini households of La Salada. Newly arriving immigrants like Nicanor, who have kin in the area, came first to La Salada in order to establish a base from which to look for work (similarly, someone who lost his job, and thus his housing, might stay in La Salada while looking for work). Many of the visitors were kin, such as Adalberto's brother, Constantino Paco, who migrated frequently and was to be found in La Salada on many weekends. On weekends, La Salada became much more of a center, as men and women on their days off would congregate at the houses of their kin to exchange news, enjoy one another's company, and eat and drink. People came from the brickworks, from construction housing, or from their own houses. Sometimes enough men would come by to put together a game of soccer in a nearby park. On Christmas and New Year's, La Salada became a major center for San Luqueños, who came from around the urban area to visit.

There was a fair each week, in the nearby commercial center of La Salada, and most of the Quirpinis I knew attended for the good prices offered by the vendors, most of whom were Bolivian. Since the 1990s this fair has grown explosively into what is now often called the largest contraband market in all of Argentina. Bolivian vendors still dominate the fair, which continues to draw buyers and sellers from throughout the urban area, although it has been the object of police repression, which in 2004 led to the death of a Bolivian (Comunidad Boliviana en Argentina 2004).

The homes of the families who live in La Salada are social centers on the weekends, although there are others, such as the brickworks, where men periodically gather to play soccer tournaments. At the same time several people were creating centers that drew people from beyond the San Luqueño migrant group; Elena Puma's vegetable stand drew customers with origins throughout Bolivia, Paraguay, and the Argentine northwest, and all of them lived within a couple of blocks of the store. In Buenos Aires there are few occasions for the sort of serial visits I described in chapter 4; the San Luqueño residents of La Salada visit back and forth a fair amount, and some weekend visitors make a point of dropping in on several houses out of politeness, but there is no dense web of serial visits and convergences characteristic of the places of Quirpini. Instead, the rather sparse social geography that the people I knew maintained in Buenos Aires found its richness in the circuit of which it formed a part; people's relations in the city were largely conditioned by the relations of their kin back in Quirpini. The place where I had arrived with Nicanor was tied to the place we had come from: an outpost, combined in a single circuit with the complex geography of Quirpini and La Salada by the back-and-forth travels of people like Nicanor, and the information and money they carried with them.

This thin network of local relations is in marked contrast to Charrúa, the Bolivian immigrant neighborhood that was the subject of Alejandro Grimson's (1999) ethnography. In the 1990s, as today, this neighborhood in the southern part of the city proper was dominated by Bolivians, most of them full-time residents, and supported a complex ritual cycle, and a fairly well-organized migrant population. Unlike Quirpinis, who are mostly temporary migrants and whose social worlds are centered on the San Lucas region, the Bolivians of Charrúa are mainly permanent residents or Argentina-born children of immigrants, significantly focused on their social and economic worlds in the city. The Bolivian community's major public celebrations take place there, and many Bolivian civic organizations are based there, too. It has been a center for Bolivians in the urban area for decades (Sassone and Mera 2007). The Quirpinis I knew in La Salada never mentioned Charrúa or showed very much interest in a community of Bolivians beyond those they knew and worked with.

Nevertheless, the space in which migrants from Quirpini acted was produced not just by Argentines and previous waves of immigrants but also by the hundreds of thousands of Bolivian (and Paraguayan, Brazilian, and Chilean) immigrants to the city, as well as their descendants.[16] As mentioned earlier, for many years Bolivians migrating to Argentina overwhelmingly did agricultural work in the neighboring and culturally familiar northwestern provinces (Whiteford 1981). In the 1950s some Bolivians began working in the fruit- and vegetable-producing farms in the north of the Province of Buenos Aires (Benencia 2006). From this marginal beginning, increasing numbers of Bolivians came to the city; with time, men moved into construction and industrial and commercial service work, and women found niches in domestic service, the garment industry, and the small-scale selling of fresh produce

(Maguid 1997). By the 1990s, and continuing to this day, although Bolivians could be found in most parts of the urban area, they were concentrated in the southern areas, particularly in the Nueva Pompeya (which contains Barrio Charrúa) and Villa Soldati sections of the city, and the partidos of Lomas de Zamora and, especially, La Matanza (Carmona 2008).

Since the mid-1990s La Salada has undergone dramatic changes, mainly as a result of the economic crisis of 2001–2002. When I passed through the area in 2004, the neat houses of the 1990s had been replaced by a shanty town. The fair, a center of commerce of dubious legality, and the massive unemployment and social dislocation that the whole country has suffered have joined to give La Salada a reputation and appearance very much like those of the villas miseria.

But, in the 1990s, residents of La Salada saw it as a safe and attractive alternative to the villas. The neighborhood where I stayed had recently been created as part of a deliberate policy to settle immigrants outside the city. The blocks and plots that I saw were laid out by provincial authorities, and the plots were made available to people who wished to live there. Over the last several years more services had been provided to residents, from electricity to police patrols and water spigots on each street corner. Everyone I talked to felt that this arrangement was a vastly better option than living in one of the villas miseria.

Although the villas offered cheap and centrally located habitation to immigrants, they were dangerous and lacked most municipal services. I was frequently warned by people in La Salada against entering them. To judge from newspaper reports in Buenos Aires in the 1990s, most urbanites viewed them as a blight on the city; not only were they ugly and unhealthy but they were also a source of crime and social disorder. Some authors have also suggested that the presence of such flagrantly "South American" populations in the heart of Buenos Aires constitute an acute display of the challenge to Argentina's self-conception represented by the new immigrants.

Efforts to eradicate the villas miseria have been under way since the late 1960s (Mugarza 1989). Initially the focus of these efforts was on "repatriation" of migrants to their home countries or provinces. In later years eradication efforts became more subtle, and La Salada appeared to be a part of them. In effect, the area was ceded to immigrants as a means to draw people from the villas miseria. In this way immigrants could be induced to live more orderly lives and, no less important, would remain invisible to the people of the cities.

Mugarza (1989) points out that the eradication of villas miseria led to a shift of immigrants to the departments outside the city of Buenos Aires; in the mid-1990s the areas immediately surrounding the city were almost half-populated by people who had come to the Province of Buenos Aires from elsewhere (Programa 1997). The central areas of Buenos Aires have for many decades been "preserved" by a policy of keeping disruptive presences such as industry and immigrant populations on the outskirts (Tulchin 1982). And although these outskirts have long been moving outward, the basic structure of the city has remained the same as it has grown (Walter 1982). The arrival of immigrants, so necessary for the economic life of the city, threatened to degrade the quality of the city; the reaction to this threat has, in the name of preserving the space of the city, provoked the ongoing spatial transformation of all of Gran Buenos Aires.

The Buenos Aires–San Lucas Circuit

In employing the term "circuit" I am adapting Rouse's use (1991); for him, a "transnational migrant circuit" is the relationship between localities in different countries transformed by people's recurrent travel as well as the movement of information and goods, into a single social space. Circuits can be inhabited; they condition people's movement, but they have no borders. One could say that they do not even have interiors. There is no place that we could call "Quirpini–Buenos Aires," but there is such a circuit. A circuit in this sense is something midway between a journey and a place, between the act of movement and a context within which people's movement is so dense, complex, and repetitive that it outlasts any particular movement. A circuit is never closed in upon itself or hermetic but rather gains its value and dynamism from the different ways that its various end points or destinations are embedded in their surroundings.

Any effort to talk about a circuit such as that which connects Quirpini to Buenos Aires must take into account its complex and ineffable nature. Yet it defines places, gives context and meaning to actions, and constrains the possible actions of those who are part of it. In addition, it is not symmetrical—a circuit connects Quirpini to Buenos Aires, but Buenos Aires is not similarly tied to Quirpini; the circuit constrains Quirpini and its residents far more than it does anyone from Buenos Aires.

In Buenos Aires and on the way there people from San Lucas participate in spaces they have played a relatively small role in creating. This means that although their passage influences those spaces, they also must adapt themselves to already prevalent norms of what can be done with spaces in other places; at times this means creating new forms of spatial practice, which might be as strange to them as they are to other people in Buenos Aires. The rise of a concentration of San Luqueños in La Salada, which on the weekends attracted people from throughout the San Lucas region, was one indication that they were beginning to localize their social bonds in the new metropolis by establishing a center of convergence. The convergence place had become part of a shared migratory circuit.

Being part of this circuit, along with the lesser ones incorporating Tarija, Santa Cruz, and other Bolivian cities, had transformed Quirpini and San Lucas. In the 1990s campesinos routinely bought and sold land among themselves, whereas in decades past most land purchases involved townspeople as either buyers or sellers. In the 1990s the land market in Quirpini was almost entirely a result of migration, as those who had made money working elsewhere returned home to buy land from others who had decided to leave the area permanently. Many of these sales were between brothers, part of a strategy to keep family lands unified.

Much as the social world of Quirpinis in La Salada depends on social relations "back home," participation in migrant circuits was becoming a necessary part of Quirpini men's social life. For instance, to sponsor a major fiesta or to climb the ladder of communal authority, nearly everyone in Quirpini had to travel elsewhere to earn money; hardly anyone had enough land to complete a normal social trajectory without access to outside income. The logic of this situation, whereby a man must travel in order to bring others to him, mirrors the dynamic of reciprocal labor in corn planting. The difference is that many of the reciprocal relations of corn planting are replaced by wage labor, and the scales involved are also quite different: in order to become a local notable of any significance, men must travel hundreds of kilometers, often to another country, and become an "unskilled" laborer in a radically different social milieu.

Buenos Aires and other migratory destinations had become omnipresent in Quirpini. We have already seen this in the bicycles young men flaunt, in the possible patterns for the circulation of corn, and the universal use of store-bought clothes. It had become impossible to be and act "in Quirpini" without doing so in some sense "in relation" to Buenos Aires. Even men who had never been to Buenos Aires were quite aware of their decision, expressing either chagrin at their lack of sophistication or pride that they had avoided the economic necessity of traveling abroad.

In the earlier decades of this century, the only orientation Buenos Aires had to rural Bolivia was one of exclusion—the world of the Argentine capital was oriented to Europe and its own agricultural hinterland, and the less-developed parts of South America were important to it only as a ground for racial, cultural, and economic differentiation. Today this has changed, and in the course of the 1990s the broader public in Buenos Aires seemed to become aware of what the governing and capitalist classes had known for some time: that a steady influx of workers from neighboring countries was becoming important to the urban area's economic fortunes. Though very few, if any, Argentines in the city have a significant orientation to Quirpini or San Lucas, many of them have become aware of the mass of migratory circuits and orient to them to varying extents.[17]

Changing Places

Traveling is not something Quirpinis do only in and around Quirpini. True to the nature of movement, it happens all over the place in such a way that it is difficult to say exactly where it happens. Casey (1996:26, 27) argues that places are "events," that they "happen." It is legitimate to ask, then, *where* a place happens; the answer is rarely simple. Quirpini considered as a place does not only "happen" in Quirpini but is made and remade by actions taken by travelers in Buenos Aires, in Santa Cruz, in Sucre, and elsewhere. As people persistently act and move in relation to Quirpini, whether or not they do so in Quirpini, the character Quirpini takes from those movements acquires a stable quality. At the same time the paths people travel, such as those tying together the small concentration of Quirpinis in La Salada, Buenos Aires, or the highways that carry people to and from Quirpini, begin to take on the character of places or, at least, come to be recognized as a route or circuit that people may inhabit. A circuit is a kind of spatial schema, characterized by recurrent, predictable movement that connects and partly defines its poles.

If we regard "places" as spaces which demand that people orient their movements in relation to them, then Buenos Aires is a crucial place for Quirpinis, and the towns and cities of Bolivia have become important places for Buenos Aires and Argentina. As such, they need to be considered and negotiated, and are subject to being treated both as unified entities and as the loci of many possible movements and blocks to movement (themselves all potential places). The region of San Lucas, for instance, can be understood as a place in the sense that it is the framework for a tremendous amount and variety of movement of a relatively consistent character; to be "in" San Lucas is to have certain recognized possibilities of movement. To be a Quirpini "in" Buenos Aires is to act within a different set of constraints, with a different set of orientations; a migrant's orientation to Quirpini is doubtless less powerful and detailed than it is when he or she is back home, but it is central to what the person is doing and why the person is where he or she is.

The sort of movement that leaves in its wake borders, households, and regional capitals, when extended across the landscape to far distant places, plays a role in the creation of social structures of correspondingly greater scale. This large-scale creation of places is an inherently dialectical process— an interaction of action and efforts to control and mold that action, the creation of structures and the transformation of those structures as they are realized in action. The business people and government officials of Argentina must attempt to understand and influence the action of thousands of people in neighboring countries so as to induce them to come and work, but to do so in an orderly fashion that does not imperil the national borders, the harmonious spatial organization of the capital city, or the smooth operation of commerce. The strengthened border, land giveaways such as La Salada, and the ambiguous legal status of many immigrants are all part of efforts to set the terms for immigrants' actions. These efforts are in turn reinterpreted by the way Quirpinis gather in La Salada, the persistence of villas miseria, and Bolivians' indifference to the immigrant amnesty. While the terms of action may be beneficial to all concerned, there is necessarily a struggle going on over the use and creation of space.

In other words, while Quirpinis travel partly as a result of the confluence of numerous political, economic, climatic, and technological events, changes, and trends, their movement forms part of the historical conditions under which other people—especially including those vitally concerned with controlling the spaces that Quirpinis traverse and occupy—operate and make their own history.

In this chapter I have tried to show that not just Quirpini but large-scale places like Buenos Aires and even Argentina, seen as a spatial entity, are products of movement and, most crucial, efforts to constrain that movement. If we keep in mind that places, though often encountered as if they were already there, are in fact constantly being created and re-created as people move about, the problem of how to talk about small-scale local spatial practice in the context of the global movement of people, goods, information, and capital becomes less vexing. One drawback to many theories of global interconnections is that by treating large-scale, already global phenomena as the dynamic source of the energy that makes things and people move about, they generate the problem that they are trying to solve. Placing dynamism all on the "big end" makes it very difficult to imagine what people might be doing on the "small end," unless it is just responding to, interpreting, or resisting what comes from outside and above.

No such problem arises if we imagine that ideas, movement, and trans-formations of all sorts are performed by and between people—in other words, fundamentally on a human scale. Nevertheless, the problem of how to relate this scale to much larger social phenomena remains. Here is where the idea of motion is so helpful: if we understand localities such as houses and small communities by means of the ways people move within and through them, it becomes evident that they are inherently dynamic, are intrinsically connected to other places, and are always, to coin a phrase, "trans-scalar." Put another way, their existence and reproduction is always tied up with the operation of places and social facts of larger and smaller scales. Not only is there no necessary difficulty in thinking about locality in a global context, but it is hard to think about locality coherently without recourse to much larger relations. By the same token, we cannot think about migration, or about small communities, as if they were sui generis or existed even for a moment entirely on their own terms or on the terms of the subjects who realize them.

Conclusion: Coming Back to Quirpini

Lives in Motion

Whitman filled his poems with lists—of people, of names—lists of types, showing their dynamism, poignancy, or just their way of being part of the universal. I will begin to draw this book to a close with a much more particular list—biographical vignettes of some people and households, showing how their lives are put together out of multi-scaled movement, their own and others. This is a good way to start synthesizing the many different scales and kinds of places and activities that we have covered. Following these vignettes, I recap the different scales of spatial actions that make up life for Quirpinis, showing how they mutually implicate one another. This extended section is followed by a discussion of how anthropologists can approach issues of scale. I close by reviewing the main techniques I have employed in this book to elucidate the dynamic and multi-scalar reality my subjects lived.

TIBURCIO PUMA

Tiburcio was one of my neighbors in the upper part of Zona Villcasana, but he was not from there. He was from Pumakuna, in the southern Zona Saka-pampa, an area (and a toponym) that appeared to be growing as families carrying the surname Puma expanded their contiguous landholdings. Tiburcio, a man in his late thirties, was born and grew up here, one of the children of Estéban Puma and Valentina Copa, both elderly by the time I did my fieldwork.

Tiburcio started migrating to Argentina as a youth, and he quickly settled into a pattern of going there several months every year, doing mostly ditch-digging in Buenos Aires, although he once went to rural Mendoza. With the money he saved from this work, he began to buy land. Rather than continuing the Puma tendency to expand in their own corner of Sakapampa, he bought land in other parts of Quirpini: two hectares in Villcasana, where he settled his family, and another two across the river in Zona Quirpini. For campesinos in Quirpini, these are very large holdings. He was even able to partly opt out of the mink'a system, planting his land in Zona Quirpini (where he neither lived nor had close kin) by hiring other Quirpinis for the standard daily wage.

Although no one was apparently bothered that he engaged in elite employment practices in addition to the socially inescapable mink'a, his land purchases had not gone without challenge. He bought the land in Villcasana from someone named Condori, who was moving permanently to Argentina; the land borders on the smaller holdings of the seller's cousin, Victor Condori, who himself had hoped to buy the land. Victor still bore a grudge because a nonfamily member bought "Condori land," and he went so far, when drunk, as to accuse Tiburcio of "stealing" the land. Everyone else, including Victor's brother, said that his argument was silly, and that Tiburcio's right to the land was not in doubt. Tiburcio's younger brother, also a frequent migrant, followed his brother's example and bought a large, abandoned house in Villcasana with about two hectares of land and moved in there with his wife. This left their parents with only a single grandchild at home: Tiburcio's daughter from a previous marriage.

When he moved out of his father's house, Tiburcio and his wife (Francisca, originally from the nearby highland community of Qhocha) set up a household on the land in Villcasana, and I knew him as a leading resident of Villcasana (by virtue of his wealth, reputation for hard work, and a friendly and generous character) and of Pumakuna (by virtue of his family's importance there, as well as the above qualities). In the lists of resident households called out for attendance at every community meeting, his was the only name called twice, once for Sakapampa and again for Villcasana.

In fact, Tiburcio complained to me that he was *too* widely respected: he was invariably one of the first people who came to mind when his fellow

Sakapampas or Villcasanas were thinking of a person to engage as a compadre or to enlist for a socially beneficial task. As a result, he felt burdened by social obligations that distracted him from working his land and migrating. He appeared to have approached some sort of limit of the benefits of prestige; given that much of his wealth came from working elsewhere, and that he seemed to have no intention of turning his prestige into a basis for covertly exploitative relationships, the demands on his time brought him limited benefit.

MIGUEL PACO, EMILIANA PUMA, AND CIRILO PACO

The members of the Paco household of Villcasana had traveled in complex but restricted paths through their lives. Cirilo Paco, the elderly uncle of my host, Miguel, had traveled by burro to northern Argentina in the 1950s, back when the journey alone took a month. There he worked harvesting sugarcane. He appeared not to have traveled much otherwise and did not buy any land with his earnings. Two of his brothers and his sister were deaf mutes and spent most of their lives working as domestic help in the household of the only resident white landowner, Rodolfo Otondo, father of Adolfo. Miguel himself worked for don Rodolfo occasionally as a youth, and it was there that he got to know his wife, Emiliana Puma.

Emiliana's father died when she was an infant, and her mother was unable to raise her alone. As a result, Emiliana developed pseudo-parental relations with a number of foster families. She lived for much of her childhood with her father's brother, Pablo Puma, in Pumakuna, and later with Filomón Villcasana, a charismatic but feckless curer who lived across the river in Zona Quirpini. As a youth, she lived full-time with the Otondos, working, like the Pacos, as a household servant. Emiliana had barely traveled outside the region, but her peripatetic childhood gave her an extensive network within Quirpini, even as it created enduring tension between her and her mother, as well as her elder sister, who was never sent to foster parents.

Miguel himself was caught in an ironic clash of national identifications, not unlike that which inconvenienced Nicanor Huarachi. His father had migrated to Argentina frequently, finally marrying an Argentine woman from the northwest. Miguel himself was born there, although he was soon brought to Quirpini. As he explained to me, ever since then he had been viewed by Bolivian officials as an Argentine, and by Argentine officials as a Bolivian; he was thus unable to acquire any sort of identity documents. He believed that his Argentine past, his transnational identity, prevented him from traveling. I found that this problem was easily circumvented when I took him to the relevant offices in Sucre, but until then he had been unable to leave Bolivia.

Instead he amassed as much land as he could without access to cash, taking over not only his father's land but the adjacent land that had belonged to his aunt and uncles—he incorporated Cirilo into his household, taking title to his land and even keeping most of the wages Cirilo received for casual labor. As a result he managed to stay put, and eked out a living by growing corn, periodically doing agricultural work in the nearby fruit- and vegetable-producing region of Camargo, and making hats, which he sold at artisanal fairs in Camargo.

Miguel's two sisters had followed completely different paths. Both migrated to Cochabamba, and he had not seen them nor heard anything of them for more than five years. He once went to Cochabamba himself, and stayed with one of them, but while I was living with him he had only a hazy idea of where they lived in the city.

I suspected that even with a Bolivian identity card, Miguel would not make the trip to Argentina. He was a nervous man, quick to imagine difficulties, and could support his family, if in a marginal way, without recourse to extended travel. It was far more likely that his children would choose to travel, and most of them would probably move away permanently as his sisters did, since the family land was of poor quality and barely enough to support one household.

HERMOGENES VILLCASANA (AND MIGUEL HUARACHI)

I met Hermo when he returned to Quirpini to live, after many years of absence. He is the youngest son of the wealthiest household in Villcasana, which holds several hectares of excellent land at the southern end of the zona. As a young man he joined his brothers doing agricultural work in northern Argentina, rarely returning to Quirpini. I was told that at least one of his brothers had bought land in Buenos Aires, a fantasy success story for a Quirpini. Hermo himself returned in his mid-thirties after nearly twenty years in Argentina, to live with his aged mother in the large house of his childhood. With him came his wife, Dominga, also from Quirpini, and their five young children, all thoroughly Argentine in language and tastes. With his savings he bought himself a large truck of the sort described in chapter 7, the standard vehicle for a long-distance trucker in Bolivia.

Hermo was determined to make the move back home permanent. Determination was what he needed, since he ran into a number of difficulties. First of all, his children hated their new home. Used to such luxuries as indoor plumbing, accessible consumer goods, and schoolmates with whom they could speak easily, they were miserable in Quirpini. Dominga was also ambivalent about the move, although willing to try it out. But perhaps a more significant challenge was economic and geographical. Quirpini lies athwart the road that connects San Lucas to the main road from Potosí to Tarija, and thence to the Argentine border. The traffic leaving the San Lucas region was not nearly enough to support the expense of operating a truck like Hermo's, and even the Potosí–Tarija route seemed to offer few economic prospects. Hermo was not eager to take the extensive absences that would be necessary if he was to make a go of the trucking business, and while I was in Quirpini he drove only in the area, even though this was not working economically.

Even if there had been enough traffic on the road from San Lucas, he probably could not have made a success of the route, precisely because he chose to live in Quirpini. This meant that he had to maintain traditional relations of generosity and reciprocity with his neighbors and kin, which in his case meant frequently giving free rides. Whenever he took his truck out Quirpinis asked him for rides, and he could never charge them. Had his plan been to become a local big shot, establishing a network of patron-client relations masked as reciprocal ties, as in the case Orlove (1974) describes for Peru, the truck might well have been a good start. But I saw few signs that this was his aim.

Although Hermo never spoke of it, I suspect that part of his motivation for moving back was the expectation that, as the youngest son, he would inherit most of his parents' land. But if his hope had been to use his long sojourn in Argentina as a way to return definitively and securely to Quirpini, it appeared that he was going to be frustrated. In order to justify the huge expenditure he had made on his truck, he would have to commit himself to being a trucker, which would mean spending months at a time away from Quirpini. As if to underscore the uncertainty of this option, while I was in Quirpini a transplanted Quirpini who had become a successful trucker was reportedly killed in Tarija by his wife and her lover, a man he had hired as a second driver. In addition, Hermo clearly understood that it is impossible to live in Quirpini as part of the community and be "rich" in any usual sense. His situation was still in flux when I left, and although he was committed to remaining, it was unclear how or whether he would find a feasible way to do so.

Both Hermogenes' situation and Tiburcio's contrasted with that of one of the wealthiest residents of Sakapampa: Miguel Huarachi. Miguel was the sole inheritor of large expanses of excellent land, so much land, in fact, that he was able to sell a large part of his corn and peach crops in Potosí, in the fashion of the landed members of the San Lucas elite. Miguel was unusual in that he had never been to Argentina, nor had he ever traveled out of the region for wage labor. Rather, he had gone to a teachers' training school in the Department of Potosí; he supplemented his income by working as a teacher in the schools of some of the more remote campesino communities. Although Miguel was undoubtedly a campesino himself, he had managed to acquire many of the cultural distinctions of members of the town elite. He had parlayed his wealth and prestige into a leadership position based largely on his ability to mediate between the zona and the representative of the regional and national elite. He had achieved this position in spite of a personality which many (including me) found to be arrogant and often hostile. One Sakapampa told me that he respected Miguel mainly because, given his advantages, he could have elevated himself into a higher social sphere but instead chose to associate with Quirpinis as an equal.

Hermogenes and Tiburcio, in their own ways, were exploring the economic mobility available through the conjunction of traditional and new forms of circulation and mediation: Hermo, by using the capital he accumulated working in Argentina to make himself into a trucker, which apparently he hoped would allow him to sustain his return to his natal community; Tiburcio, by using money from labor in Argentina to underwrite large land purchases in Quirpini. In contrast, Miguel's wealth allowed him to live through much more traditional (and traditionally elite) forms of circulation: a combination of participating in regional agricultural markets, helping to mediate his zona's patron-client relations, and working in a government job.

FELIX VILLCASANA AND ANISA IBARRA

Felix and Anisa were both in their fifties when I was in Quirpini. They had five children, ranging in age from a fourteen-year-old to a newborn; their eldest son had died shortly before I arrived. They both had some travel experience.

Anisa, a thoughtful, capable, and well-respected woman, had traveled when she was young, spending two years working as a domestic servant in La Paz and another two years in Sucre. She traveled, she told me, to "see the world," and her travels seemed to give her a sense of what the cities were like, although she had retained almost no Spanish. She still made occasional short trips to Potosí.

Felix had been traveling for work since 1963, when he went to Mendoza in the northwest of Argentina and stayed for nine years. Since then he had worked throughout northwest Argentina as well as in Sucre and Buenos Aires, where he still spent nearly half of every year. He worked in various jobs, from digging ditches to making bricks to construction to agricultural work. The income he brought home had enabled him to add some good land to his inheritance and Anisa's, and his hard work and even temper earned him wide respect in Quirpini, which was manifested in his ascent up the kurajkuna hierarchy.

He would likely have had more prestige, and climbed the authority hierarchy more rapidly, were he not maintaining a second household in Argentina. I consistently heard that he had another family outside Buenos Aires, with a woman he had married before Anisa. This was a source of constant irritation to Anisa, and she occasionally complained publicly about it, once loudly announcing the existence of Felix's second family while I was videotaping her and Felix at work in a field. The general feeling in Quirpini was that having a second family was something Felix ought not to be doing, but also that it was no one's business. Felix claimed, without much energy, that the rumor was untrue, and when I was in Buenos Aires he never spent time with other San Luqueños. After some initial doubt, I became convinced by the unanimity of the gossip and his listless denials that it was true.

CARMINSA SANTOS AND GENARO MAMANI

Carminsa and Genaro no longer traveled much. Genaro, an energetic and cheerful man nearing forty, had made only one trip to Argentina, returning after more than a year when Carminsa, as energetic as he and of a very determined character, went to get him and found that he had set up house with an Argentine woman. She "dragged him back by the ear," as she put it (but not before they lived there together for six months), and he had not traveled very far since then.

They met when he was traveling. As a young man, Genaro learned how to drive a tractor; during my time in the area he was sometimes hired to drive the valley's sole tractor. He used to travel from place to place, hiring himself out as a tractor driver, and on one such trip, when he was working in Likisana (a large potato-producing plain far to the north of San Lucas), he met Carminsa. Together they came to Quirpini and settled on his mother's land in Villcasana.

On his single trip to Argentina, Genaro learned the construction trade in Mendoza by bluffing his way into an assistant's job, and he frequently worked as a builder in San Lucas. Although the wages were nothing like what an unskilled worker can make in Buenos Aires, the work came often and on his terms. Between that work and his more than adequate landholdings, his family lived well. He was able to buy some land of his own next to his mother's and expected to inherit hers. Already, he and his father farmed their lands jointly.

A few years before I came to Quirpini, Carminsa's brother, Alejandro, had bought land there, thinking to settle. Some people resented having an outsider buy land, and there was a fight when he tried to draw water directly from the river to irrigate his land, disregarding the elaborate system for sharing irrigation water. Eventually he decided that he preferred Likisana and returned there, but he still visited from time to time; Genaro and Carminsa worked his land.

In the 1990s Genaro's travels were limited to the region, which permitted him to take a more active part in local social obligations and roles than he would find convenient otherwise. Although Genaro and Carminsa were not nearly as wealthy as Tiburcio's family, let alone Hermogenes', they were well respected for their generous and responsible character and their willingness to work hard. Genaro had not participated in the kurajkuna hierarchy, focusing instead on the school committee, in which he had achieved the position of treasurer.

JUSTO CRUZ AND JUSTINIANO CRUZ

Justo Cruz was in his sixties, widowed, and had fairly sizable fields right by the road in Zona Quirpini. He had followed an old-fashioned migration trajectory, traveling to northwest Argentina for the first time in the 1950s and making a total of three trips to the agricultural regions of the northwest. Since then he had done some agricultural work in Tarija and had traveled to

Santa Cruz in 1991, as much to visit one of his daughters as to work. His son, Justiniano, was about thirty when I lived in Quirpini, married to Leonarda Colque, with four small children; they lived in a house near his father, and the two men's land was adjacent.

Like Hermogenes Villcasana, Justiniano was the youngest son and thus could expect to inherit the bulk of his father's land; however, it was also anticipated that he would stay around to take care of his father as Justo aged. For instance, Justo served as corregidor (a demanding ritual and political role) in 1993, and he never would have been able to fulfill the obligations involved without the aid of his son's household. As a widower, Justo was already more reliant on his son's family than he might have been, even though he was still physically and mentally fit.

Justiniano was an ambitious and energetic man who had been a local peasant union leader in his twenties, and he played a key role in some of the political changes described in chapter 6. He frequently complained to me that his father, rather than giving him enough land to raise a family, held all of his land in his own name. Justo himself was frustrated that all his other children had moved elsewhere, blocking his efforts to achieve the universal value for men in Quirpini: being the head of a large, multi-household family. It seemed to me that Justo wanted Justiniano to remain dependent on him so that he could hang onto at least one son. But his plan had backfired, because Justiniano felt that, in order to establish even minimal independence for himself, he needed land of his own. As a result, he had taken to migrating to Buenos Aires for several months of every year and had managed to buy a small but adequate plot of land next to his father's. His trips provided both cash to sustain his family and savings for future land purchases. Thus Justo's efforts to exercise maximum control over his son had driven Justiniano to establish his economic independence through access to an economic sphere where Justo could have no influence at all over his son.

Justiniano constantly talked about the option of moving permanently to Buenos Aires or to a Bolivian city, but he always decided against it. Although work in Quirpini was hard and there was no money, he told me, in Quirpini he could work when he wanted to rather than following someone else's schedule.

Everyone in Quirpini cobbled together an existence by taking part in and influencing movement at many different scales. I was unable to see this on my initial walk around the community and learned it only over time. One thing I have striven to do in this ethnography is to examine the relationships between different places by focusing on various aspects of my subjects' actions and movement, paying particular attention to the patterns these actions follow, such as circuits, concentric visits, the circular movement of corn, and so on. These patterns exist at various scales. The reciprocal interactions between two households, for instance, can be roughly described by referring to the actions of a small number of people who reside in those households as well as certain other key mediators of their relations. The concentric coming together of Quirpinis at the school and at the corregidor's house for reuniones and Carnival necessarily occurs on a larger scale and involves a greater range of people. The circuit connecting Quirpini and Buenos Aires can only be understood with reference to the travels of dozens of people (which happen in geographical and social contexts constituted by the travels of hundreds of thousands of people), the efforts of two national governments to influence those travels, the condition of the labor market in Buenos Aires, and so forth. This circuit is an irreducibly large-scale phenomenon.

In migrating, Quirpinis extend tremendously the circuits that animate their community and their households. They have varied motives and widely different means, and follow divergent strategies. Those who go to Buenos Aires enter the migratory circuit in different ways, and situate themselves at different points within it. Yet what they do, taken together, is a significant part of that circuit. Just as it is difficult to say "where" travel takes place, circuits of mass movement resist any single characterization. As I emphasized in my discussion of the way goods are moved about in corn planting, such circuits are not an utter novelty but the length and contents of the circuits connecting Quirpini to Buenos Aires are unprecedented.

Coming Back to Quirpini

In the course of this book I have had frequent recourse to words that invoke uncertainty, illusion, and a lack of solidity. I have extolled disorientation, referred to places and social relations as "evanescent" or "ineffable," and argued that Quirpini and even Bolivia have only a contextual reality. One reason why place is such a useful idiom for talking about social reality is that it seems so real, so solid. Places are where our bodies are, the location of our intentions and our memories. Yet when we look at places, they quickly become hazy, and we easily see that not only have they been invented but they are necessarily reinvented all the time. Places—hometowns, nation-states, neighborhoods—seem simple, but they are always complex amalgams of geography, memory, movement, and power. As I have emphasized, they can never be restricted to their own scale but are defined by the places they contain, the places they are linked to, and the places that contain them.

A place with some depth and reality, like Quirpini, comes in and out of focus depending on what people are doing in relation to it; it presents itself as very different things according to how it is enacted. Places can start to seem impossible once we look at them closely. For this reason, it has been essential not to let any space or place appear as a "given" container for people's actions. For an anthropological work, the location that must be most carefully problematized is the "community."

The ethnographic focus of this book has been on successively larger scales of action and locality in which Quirpinis act and through which they move. There is something artificial about this small-to-large organization, simply because, as I have shown, every scale of activity and place that I have described is implicated in all the others.

We have seen how directly the establishment and reproduction of households were connected to sources of wages such as Buenos Aires in many different ways. The image of sophistication and wealth that helped young men attract girls, the resources to piece together an adequate landholding, the cash income that enabled them to buy clothes, noodles, tools, and school supplies, even corn (if they have not succeeded in assembling large enough fields)—all these inextricably entangled households with distant cities. But even these connections presupposed the far closer link between a wasi and its chajra—the embeddedness of a house in the fields that produce the family's basic subsistence. And houses, of course, were intimately tied to other households through networks of shared labor, food, and drink, not to mention the circulation of young people in marriage, the prerequisite for the existence of any household. The money earned in Buenos Aires enabled Quirpinis to buy all sorts of things, to participate in the long-distance circulation of commodities produced as close by as in San Lucas (relatively few items such as doors, simple furniture, bread, or, most important, trago) and as far away as China (for example, the bicycles that were so important in advertising one's travels).[1] Also crucial to the lives of households were ongoing connections, mediated by kinship or barter, with households in other ecological zones, such as the highland herders to whom they sent their cows for pasturing, the llameros who brought freeze-dried potatoes and salt from Potosí, and the pepper growers of the Pilcomayo River valley in eastern Chuquisaca. Many of these distant connections were incorporated into ritual life, as the llameros brought a variety of crucial ritual substances including q'uwara and the valleys provided reeds for the celebration of Palm Sunday. Similarly, the fields each house relied on were worked through multi-scaled circulations of corn, money, q'uwara, and people.

One could argue, perhaps, that no one really starts from Quirpini when they go to Buenos Aires or Santa Cruz but rather that people migrate from households. With the exception of the border rituals described in chapter 4, migrants make no obvious gesture to the community when they plan their trips and when they travel. In fact, there was a turn of thought among Quirpinis that opposed migration and communal values. Several people mentioned that the rise of migration was undermining local fiestas, as people had less time to organize them or attend. I was also told that the community's soccer team was not what it had been, since most men in their twenties spent much of the year away. A constant challenge to efforts to recruit men for the kurajkuna was that many of the most enterprising and effective men made regular and lengthy trips away, and were not inclined to put off a year's lucrative work for the sake of an authority position. In addition, as demonstrated by Felix Villcasana's second family in Argentina and the murder of the trucker in Tarija, the threatening aspects of secrecy were intensified in migration. It was very hard to know where someone had been or what they had done there, and virtually no way to know what he had earned, whether he planned to sell his land and move away, or if he would begin to buy land throughout the community. People seemed to feel a tension between the implicit individualism and secrecy of migration and the practice of community life.

In Buenos Aires, to be "from Quirpini" was a meaningful designation only in very restricted circles—among Quirpinis or others from the San Lucas region. Just as they were turned into indios in Bolivian cities, the most encompassing identity they became enmeshed with when in the Argentine city was that of "Bolita." A final irony of the way that the mastery of criollo cultural norms escaped the Bolivian nationalizing project because of the proximity of Argentina was that Argentines' casual exclusionary practices were perhaps more effective at making indigenous migrants experience themselves as Bolivians than were all the Bolivian state's ambivalent gestures of inclusion.

The question arises, then, whether "Quirpini" really matters at all. Does anyone actually "start from Quirpini," or do they start from a household, from a class position, from an ethnic identity, or from their personal interests? By allowing the full vagueness of places into my text, have I dispelled them entirely? My aim has been to show not that places like Quirpini or the San Lucas region are unreal but that their mode of reality is one of barely existing, of always being provisional, of presenting themselves at certain moments and in certain ways, and of constant dynamism.

For all its ethereality, Quirpini was without doubt a place that people came back to. Successful migration allowed them not only to sustain their families but also to take on advanced authority positions and the heavy costs they entailed, one of the most important ways to turn the fruits of travel into prestige. For those who returned, Quirpini seemed to be a crucial site in which to realize the potential value they had accumulated in Buenos Aires, even as migration had transformed both their individual values and the communal values that often seemed to stand in contrast to them. The youths on their bicycles, for instance, were displaying their cash and sophistication before the audience that mattered most to them.

The place they return to is replete with ironies. Coming home to Quirpini from Buenos Aires or any Bolivian urban center means going from a marginal position in a regional (or, in the case of Buenos Aires, continental) center to a position of relative centrality in a place that is clearly on the margins of any larger worlds of which it is a part. This dichotomy seemed to frame many people's attitudes about whether to maintain Quirpini as their home or to move their family elsewhere and pull up their roots. Justiniano Cruz, for instance, put great importance on the fact that he controlled his own time when he was in Quirpini—he did not work for anyone besides himself. Nevertheless, as I pointed out above, frequent travel to Buenos Aires was a necessary part of his efforts to gain some autonomy from his father. Were it not for his travels to Argentina, he virtually would be working for his father while he awaited his inheritance. Migration had become a necessary requisite of an autonomous adulthood, and coming back to Quirpini was in many ways an experience of freedom.

In some ways this meant that Quirpini, like a house during corn planting, was becoming gendered as a feminine space. At a certain point in my fieldwork I began to ask myself what the community of Quirpini was for the people I knew. The best answer I could come up with only applied to men.

Wherever an adult man went outside Quirpini, he found himself at the bottom of just about every hierarchy he encountered. In other communities he was either an outsider with no standing, or if he had married into the community, he was a *tullqa*, a son-in-law, bound to years of service to his wife's parents. In San Lucas, as in Bolivian cities, he was a campesino, an indio, poor and at the bottom of the prevailing ethnic hierarchy. In Argentina he was a Bolita, a foreigner occupying a marginal position both socially and economically, subject to the demands of employers and, increasingly in the mid-1990s, the object of resentment and scorn.[2] Back home in Quirpini, however, he was a man among his peers, directly subject to no one. And, normally, he was, or could aspire to be, the head of a household. Moreover, because of the way households are gendered, a man was almost certain at some point to occupy the dominant half of a complementary pair.

As migration and the flight of the regional elite were gradually shifting the power balance between San Lucas and the communities, villages like Quirpini were taking on more political and ritual importance, not less. In the early 1980s Quirpini's only shared property was the school; by the middle of 1994 the community also had its own cemetery and a new chapel, with officials in charge of each. Even the tension between the zonas, as long as it did not lead to further fission, reinforced the fact of the community as the framework within which the zonas contended.

As we have seen repeatedly, much of Quirpini's existence as a community was synonymous with its inclusion in larger social and political realms, and its subordination to the dominant element of those realms. The school was a central defining feature of Quirpini, not least because of its role in subordinating the community as a whole to the regional elite and the national government and Bolivian criollos. The meetings, fiestas, and pageants in the school, not to mention the students' daily attendance at classes and their parents' multifaceted involvement with the school, all had the secondary effect of placing the region and the Bolivian nation at the center of Quirpini.

Quirpini exists as a realm where values are transformed, where potentials are made real. It is in Quirpini that the work a man does in Buenos Aires can be transformed into a household, prestige, and the achievement of full personhood. This is where the Bolivian nation-state can make subjects into citizens. Quirpini exists as a place people leave and return to, as an articulation of regional and national power relations, and as an arena in which the forms of value produced or acquired elsewhere, such as cash, the power of saints, and official political power, can be realized as social goods such as status and the capacity (limited, in this case) for collective action. Seen in this way, Quirpini is nothing but its own inside and outside, that which it contains and that which contains it, and the interplay between them. Yet the place to which Quirpinis return is undergoing constant transformation, not least as a result of their travels. The rise of Quirpini's internal market in land and labor, as Tiburcio's situation shows, were radically changing the possibilities for action back home. Other related phenomena, such as the fact that most adult men's siblings had permanently moved away, were also changing the terms on which people formed their networks, and thus affecting the area's social terrain.

As we saw in chapter 5, the regional elite are even more ephemeral than Quirpini, and even more reliant on the constant interplay of processes at different scales. They are an elite only to the extent that they can dominate movement of all sorts of value between the communities and various distant or putatively inclusive realms, such as the Bolivian government and the world of commerce, as well as their capacity to dominate the terms on which the different actors in the region are able to combine into effective alliances. Their increasingly tenuous position relies on their ability to keep different scales of action and movement apart, and control their interaction. As a result, they are an entirely reactionary force in relation to rising campesino migration and the individual social mobility to which it is giving rise, the growing strength of the campesino union, and even the Bolivian state's increasing efforts to establish more direct relationships with its citizenry.

Like all nation-states, Bolivia, as an "imaginary community" (Anderson 1991), must sustain itself internally in part by making itself real at the level of experience. In other words, it has to produce itself at multiple scales throughout the national territory, insisting on being the context for all sorts of action. Nationhood and citizenship must be evoked and simulated repeatedly, through schools, public offices, plazas, and borders. Quirpini, especially the school, is just one of the myriad sites in which national values are realized. Put differently, Quirpini is not only a place where individuals transform value but is also where the Bolivian state realizes itself as one condition (a context) under which people transform value. So the values being transacted as families pass through the authority hierarchy, show off their bicycles, and so on, cannot be usefully called "local" in contrast to "national" values. Quintessential expressions of Quirpini's political wholeness such as the kurajkuna and the junta escolar are constituted in collaboration with the community, the town elite, and the state, and remain subject to all three.

If a nation-state must create the circumstances under which people collaborate in their own creation as citizens, both administratively and at a personal and emotional level, then the situations of Miguel Paco and Nicanor Huarachi suggest that Bolivia has achieved only spotty success. Although Miguel actively engaged in patronage relationships tied to national elections, he made no efforts to make himself a proper Bolivian citizen. Nicanor, similarly, was largely unconcerned about having no Bolivian documents, as this was only an inconvenience when he wanted to travel. Their stories, along with the heightened tendency of Quirpinis abroad to identify with other Bolivians, suggest that the Bolivian state is least able to make itself real to those who remain in rural villages. In distinction to the Jeffersonian fantasy of a sedentary citizen-yeomanry, the subjects most likely to actively embrace citizenship are migrants and cosmopolitans. The ideal Bolivian citizen is in motion.

Buenos Aires has always existed as the product of long-distance, multi-scaled circulation of goods and people. It has also long been the site of struggles over the control of movement. During the colonial period, much of the city's prosperity came from its Atlantic port and the willingness of authorities to skirt or ignore Spanish controls on trade; it was particularly important as a nexus of trade between Britain and the mining city of Potosí. From the mid-nineteenth century, after independence had cut the city off from Bolivian mining centers, Buenos Aires came to dominate the export of beef and related products from the Argentine interior to Europe. Later in the century the city became the main destination of a huge influx of overseas immigrants, the product of an elite effort to fill the "empty" pampas with Europeans. As such, and in an ironic reversal of the city's colonial defiance of borders and controls on movement, Buenos Aires became the center of Argentine efforts to regulate immigrants' movement and their impact on Argentine society. In short, Buenos Aires has always been elsewhere.

Bolivians are writing a new chapter of this long history of outward focus. They at once represent a new dimension of translocal integration and the return of an old one: Buenos Aires was founded by expeditions sent from what is now Bolivia, and was long connected to the southern Andes by commercial and political ties. In addition, the sudden appearance of Bolivians as a national issue in the 1990s represented the return of immigrants to the center of the national consciousness, after decades of absence. Quirpinis make up a tiny part of the most recent development in a long history of circulation, connection, and division. The Quirpini–Buenos Aires circuit is one of thousands of linkages—migratory, financial, and commercial—that appear to be constituting the Southern Cone as a region in a new and more meaningful sense (see Grimson and Kessler 2005).

Historically Buenos Aires drew resources from its hinterlands; later it found markets there and, after the great waves of European migration ended, a source of labor. One aspect of the growing integration of the Southern Cone is that in many ways Bolivia in the 1990s was beginning to seem like a part of the hinterland of Buenos Aires. Today places like Quirpini, which are largely beyond the political control of the Argentine state, play a significant role in the economic and spatial life of Buenos Aires. The disjunction of political and demographic hinterlands is part of why the international border has become such a vexed issue.

That hinterland, and the Southern Cone as a whole, is made up of complex paths of circulation of people, goods, money, and information. Just one small strand of these complex linkages is the circuit between Quirpini and Buenos Aires. Quirpinis who travel the circuit, and inhabit Buenos Aires, do so largely through extensions of the kin and reciprocity networks they established at home. Although one perspective in Quirpini viewed migration as an individual phenomenon, migration depended entirely on local networks.[3] It is through these networks that households can replace the labor of a migrating son or husband, learn about job prospects in the city, and stay informed about goings-on back home. In addition, as we have seen, Quirpinis in Buenos Aires frequently felt the need to turn to local dispute-resolution strategies and mediating figures in order to navigate conflicts among Quirpinis, or even between Quirpinis and other Bolivians.

To return to Lefebvre's declaration about "the worldwide" and "the local," he did not go far enough. In fact, on the contrary, the worldwide, like the national, can only exist through localities. It is the very ineffability of such large-scale phenomena that requires them to exercise as much control as possible over local actions and meanings if they are to exist at all. As a result, if we are to understand them, we must focus both on the tenuousness of their existence and on the extreme level of control they must exercise on actors, actions, and experiences in order to fend off oblivion.

Methodological Reflection

In writing this book I have employed a number of techniques that allow me to understand the inter-relation of differently scaled activities, and to represent the ceaselessly dynamic and multi-scalar nature of the places in and through which Quirpinis act and move.

My starting point is always the small-scale; in fact, I would argue that starting at the small-scale one can grasp the large, but if we start by looking at states, transnational economic forces, and the like, we will never actually be able to understand what happens in particular situations. To rephrase the comment of a fictional resident of Maine, "You can't get here from there." Instead, I have tried to show how large-scale structures such as nations must exist locally, and incorporate themselves into all sorts of small-scale practices in order to exist at all. In one sense, the progression of chapters went from the small-scale to the large, but this was not so much a change of scale as a matter of addressing the incorporation of Quirpinis into successively larger-scale phenomena.

My most omnipresent technique has been to focus on practice and action. Here I follow the phenomenological preference to grasp structures through the actions that realize them, rather than following Durkheim in treating action as a playing out of structure. Given the spatial theme of the book, I have concentrated most persistently on movement: the mobility of information, things, and, most important, people, considered as subjects and as bodies.

There are excellent phenomenological ethnographies (e.g., Stoller 2002) that train their attention on the particularities and the experiences of subjects. Such an approach can do a matchless job of showing what the world looks like for certain people, but it is not, in itself, an approach to multiple scales. In contrast, this book has been concerned with how small-scale action becomes part of, and is constrained by, large-scale structures of action. A key way that I move from action to the structures that constrain action, and from experience to elements of the larger orders that govern experience, is through attention to patterns of repetitive action. Much of the book, then, is intended as a poetics of movement, on the principle that it is largely through repetition that movement is creative of social space. From the patterns of movement and transformation that people, food, and information follow through households, to the patterns traced by corn in corn planting, to people's recurrent visits to authorities and one another in an event like Carnival, and to a large-scale demographic phenomenon like mass migration, experience and space are structured by recurrent movement. Schemata, as discussed in the introduction, can be understood as the permanent effect of such repetitions.

My reading of Lefebvre's spatial dialectic is central to my understanding of how places are produced through struggle. A place like Quirpini, with its complex history impacted by a variety of imperial, colonial, and national policies, always entangled in multifaceted and conflicting economic connections, cannot of course be seen as the simple product of the actions of Quirpinis. On the contrary, what people like Quirpinis are up to, and what they are creating with their actions, is always of vital importance to those who exercise power at a far larger scale. At every turn, even as people are willy-nilly creating places through action, those actions, and thus the places they create, are being constrained and influenced by projects of those who wield power at what appears to be a larger scale. This is the main import of my chapters on the regional power structure and the ways the Bolivian nation-state strives to realize itself through Quirpinis' ritual action, as well as my discussion of the Argentine-Bolivian border. Agents of power bring forth structures (such as the Día del Estudiante or control of the circulation of goods) which act as representations (sometimes imperative representations) of people's "spatial practice"; these representations are in turn realized in the lived space that results as people incorporate (or do not) these new constraints into their spatial practice. The imposition of power is rarely as direct as it may appear, but rather in most situations depends for its realization on people's creative responses to its imposition.

One important means by which power is applied, and also a crucial way that large-scale realms are made real in localities, is through the manipulation of context; attention to these manipulations has been another main element of my approach. Concern with context is not restricted to states and regional elites; even the young men riding bicycles in urban clothes are trying to invoke a number of distant realms (Buenos Aires, urban Bolivia, even San Lucas and Padcoyo as destinations for bicycle travel) as a relevant context for themselves and for the girls they are trying to impress. Understanding the deployment of context—or, in Weber's (1999:2) phrase, attention to what action is "oriented to"—is crucial to grasping the meanings, the multi-scalar nature, and power-ladenness of movement and places.

In some way, the nature of any place is found elsewhere. The techniques I have used in this volume have allowed me to develop an approach to place as something intimately related to movement, and thus inherently multi-scalar and expansive. The identification of place and territory, a common starting point for many anthropologists, obscures this dynamism and inter-connectedness. Another point I have attempted to make is that "territory," understood as a space defined by its boundaries, is only one moment of "terrain," by which I mean a space defined and structured by internal features and qualities that facilitate and constrain movement. I employ "terrain" as an analogue of Lefebvre's "social space." If we are to problematize "territory," it follows that the anthropological staple, "community," must be cast into doubt as well, both as a social and a geographical given. In this book, I have explored ways to usefully and concretely grasp places as spaces which do not exist constantly for everyone involved with them, and which definitely do not look the same for all their inhabitants. In refusing space as something stable, a given condition for action, in favor of multifaceted, even contradictory places, we move not into unreality or vanishing places but rather closer to the actual ways in which both we and our subjects dwell.

GLOSSARY

Terms in the glossary are identified as Spanish (Sp.), Quechua (Qu.), or a place name (pl.). Most terms are defined according to their usage in Quirpini in the 1990s.

ahijado (Sp. and Qu.) — Godchild.

alcalde mayór (Sp. and Qu.) — The fourth-highest authority position among the Quirpini kurajkuna. See also **kurajkuna**.

alcalde segunda (Sp. and Qu.) — The fifth-highest authority position among the Quirpini kurajkuna. See also **kurajkuna**.

alferéz (Sp. and Qu.) — The sponsor of a fiesta.

almilla (Qu.) — Traditional woolen women'sclothing in Quirpini. At the time of my fieldwork, only two old women still wore it daily. See **traji**, **pollera**.

aqha (Qu.) — A beer made from corn; the most common alcoholic beverage in the San Lucas region. Called **chicha** in Spanish and English.

Avichuca (pl.) — Formerly a zona of Quirpini, it broke away to form a separate community in the late 1980s. See also **zona**.

ayllu (Qu.) — The most common name for the main territorial and political subdivisions of indigenous Andean polities. Also means "family." See **zona**.

ayni (Qu.) — A form of labor reciprocity whereby two people, normally close relatives, exchange equal amounts of the same kind of labor. May be used as a verb or a noun. See **mink'a**.

caballero (Sp.) — Gentleman (lit., "horseman"). In Quirpini, the term refers to men of the San Lucas elite.

cacique (Sp. and Qu.)	Second-highest authority position among the Quirpini kurajkuna. Had been the highest until political reforms in the 1980s created the position of corregidor auxiliár. See also **kurajkuna**.
caminero (Sp. and Qu.)	The lowest position among the Quirpini kurajkuna. The caminero is nominally in charge of Quirpini's annual day of path-cleaning. See also **kurajkuna**.
campeonato (Sp.)	Soccer tournament involving teams representing several communities. These tournaments are often major social events.
campesino (Sp.)	In Bolivia, this Spanish word for "peasant" or "country dweller" has also come to refer to indigenous people, especially agriculturalists.
ch'alla (Qu.)	Variously a ritual including libations, an offering of a few drops of any alcoholic drink to the Pachamama, and any event at which people drink alcoholic beverages. Often used as a verb, meaning to perform or take part in any of these activities. See also **Pachamama**.
chajra (Qu.)	Agricultural field. Also, countryside.
chicha (Sp.)	Beer made from corn. Called **aqha** in Quechua.
cholita (Qu. and Sp.)	Young girl. The word suggests a person of highland indigenous origins in some way distanced from those roots, as by residence in a city or adoption of nontraditional clothes. Can be opposed to **imilla**.
chujllu (Qu.)	Corn-on-the-cob.
compadre/comadre (Sp. and Qu.)	"Co-father"/"co-mother;" the terms parents and godparents use to address each other.
comparsa (Sp.)	A group of dancers. Usually applied to the Carnival dance groups from the town of San Lucas.
corrégidor auxiliár (Sp. and Qu.)	Highest position among the Quirpini kurajkuna. This position was created in the 1980s. See also **kurajkuna**.
criollo (Sp.)	In Spanish American colonies, this word denoted those of Spanish ancestry born in the Americas. Today it refers to the dominant Eurocentric elements of most Latin American societies, as well as their cultural and racial values.
Cumuni (pl.)	A former zona of Quirpini that was in the process of breaking away while I was in the area. See also **zona**.
gente decente, gente de corbata, gente del pueblo (Sp.)	"Decent folk," "folks with ties," "townspeople." Terms for members of the Spanish-speaking elite of San Lucas.
hacendado (Sp.)	Owner of a **hacienda**.

hacienda. (Sp.)   A large landholding, usually worked by laborers bound to the land by law or by debt; haciendas were established throughout the Spanish colonies of the Americas. In the highlands of Bolivia most haciendas (all of which were worked by indigenous campesinos) were dissolved in the course of the Land Reform beginning in 1952.

imilla (Qu.)   Young girl. The word suggests highland indigenous identity and can be opposed to **cholita**.

Jatun Kellaja (pl.)   The traditional name of the ayllu encompassing what is now the community of Quirpini, plus the breakaway communities of Avichuca and Cumuni. The name ("Great Kellaja") suggests that the ayllu was once the dominant part of the larger ayllu called Kellaja. See also **ayllu**.

junta escolar (Sp.)   The committee that runs the Quirpini school. Members hold office for one year.

karnawalkuna (Qu.)   "Carnivals." The musicians and dancers who go from house to house during Carnival.

kurajkuna (Qu.)   "Elders." The nominal political authorities in Quirpini, known as *autoridades políticas* in Spanish; the authorities hold office for one year.

kuraka (Qu. and Sp.)   Third-highest authority position among the Quirpini kurajkuna. See also **kurajkuna**.

kusina (Qu.)   Kitchen (from the Spanish *cocina*).

larqha (Qu.)   Irrigation canal. Also, the group of households that draw water from a given canal.

llameros (Qu. and Sp.)   Itinerant traders from the highlands of Potosí, who carry highland goods into the temperate and lowland areas on their llamas in the course of trading journeys that may last months.

llank'ay (Qu.)   Ploughing. Can also be a general word for "work."

mallku (Qu.)   Condor. Also refers to powerful mountain spirits, identified with condors.

mestizo (Sp.)   A person of mixed European and indigenous heritage (biological or cultural or both). The term is little used in the San Lucas area.

mink'a (Qu.)   A system of labor reciprocity whereby a household invites people to contribute labor, giving them copious food and liquor in exchange; in principle, the transaction must later be reversed. See **ayni**.

mujun (Qu.)   A pile of rocks marking a boundary; from the Spanish *mojón*.

mulli (Qu.)   A spiny tree that grows widely in the San Lucas region.

Pachamama (Qu., also used in Sp.)   "Earth mother"; chthonic female deity whose cult is practiced throughout the rural Andean highlands. See chapter 2 for more details.

Padcoyo (pl.)   The community at the spot where the roads to San Lucas and to the eastern highlands of the region separate from the main Potosí-Tarija road. This is where people of the region go to catch rides to other places.

pantilla (Qu.)   A group of Carnival musicians and dancers; from the Spanish *pandilla*, or "gang."

patakuna (Qu.)   During Carnival, the group of musicians and dancers who make house visits in the upper (*pata*) part of Quirpini.

pikanti (Qu.)   A dish of chicken prepared with hot (Sp. *picante*) peppers. This was the dish that people in Quirpini expected to be fed during a corn-planting mink'a. See also **mink'a**.

pollera (Sp., also used in Qu.)   A pleated skirt worn with petticoats, often seen as the signature garment of **cholitas**, or urban and town women of indigenous background. In the generation before my arrival in Quirpini, campesina women had abandoned the traditional **almilla** for polleras.

puñuy wasi (Qu.)   Bedroom.

q'uwara (Qu.)   A concoction of coca leaves, herbs, animal fat, and a mineral called *q'uwa*, which is burned as an offering to the Pachamama.

Qhocha (pl.)   A community near Quirpini situated in a plateau of the same name in the highlands west of the San Lucas River valley.

quinoa (Qu. and Sp.)   A grain native to the Andes. Around San Lucas, quinoa is grown mainly in highland areas but is rarely seen in Quirpini.

reunión general (Sp.)   A meeting of all the households of Quirpini, held roughly once a month. In principle, Quirpini's highest decision-making body.

San Lucas (pl.)   The largest town of the area, and capital of the provincia of Nor Cinti. The Spanish-speaking regional elite live almost exclusively in San Lucas.

sara (Qu.)   Corn.

sindicato (Sp.)   Common name for the Confederación Sindical Única de Trabajadores Campesinas Bolivianas, the national campesino union, which is a major political force in the highlands surrounding San Lucas.

Tambo Khasa (pl.)   A small community between Quirpini and San Lucas.

tata/mama (Qu.)	Father/mother. Honorific forms of address for respected adults and especially communal authorities, e.g., "Tata Kuraka."
trago (Sp. and Qu.)	A powerful drink made of diluted cane alcohol, often drunk alongside corn beer. Sometimes known as *qhari aqha*, or "male corn beer."
traji/traje (Qu./Sp.)	Traditional men's homespun clothing; also can be called "cultura." Compare to **almilla**.
uchu (Qu.)	Chili pepper. In the San Lucas region, uchu grows in the Pilcomayu River valley.
urakuna (Qu.)	During Carnival, the group of musicians and dancers who make house visits in the lower (*ura*) part of Quirpini.
wasi (Qu.)	House, room, residence, or household. See chapter 2 for a discussion of this term.
wirkhi (Qu.)	A ceramic container, commonly used to hold chicha during Carnival.
yaku alkalti/juez de agua (Qu./Sp.)	The person in charge of maintaining an irrigation canal. Each canal has a yaku alkalti, which is a one-year responsibility.
zona (Sp. and Qu.)	One of the three spatial and political subdivisions of Quirpini. See **ayllu**.

NOTES

Introduction

1. As Williams (1973:120) puts it: "A working country is hardly ever a landscape. The very idea of landscape implies separation and observation."

2. All the ethnographic information alluded to here is elaborated upon in chapter 1.

3. They were brothers, from another part of Bolivia.

1. Places and History in and about Quirpini

1. For an account of the complex dualistic world of race in the Andes, see Weismantel 2001. Toranza (1992) and Albro (2000) critique the dualistic view of Andean ethnic difference, arguing that what prevails today is a multipolar system of social distinction based on race, culture, class, and geography.

2. The best herding areas are further south in the high fields of the Tarachaka mountain range.

3. Ulpana Vicente (1981) gives his impression of regional agricultural techniques and knowledge, focusing on the highland region.

4. The plain of Qhocha, which is on the far side of the hills lining the west side of the San Lucas River valley, is not connected by road to the rest of the region. For this reason, and because it was all owned by a single *hacienda*, it has more tenuous ties to the valley than do the highlands to the east. In climate and history, however, it is similar to the eastern highlands.

5. In Bolivia the term *valle* is usually reserved for a tropical ecological zone characterized by steep valleys on the eastern slopes of the Andes Mountains. What I am calling the San Lucas River "valley" is called a *cañón* in Bolivian Spanish.

6. Water is plentiful, however, only compared to the arid highlands. Lack of water (rather than lack of land) is still the main constraint on the expansion of farming in the valley. Although the valley is less dependent on seasonal rain to grow crops than are the highlands, it had experienced the same lack of rainfall, and in the early 1990s nearly all the un-irrigated fields in Quirpini had been abandoned.

7. In the Spanish colonies, *criollo* was a term applied to those of Spanish descent born in the Americas; this class of people comprised most of the local administration and held great economic power but was always politically subordinate to *peninsulares,* or those who came from Spain itself. In the Andes, both groups had higher status and greater power then *indios* (those of indigenous extraction) and *mestizos* (those of mixed Spanish and indigenous ancestry). The wave of early-nineteenth-century struggles over independence that led to the independence of most of Spain's American colonies are generally taken as a seizure of power by criollos, who became, and have largely remained, the dominant political and economic group in the new nations.

8. For more extensive information on the relation of the San Lucas region and the Quillaca Federation, see Abercrombie 1998. Unless otherwise indicated, I draw on Abercrombie for information about the region's colonial history.

9. There appears to be no record of the year in which San Lucas was founded, as many historical documents were lost when the town was burned by Spanish soldiers during the War of Independence. This lacuna troubled some of the more historically minded townspeople. Furthermore, it is not completely clear that the town of San Lucas is sited on the location of the original reducción. A few kilometers below San Lucas, there are ruins of what appears to have been a village; some residents believe that this was the original location of the town, perhaps abandoned after it was burned in the war.

10. One example is the "vertical ecology" described above.

11. Larson (1998:chap. 3) discusses the impact of mita on indigenous mobility.

12. For a general account of the mid-century social and political transformations in Bolivia, see Malloy 1970.

13. For contrasting accounts of the relationship between indigenous campesinos and town elites, see Abercrombie 1998 and Gose 1994.

14. These are mostly used during the rainy season, when a heavy downpour can turn the streets into raging streams.

15. While I was doing my fieldwork the court bought the house of a nonresident elite family and moved its offices there.

16. Early in my fieldwork a member of the town elite told me that she had heard from a campesina that I was "nice" because I responded when campesinos greeted me. I took this to mean that members of the elite felt no need to respond to the polite greetings of campesinos, and that the latter noticed and resented this behavior.

17. This practice seemed to me to have something to do with the conviction, among both elites and campesinos, that members of the other group were lazy (*qhilla* in Quechua, *flojo* in Spanish). Campesinos rarely saw elites doing manual labor, and elites spent much of their time exhorting campesinos to work.

18. For a discussion of the ways in which "civilized" domestic spaces are differentiated from campesino houses in Bolivia, see Stephenson 1999.

19. It is not possible to be exact about the population of a community, because people of the area do not necessarily live in precisely one community. In addition to the five hundred people who live in Quirpini, about one hundred people in twenty households had some claim to "membership" in the community. Some simply owned land there and did no more than hire laborers to do their share of the work cleaning the irrigation canal (see below) and periodically plant or harvest their fields. Many married couples had land in both partners' home communities, and lived only part-time in Quirpini and the rest of the time elsewhere.

20. To distinguish it from the community as a whole, I refer to the first of these as "Zona Quirpini" but follow local usage in referring to the others simply as "Villcasana" and "Sakapampa."

21. I should emphasize that Platt's is an ideal model and the terminology employed may vary considerably from community to community. In my fieldwork I never heard the term "ayllu"

applied spontaneously to zonas or to Quirpini as such, but when I asked if these were "ayllus," the response implied that this identification was so obvious as hardly to merit mention.

The greatest weakness of Platt's model, in my view, is that no Andean ethnic group, including the Macha, appears to actually call the most inclusive level of political integration an "ayllu."

22. While I was in the area, one small canal was eliminated when San Lucas took over its spring in order to expand the town water supply.

23. Such figures are prominent in the sacred landscapes of many highland Andean communities, and ethnographic discussions of them abound. Some highlights can be found in Platt 1978; Isbell 1985; Martínez 1983, 1989; Abercrombie 1998; and Arnold 2006.

24. In Quirpini "ch'alla" can refer to the act of libation, to certain rituals incorporating libations among other actions (particularly offerings and prayers), to the act of drinking alcoholic drinks, or to a party. For insightful work on ch'allas in Bolivia, see Abercrombie 1998 and Arnold 2006.

25. Elsewhere in the region these ch'allas are held on various nights but always in August, when the mallkus are generally believed to be most active.

26. There was one tractor in the valley, bought in the 1980s by a local cooperative association. The larger landowners of the valley, mostly townspeople, sometimes hired it for planting. I only saw it come to Quirpini once.

27. In Quirpini the terms *originario* and *hacienda* are still used to distinguish communities that had always been independent and those that had been owned by a hacendado.

28. Although it might seem odd to talk about finance in a Bolivian campesino community in terms of dollars, I found that most people in Quirpini, and nearly everyone in San Lucas, had a rough idea of the current dollar exchange rate. Many people brought home their wages from Argentina in dollars, and everyone knew of a way to exchange dollars; the local cash economy was permeated with dollar values.

29. For a fascinating and exhaustive account of why this collapse happened and some sense of what it meant for Bolivian mining communities, see Crabtree 1987.

30. They specifically mention the lack of land, lack of rainfall, poor ecological conditions, or an excess of people with claims to the same land.

31. See, for instance, Hinojosa Gordonava et al. 2000; Caggiano 2005; Grimson and Jelin 2006; Magliano 2007; and Carmona 2008.

32. Since the mid-1990s the neighborhood has changed dramatically. The sluggish employment situation of the late 1990s gave way in 2001 and 2002 to utter economic collapse, throwing millions of people in Argentina out of work. In 2004 I again visited La Salada, and it appeared to have become similar to the urban squatter settlements, or *villas miseria*, for which it was originally conceived as a solution (see chapter 7). At the same time a major market, in which Bolivian vendors play an important role, has grown out of the small weekly market that existed when I was in the area.

33. In the form of support from the Organization of the Petroleum Exporting Countries (OPEC) for the government's regional development project.

2. Bicycles and Houses

1. See Harris 2000 on the conjunction of houses and married couples in the rural highland of Bolivia.

2. In Quirpini the main exception is *ayni,* usually seen as a debt between two individuals, normally close kin.

3. Many houses in Quirpini had no *wirjin,* or their residents had "forgotten" her name and no longer made offerings to her. Even in such homes, people said there actually was a wirjin in the patio, although perhaps a neglected one. I knew of no Catholic family that did not put a *wirkhi*, a

pitcher of corn beer decorated with flowers and said to be "for" the wirjin, in the center of their patio during Carnival. As with all manifestations of the Virgin, this figure is explicitly identified with the Pachamama.

4. That the household of Fabián and Augustina was referred to by his name rather than hers is an indication of the strength of the local preference for designating households with male names: all the couple's land in Quirpini was her inheritance; Fabián had some fields in the nearby community that he came from.

5. This may have to do, in part, with the different questions that I brought to the field.

6. It is possible that some houses are continuously repaired and renovated until little remains of their original walls, but I never heard of this happening.

7. Most of the men in Quirpini had a craft, such as making and repairing sandals, carpentry, repairing radios, or making hats. Nearly all the women of Quirpini were at least competent weavers, but I never knew a house to include a room dedicated to weaving; all adult women cooked, and all houses had a kitchen.

8. Evangelical Christians in the area deny that she exists, just as they deny the importance of the closely related Virgin Mary.

9. Among indigenous people of the Andes, ore is widely held to grow underground, like a tuber.

10. But the q'uwara, the center of a chajra during corn planting, is more a space of avoidance than convergence; it is the men who have converged at the field who have to stay away from the q'uwara.

11. Harris (2000:212–213) points out that *pacha* can be used to indicate emphasis and completion. At the time I was revising this manuscript, I received the sad news that Harris had suddenly died after an extraordinarily fruitful, if too short, life devoted to understanding the people of Bolivia and the Andes. I first met her when she served dinner to me and some mutual friends; she made us pasta, and accordingly was dubbed "La Pastamama." Like many working in the area, I have benefited immeasurably from her insight, hard work, and wisdom.

12. In late 1993 specialists from a government program dedicated to eradicating *chagas*, an insect-borne disease endemic to most of Bolivia, urged all the households in the valley to separate their animal pens from the main residence. Though many were inclined to follow the advice, no one had done so by the time I left in 1994.

13. Quirpinis do not generally drink water, preferring corn beer, soda, and herbal teas.

14. Within the irrigated valley bottom, all land and whatever grows on it belongs to someone. The owner of a tree or plant can, in principle, forbid others from taking any part of it; in practice, this is not an issue for common herbs, but property rights are more strictly observed when it comes to firewood.

15. I elaborate on the spatial basis of the power of the San Lucas elite in chapter 5.

16. The suffix -*man* can denote the purpose of action as well as the destination of movement. *Imaman,* or "to what," is a common way of asking "for what purpose?" or "to what end?"

17. In Quechua, *yuraj qulqi*. People in Quirpini told me that this is an extraordinarily valuable mineral that was freely available before the Spanish conquest but disappeared afterward. Now foreigners search for it, avaricious for the unimaginable wealth its discovery would bring, but they have yet to discover it.

18. There were two exceptions. Toward the end of my stay in Quirpini, a recently returned immigrant began building a house with two stories on a small plot alongside the road. It was not clear when I left whether the house would have a traditional patio or a yard to the side of a single compact house. The other exception was the house of Adolfo Otondo, the sole elite landowner resident in Quirpini. His was a sprawling hacienda-style house, with a sharper distinction between productive and residential spaces than in other houses of the area, several patios, and rooms for

domestic servants. No one regarded Otdondo or his family as "Quirpinis" in the sense that Miguel and his family were, and his house was treated as a different kind of structure from the "normal" houses of the community.

19. This term is from Nicholson-Smith's translation (1991). Shields (1999) objects to this English rendering of Lefebvre's French, preferring "spaces of representation."

20. It is not entirely clear if Lefebvre thinks of "lived space" as a rarified ideal achieved only by artists and philosophers, or as the true lived space of "inhabitants."

3. The Geography of Planting Corn

1. Poole (1984) takes this point so seriously that in her discussion of agricultural calendars in Paruro, Peru, she distinguishes the time of labor and the time of production: the latter is the period when plants themselves are producing, with relatively little help from people.

2. For more on textualization, see Rockefeller 1998.

3. I should emphasize here that the actions are *relatively* paradigmatic. People do not treat corn-planting as a pure form of activity and are perfectly able to carry out the familiar actions that constitute sara llank'ay in a way that is appropriate to any number of particular and contingent factors, such as the size of the field, the household's current and anticipated needs, what was planted in the field in years past, and the social positions people occupy or would like to occupy.

4. In the cold highlands to the east and west, where corn is rarely planted, potatoes, wheat, and barley are much more important crops and are planted in mink'a, I was told.

5. For more on how irrigation water is distributed, see chapter 5.

6. One agronomist I talked to suggested that people in the San Lucas valley could be seen as doing hydroponic farming; the soil is nearly devoid of nutrients, and crops grow almost entirely because of the fertilizer they are given.

7. The most general Quechua word for "plowing" is *llank'ay,* but in corn planting this word is used only for the final plowing of furrows as they are seeded. In contrast, *barbecho,* borrowed from Spanish, refers only to plowing done in preparation for planting.

8. This strengthening of a relationship can even be done when there is no child to baptize: Constantino and Justiniano baptized a "bread baby" (*t'anta wawa*), so that they could call each other *compadre.*

9. For an excellent general account of Andean reciprocity, see Mayer 1974, 2001. The articles collected in Alberti and Mayer (1974) also give an informative range of perspectives on reciprocity.

10. I suspect that this shift of terminology had to do with the more strongly egalitarian connotation of "ayni." Before I was well known in Quirpini, people frequently made efforts to present the community as internally undivided and perfect in its realization of egalitarian ideals.

11. The term derives from *khuli,* Quechua for "clod."

12. A *costal* is a measure of weight equivalent to the English hundredweight.

13. "Houseowner." The senior man of the planting household is usually given this designation, regardless of who has title to the field.

14. His words were "watapaj ujyanapaj," which can also be glossed "in order to drink for the year."

15. Or *mujira.* The first term combines *ilu-,* the Quechua root for "sow" with an Aymara suffix *-ri* indicating the person who habitually performs the action; the second combines the Quechua word for seed (*muju*) with the Spanish suffix for a person who does the action (*-ero/-era*). Medlin (1983) says that in Calcha, not far from the San Lucas region, the woman dropping the seeds must be an unmarried maiden, but there is no such preference in Quirpini.

16. Apparently from the Spanish word "buey," meaning "ox." A common way people in Quirpini communicated with animals was to call out a stylized version of the name of the kind of animal they were addressing, for example, "Wiy!" for oxen, "Wija!" (from the Spanish *oveja*) for sheep.

17. I was told that in the past both the plowman and sower carried bread babies on their backs, but while I was in the area the only people to continue this custom were the Spanish-speaking landowners of the town.

18. Another hybrid word, combining the Quechua word *pampay*, or "flatten," with the Spanish agentive suffix *-ero/-era*, to mean "one who flattens the ground."

19. Sometimes they use large enamel chicha cups instead.

20. Usually there are more men present than women, so when all the women have drunk, the men pressure some of them to drink again; eventually the game ends with pairs of men drinking together, which everyone finds less funny.

21. For more on gender dualism in the Andes, see Platt 1978; Silverblatt 1987; and Stephenson 1999.

22. In the course of a lifetime, it would not be extraordinary for someone to take part in four or five hundred such plantings.

23. Orlove (1974) long ago showed how supposedly egalitarian forms of exchange can be manipulated by campesinos with access to capital to become a means of exploitation. This did not happen with any consistency in Quirpini.

24. That the people who respond to a household's invitations see themselves as sharing a relationship with the inviting family is made clear when someone is not invited or does not turn up. Then people look for an explanation, seeking some story of ruptured relations to explain an individual's or a family's exclusion from the provisional group.

4. Carnival and the Spatial Practice of Community

1. This tendency is doubtless strengthened by the fact that some key components of many places, such as large-scale geographical and climatic features, actually do exist prior to and independent of human action.

2. Much of the debate going on today in the United States concerning the control of undocumented immigration is about the *kind* of deference immigrants should show the border and, by extension, the nation-state. Crossing the Rio Grande at night, or sneaking through miles of desert, are certainly forms of deference but not ones that invoke the territoriality of the U.S. or the government's ability to fully inhabit it.

3. Property lines divide not only the earth but also what grows on it and most goods found on it. One of Miguel Paco's children pointed out a tree on the border between Miguel's land and a neighbor's; Miguel had the right to use firewood from one side of the tree, and the neighbor had the right to the other.

4. The *Shorter Oxford English Dictionary* defines "territory" as "the land or district lying round a city or town and under its jurisdiction" or "the land or country belonging to or under the dominion of a ruler or state" (1979:"territory"), where "terrain" is said to mean "a tract of country considered with regard to its natural features, configuration, etc." (1979:"terrain"). In other words, in English, "territory" is land considered as extension, whereas "terrain" is land considered as a collection of features and internal attributes. One possible etymology of "territory" underlines the extent to which the word is concerned with the outer borders of a space: though it may well share with "terrain" the Latin root *terra*, meaning "earth" or "land," it might just as well arise from *terrere*, "to frighten," in a derivation that would have meant "a place from which people are warned off" (Ayto 1993:"territory").

5. I have heard anecdotally that people make the trip from as far away as Betanzos, a town outside the city of Potosí.

6. Many of these women actually showed off weavings made by their mothers or by women from other households.

7. This sort of substitution was common in Quirpini, it being more important that a role be filled than that it be filled by a particular person.

8. From the Spanish *pandilla* (gang).

9. To say that "everyone" took part required eliding two kinds of absence. First of all, it implied that the members of the households who come to the *corregidor*'s house are able to represent the household members who do not come. Second, it leaves the non-Catholic Quirpinis out of the picture entirely—no one ever commented on their absence or tried to induce them to take part. My sense was that evangelicals in the community colluded in their own erasure by lying low during Carnival.

10. The Spanish word *alcalde* can refer to several political roles, such as the *alcalde mayor* and *alcalde segunda* of the Quirpini authority system, but in the case of the *alcalde* of San Lucas it refers to an elected executive of a town and can be translated as "mayor."

11. Quirpini, and other communities, used to own houses in town, which served as bases during the frequent ritual visits to San Lucas. As I detail in chapter 5, the number of ritual visits to San Lucas had been drastically reduced in recent decades, and all these houses were sold.

12. Apart from the house, most of these goods are expensive and fairly durable manufactured goods, such as ploughs, bicycles, radios, propane stoves, and so on.

13. This was very stressful.

14. I was never able to establish whether there was normally a comparsa for Sakapampa. In 1994 there was none; although people in Villcasana told me that this was because the person named as alferéz that year had died, a Sakapampa heatedly claimed that Sakapampas did not form comparsas because it was not part of "our" tradition.

15. Although evangelical Christians were systematically excluded from the "whole" of Quirpini in this enactment, individual Catholic households might exclude themselves simply by not being home that day. The most common reason to avoid hosting the Carnival visitors was that too many members were abroad; in this case, the remaining household members would generally help out another household. Alternately, they might stay quietly indoors and not respond when the dancers appeared at the house.

16. I say "most" relationships are trumped in this way because some households, particularly those short of adult members, may invite friends or kin to help them serve the visitors; in this situation a friendship takes precedence over the uniform relationship between community members. In addition, every household prepares for these visits with the help of their unique network of reciprocal aid.

17. Of course, different people traverse different amounts of terrain: those who live at the upper and lower extremes of Quirpini, as well as those who dance and play flutes, cover almost half the community's inhabited land. Those living near the school do not travel far, unless they choose to join the visits early.

18. The Quechua verb *samay* means "breathe" and, by extension, "rest" and "wait."

19. I contend that this complex of ideas and actions does not define a place because the distinction it marks—between inhabited agricultural areas and the wild, dangerous mountains—is valid for the entire valley, and indeed for any highland area; it lacks geographical specificity.

20. They cannot, of course, completely ignore the boundaries of all households, since some are defined by walls with gates or doorways. Insofar as is practical, however, the pantillas ignore the bounded aspect of households.

5. Ethnic Politics and the Control of Movement

1. While I was in Quirpini there was no specific date on which the offices changed hands; rather, the transition was gradual, as marked by the presence of both old and new authorities at the weekly meetings of authorities for some weeks after the vote.

2. For a biting parody of this view, see Mark Twain's "To the Person Sitting in Darkness" (1992).

3. Members of the town elite were never called *vecinos, mestizos,* or *mistis,* terms commonly used in other parts of the Andes. Campesinos living in San Lucas sometimes called them *llajta ukhu runas* ("people of the town center"), reflecting the prevailing ethnic division of space in the town.

4. Racialized two-part hierarchies such as this are very common in the rural Andes, although the precise terms on which race, power, identity, and economics are worked out within these hierarchies can vary considerably from situation to situation. See, for instance, Isbell 1985; Rasnake 1988; Gose 1994; and Abercrombie 1998.

5. The head of the local development agency while I was in the area was never accused of any impropriety, not even in gossip, but I took this to be an exceptional situation.

6. When I remarked to one of the more radical Quirpinis that it would be great to have a campesino as mayor, he reacted as if this were a pleasant fantasy.

7. Sometimes the priest would perform these sacraments on his visits to the villages of the area.

8. This would not be the first time this occurred. I was told that the elite townspeople had run a priest out of town on a donkey in the early 1970s, although I never knew what he had done to upset them. As punishment, the town was left without a priest for a decade.

9. Quirpinis generally talked as if the positions were passed by men, although, in a very real sense, they are passed by households or even extended families. When the kuraka, for instance, acts in his official capacity, he is often referred to as *tata kuraka* ("father kuraka"); his wife is then called *mama kuraka* ("mother kuraka"). At meetings either member of the couple is sufficient to fulfill the obligation for an authority to be present, although in rituals they appear together, and if either one is absent, the absentee's place is taken by someone of the same sex.

10. This arrangement has the additional effect of allowing the authorities to serve as de facto representatives of their zona at the weekly authority meetings.

11. I suspect that it was in order to rectify this situation that the couple's godmother made a point of taking the girl's side in all disputes.

12. One of the clearest expressions of this transcendent role was the common custom, during many fiestas, of addressing any member of the kurajkuna as *tatanchis,* or "our father." Quechua distinguishes two first-person plurals—the exclusive form refers to the speaker and unspecified others, but excludes the addressee; the inclusive form encompasses the addressee as well as the speaker and, potentially, others. Were the authorities simply styled as "fathers" of the community members, we could expect them to be addressed as *tatayku,* meaning "father of me and some other people." But *tatanchis* incorporates the *inclusive* suffix; in other words, it interpellates the authority as father of the speaker *and of himself.*

13. Quirpinis gathering indoors nearly always conform to this general pattern, whereby women sit low and near the door and men sit higher across from it.

14. In the highland areas the peasant union takes on much of this role as well.

15. This form of mink'a and the daily wage were not as different as it might seem, since jornal had to include lunch for the workers and dinner in the evenings, with alcohol. In mink'a no money changed hands, but the food was more plentiful and the landowner had to throw a real party in the evening.

16. "Los Quirpinis son mis hijos predelictos" was the phrase he used.

17. The minor canals each had exclusive access to its own water source.

18. A possible exception is Castillo Mayu Larqha, which watered the land of only a handful of families.

19. This appears to be an atypical relationship between cross and canal for rural Peru and Bolivia.

20. One member of an old San Lucas family assured me, in 1993, that "no one" lived in the town anymore, although in fact the town's population had doubled over the previous two decades.

6. Placing Bolivia in Quirpini

1. This is the vernal equinox, and the day is also called *Día de la Primavera,* or Day of Spring. If September 21 falls on Saturday or Sunday, the celebration is moved to a weekday.

2. One theme of Gupta's illuminating forays into the anthropology of states (see, for instance, Gupta 1995; Ferguson and Gupta 2005; and Gupta and Sharma 2006) is that it is the distinctive contribution of anthropology to look at this aspect of governance.

3. Arnold (2006) describes a similar Bolivian school ceremony in the altiplano.

4. Of course, participation in events before an audience is hardly something new for Quirpinis; the Catholic Mass is a form of spectacle, and even students in a classroom can be considered a kind of audience, although they lack the anonymity that usually comes with the role. But the civic rituals are distinctive in that campesinos can occupy both sides of the spectacle. Rather than being the passive or managed recipients of spectacular instruction, they can, in the tradition of Passion Plays, take an active role in both putting on and witnessing the rituals.

5. Meaning "this world," a Quechua expression that refers to the world as opposed to heaven (*janaq pacha,* or "upper world") and the underworld (*ukhu pacha*), as well as to other epochs, which are sometimes called *ñawpa pacha,* or "olden times."

7. Where Do You Go When You Go to Buenos Aires?

1. For an analysis of how the crisis affected immigrants, see Grimson and Kessler 2005; and Grimson and Jelin 2006.

2. I avoid using percentages in referring to the results of my survey so as not to present the data as more exact or generalizable than my simple methods and small sample size permit. The fifty households I sampled had 282 members, of whom 174 were adults. The quality of information in each household was slightly different, as some of my interlocutors told me about dead members of the household, others told me about people who were absent, and some did not know the whereabouts or full travel histories of absent household members. In addition, my survey recorded no trace of people who had left Quirpini permanently and whose parents were no longer alive (i.e., those who did not even theoretically "belong" to a specific household); thus the survey understates the scale of migration from Quirpini.

3. Of ninety-one adult males surveyed, seventy-seven had migrated at some point, sixty-six to Argentina in general and fifty-seven to Buenos Aires.

4. Of the men surveyed, twenty-seven had been to Santa Cruz and twenty-six to Tarija.

5. Of eighty-three women surveyed, thirty-six had migrated; thirteen had been to Argentina and only five to Buenos Aires.

6. Twelve women had been to Santa Cruz, nearly the same number as had been to Argentina.

7. See Munn 1996 on trucks as sacred places in Australia.

8. This is not to suggest, of course, that people do not play with and manipulate representations of themselves and others in Quirpini. Such play is a crucial part of social relations, but the

terms and limits under which such play occurs are very different from those on the border or in officialdom.

9. Since the main function of the border crossings between Bolivia and Argentina, from the Argentine point of view, is to separate Argentines from Bolivians, I could even say that the border had, for a moment, made me into a Bolivian. I was not a very good Bolivian, as I had learned countless times already, and my presence at the border crossing perplexed and irritated the Argentine officials I encountered.

10. The Bolivian–Argentine border, however, is not as fearsome a power as the U.S.–Mexican border, which in the social science literature has at times appeared to be the one "true" border, as it separates so much, and the crossing of it creates and confounds so many categories and social realities (see Alvarez 1995). If national borders are treated as the types for spatial borders in general, the U.S.–Mexican border, for U.S. social scientists, is the type for national borders.

11. Apparently the number of migrants increased. Although all anecdotal evidence suggests that cross-border migration has increased dramatically from the fifties to the nineties, there are no firm numbers to establish that this has actually happened. Census figures (Programa 1997) suggest that whatever increase has occurred has been limited, but these numbers are not reliable.

12. "El gobierno federal fomentará la inmigración europea y no podrá restringir, limitar ni gravar con impuesto alguno la entrada en el territorio argentino de los extrangeros que traigan por objeto labrar la tierra, mejorar la industria e introducir y enseñar las ciencias y las artes."

13. This reading material, full of news of economic policy, the legal troubles of the son of then president Carlos Menem, the exploits of a scandalous entertainer, and the upcoming exodus of the beautiful people to Uruguay for Christmas vacation, left me relatively well informed about a world I would never see, and whose existence none of my Bolivian friends ever seemed to notice.

14. The Provincia of Buenos Aires includes only areas outside the city proper, which has its own government. Similarly, the term "Gran Buenos Aires" ("Greater Buenos Aires") refers not to the whole conurbation but only to the outlying partidos (Sargent 1974:xvii).

15. While I was there I never heard this neighborhood distinguished from the rest of La Salada by a distinct name, but some map research has convinced me that this was Barrio José Hernández, just over the Riachuelo from the center of La Salada, in La Matanza.

16. The spaces of Bolivians in Buenos Aires are being increasingly well documented by a growing wave of ethnographic and other research, particularly since 1999. This growth in interest in new migrants to Buenos Aires is part of a general increase in attention to migration within Latin America; see, for instance, Salman and Zoomers 2002; and Novick 2008.

17. The changing awareness of Bolivian and other cross-border immigrants is reflected in scholarly work in Argentina. In the early 1990s research on cross-border immigration was relatively scarce, and the study of immigration was mainly concerned with historical research into European populations that constituted Argentina's immigrant heritage. In contrast, today there is a growing community of scholars working on South American populations in the Buenos Aires area and in the country as a whole. An excellent selection of recent work on these migratory populations can be found in Grimson and Jelin 2006.

Conclusion

1. The extensive supply chains that bring a multiplicity of goods to the San Lucas region is one of the most important multi-scalar phenomena that I have not been able to address adequately in this book.

2. Yet, as much as they were excluded from Argentine society as Bolivians, Quirpinis seemed to find the terms of their exclusion in Argentina less onerous than those they experienced as

"indios" in Bolivian cities. The condescending misrecognition they received as members of an undifferentiated Bolivian laboring class appeared to be part of their experience of Buenos Aries as a place where they were liberated from many of the constraints of life in their home country.

3. This is the main reason why the Argentine film "Bolivia" (Caetano 2001) is unconvincing as an image of the lot of Bolivian migrants to Buenos Aires: the immigrant character appears to be completely isolated in the city, unconnected to any Bolivian networks. To my knowledge, this rarely happens among rural Bolivians in the Argentine capital.

BIBLIOGRAPHY

Abercrombie, Thomas Alan. 1991. "To Be Indian, to Be Bolivian: 'Ethnic' and 'National' Discourses of Identity." In G. Urban and J. Scherzer, eds., *Nation-States and Indians in Latin America*. Austin: University of Texas Press.

————. 1998. *Pathways of Memory and Power: Ethnography and History among an Andean People*. Madison: University of Wisconsin Press.

Alberti, Giorgio, and Enrique Mayer. 1974. *Reciprocidad e intercambio en Los Andes Peruanos*. Lima: Instituto de Estudios Peruanos.

Albó, Xavier. 1987. "From MNRistas to Kataristas to Katari." In S. Stern, ed., *Resistance, Rebellion and Consciousness in the Andean Peasant World: 19th to 20th Centuries*. Madison: University of Wisconsin Press.

Albó, Xavier, Tomás Greaves and Godofredo Sandoval. 1981–1987. *Chukiyawu: La cara aymara de Nuestra Ciudad*. La Paz: CIPCA.

Albro, Robert. 2000. "The Populist Chola: Cultural Mediation and Political Imagination in Quillacollo, Bolivia." *Journal of Latin American Anthropology* 5(2): 30–88.

Allen, Catherine. 1988. *The Hold Life Has: Coca and Cultural Identity in an Andean Community*. Washington, D.C.: Smithsonian Institution Press.

Alvarez, Robert R., Jr. 1995. "The Mexican–US Border: The Making of an Anthropology of Borderlands." *Annual Review of Anthropology* 24: 447–470.

Anderson, Benedict. 1991. *Imagined Communities: Reflections on the Origin and Spread of Nationalism*. London: Verso.

Appadurai, Arjun. 1996a. "Disjuncture and Difference in the Global Cultural Economy." In *Modernity at Large: Cultural Dimensions of Globalization*. Minneapolis: University of Minnesota Press.

————. 1996b. "Global Ethnoscapes: Notes and Queries for a Transnational Anthropology." In *Modernity at Large: Cultural Dimensions of Globalization*, 48–65. Minneapolis: University of Minnesota Press.

————. 1996c. "Patriotism and Its Futures." In *Modernity at Large: Cultural Dimensions of Globalization*. Minneapolis: University of Minnesota Press.

———. 1996d. "The Production of Locality." In *Modernity at Large: Cultural Dimensions of Globalization*. Minneapolis: University of Minnesota Press.

Arnold, Denise. 1987. "Kinship as Cosmology : Potatoes as Offspring among the Aymara of Highand Bolivia." *Canadian Journal of Native Studies* 7(2): 323–337.

———. 1992. "La casa de Adobes y piedras del Inka: Género, memoria y cosmos en Qaqachaka." In Denise Arnold, Domingo Jiménez, and Juan de Dios Yapita, eds., *Hacia un orden andino de las cosas*. La Paz: Hisbol/Ilca.

Arnold, Denise, with Juan de Dios Yapita. 2006. *The Metamorphosis of Heads: Textual Struggles, Education, and Land in the Andes*. Pittsburgh: University of Pittsburgh Press.

Ayto, John. 1993. *Dictionary of Word Origins*. New York: Arcade.

Balán, Jorge. 1990. "La economía domestica y las diferencias entre los sexos en las migraciones internacionales: Un estudio sobre el caso de los Bolivanos in la Argentina." *Estudios Migratorios Latinoamericanos* 5: 25–26.

———. 1992. "The Role of Migration Policies and Social Networks in the Development of a Migration System in the Southern Cone." In Mary Kritz, Lin L. Lim, and Hania Zlotnik, eds., *International Migrations Systems: A Global Approach*. New York: Oxford University Press.

Balán, Jorge, and Jorge Dandler. 1986. *Marriage Process and Household Formation: The Impact of Migration on a Peasant Society*. New York: Population Council.

Bastien, Joseph. 1978. *The Mountain of the Condor: Metaphor and Ritual in an Andean Ayllu*. St. Paul: West.

Bateson, Gregory, and J. Reusch. 1951. *Communication*. New York: Norton.

Bauman, Richard, and Briggs, Charles L. 1990. "Poetics and Performance as Critical Perspectives on Language and Social Life." *Annual Review of Anthropology* 19: 59–88.

Bell, Vikki. 1999. "Mimesis as Cultural Survival: Judith Butler and Anti-Semitism." *Theory, Culture and Society* 16(2): 133–161.

Bello, Walden. 2001. *Future in the Balance: Essays on Globalization and Resistance*. Oakland: Food First.

Benencia, Roberto. 2006. "Bolivianización de la horticultura en ala Argentina." In Alejandro Grimson and Elizabeth Jelin, eds., *Migraciones regionales hacia la Argentina*. Buenos Aires: Prometeo Libros.

Bergson, Henri. 1946. *The Creative Mind: An Introduction to Metaphysics*. Translated by Mabelle L. Andison. New York: Philosophical Library.

Bestor, Theodore C. 2003. "Markets and Places: Tokyo and the Global Tuna Trade." In Setha M. Low and Denise Lawrence-Zúñiga, eds., *The Anthropology of Space and Place: Locating Culture*. Oxford: Blackwell.

———. 2004. *Tsukiji: The Fish Market at the Center of the World*. Berkeley: University of California Press.

Blustein, Paul. 2005. *And the Money Kept Rolling In (and Out): Wall Street, the IMF, and the Bankrupting of Argentina*. New York: Public Affairs.

Bouysse-Cassagne, Thérèse. 1978. "L'espace aymara: *Urco* et *uma*." *Annales E.S.C.* 33: 5–6 (1057–1080).

Briggs, Charles L. 1996. "The Politics of Discursive Authority in Research on the 'Invention of Tradition.'" *Cultural Anthropology* 11(4): 435–469.

Briggs, Charles L., and Richard Bauman. 1992. "Genre, Intertextuality, and Social Power." *Journal of Linguistic Anthropology* 2(2): 131–172.

Butler, Judith. 1988. "Performative Acts and Gender Constitution: An Essay in Phenomenology and Feminist Theory." *Theatre Journal* 40(4): 519–531.

———. 1993. *Bodies That Matter: On the Discursive Limits of "Sex."* New York: Routledge.

———. 2006. *Gender Trouble: Feminism and the Subversion of Identity*. New York: Routledge.

Caetano, Israel Adrián. 2001. *Bolivia*. 75 min. Argentina.

Caggiano, Sergio. 2005. *Lo que no entra en el Crisol: Inmigración boliviana, comunicación intercultural y procesos identitarios*. Buenos Aires: Prometeo.

Canessa, Andrew. 2005. *Natives Making Nation: Gender, Indigeneity, and the State in the Andes*. Tucson: University of Arizona Press.

Carmona, Alicia. 2008. "Bailaremos: Participation in Morenada Dance Fraternities among Bolivian Immigrants in Argentina." Ph.D. dissertation, University of Chicago.

Casey, Edward. 1996. "How to Get from Space to Place in a Fairly Short Stretch of Time: Phenomenological Prolegomena." In S. Feld and K. Basso, eds., *Senses of Place*. Santa Fe, N.M.: School of American Research Press.

———. 1998. *The Fate of Place: A Philosophical History*. Berkeley: University of California Press.

Castells, Manuel . 1989. *The Informational City: Information Technology, Economic Restructuring, and the Urban-Regional Process*. Oxford: Basil Blackwell.

———. 1996a. "The Net and the Self: Working Notes for a Critical Theory of Informational Society." *Critique of Anthropology* 16(1): 9–38.

———. 1996b. *The Rise of the Network Society*. London: Blackwell.

Castro, Donald S. 1991. *The Development and Politics of Argentina Immigration Policy, 1852–1914: To Govern Is to Populate*. San Francisco: Mellen Research University Press, 1991.

Clarín. 1999a. "Inmigracion ilegal: Proyecto para cambiar la ley de migraciones: Menem dijo que los inmigrantes ilegales deberán irse del país. (January 21)." Available at http://www.clarin.com.ar/diario/99-01-21/e-03401d.htm (accessed February 22, 1999).

———. 1999b. "Un sistema informatizado controlará pasos fronterizos. (January 23)." Available at http://www.clarin.com.ar/diario/99-01-23/e-04502d.htm (accessed February 22, 1999).

Cole, Jeffrey A. 1985. *The Potosí Mita, 1573–1700: Compulsory Indian Labor in the Andes*. Stanford, Calif.: Stanford University Press.

Comunidad Boliviana en la Argentina. 2004. "Impresionante operativo policial para el desalojo de los puestos de la feria 'La Salada.'" Available at http://www.comunidadboliviana.com.ar/shop/detallenot.asp?notid=445 (accessed April 26, 2007).

Cook, Noble David. 1981. *Demographic Collapse: Indian Peru 1520 to 1620*. Cambridge: Cambridge University Press.

CORDECH (Corporación Regional de Desarrollo de Chuquisaca). n.d. (1993). "Informe de evaluación (1989–1991) Proyecto de Desarollo rural Chuquisaca Sur. Sucre."

Cornaglia, Miguel Angel. 1994. *La inmigración: Grave problema nacional*. Buenos Aires: Faro Editorial.

Crabtree, John. 1987. *The Great Tin Crash: Bolivia and the World Tin Market*. New York: Monthly Review Press.

Dandler, Jorge. 1984. "Campesinado y reforma agraria en Cochabamba (1952–1953): Dinámica de un movimiento campesino en Bolivia." In J. Dandler, ed., *Bolivia: La fuerza historica del campesinado*. La Paz: CERES.

Dandler, Jorge, and Carmen Medeiros. 1991. "Migración temporaria de Cochabamba, Bolivia, a la Argentina: Patrones e impacto en las áreas de envío." In Patricia R. Pessar, ed., *Fronteras permeables: Migración laboral y movimientos de refugiados en América*. Buenos Aires: Planeta.

de Certeau, Michel. 1984. *The Practice of Everyday Life*. Translated by Steven Rendall. Berkeley: University of California Press.

De Marco, Graciela, and Susana Sassone. 1983. *Movilidad geografica de los inmigrantes limitrofes: Su impacto en la frontera Argentina*. Buenos Aires: OIKOS.

Derrida, Jacques. 1971. "Signature Event Context." In *Limited Inc*. Evanston, Ill.: Northwestern University Press.

Dilley, Roy, ed. 1999. *The Problem of Context*. New York: Berghahn Books.

Escobar, Arturo. 2008. *Territories of Difference: Place, Movements, Life,* Redes. Durham, N.C.: Duke University Press.

Escudé, Carlos. 1988. "Argentine Territorial Nationalism." *Journal of Latin American Studies* 20: 139–165.

Evans-Pritchard, E. E. 1969. *The Nuer: A Description of the Modes of Livelihood and Political Institutions of a Nilotic People*. Oxford: Oxford University Press.

Favero, Paolo. 2003. "Phantasms in a 'Starry' Place: Space and Identification in a Central New Delhi Market." *Cultural Anthropology* 18(4): 551–584.

Ferguson, James, and Akhil Gupta. 2005. "Spatializing States: Toward an Ethnography of Neoliberal Governmentality." In Jonathan Xavier Inda, ed., *Anthropologies of Modernity: Foucault, Governmentality, and Life Politics*. Malden, Mass.: Wiley-Blackwell.

García, María Elena. 2005. *Making Indigenous Citizens: Identity, Development and Multicultural Activism in Peru*. Stanford, Calif.: Stanford University Press.

García Canclini, Nestor. 1995. "Hybrid Cultures: Strategies for Entering and Leaving Modernity." Translated by C. L. Chiappari and S. L. López. Minneapolis: University of Minnesota Press.

Gennep, Arnold van. 1977. *The Rites of Passage*. Translated by Monika B. Vizedom. London: Routledge and Kegan Paul.

Gibson, James J. 1979. *The Ecological Approach to Visual Perception*. Hillsdale, N.J.: Lawrence Erlbaum.

Gose, Peter. 1994. *Deathly Waters and Hungry Mountains: Agrarian Ritual and Class Formation in an Andean Town*. Toronto: University of Toronto Press.

Graeber, David. 2001. *Toward an Anthropological Theory of Value: The False Coin of Our Own Dreams*. New York: Palgrave.

Grimson, Alejandro. 1999. *Relatos de la diferencia y la Igualdad: Los Bolivianos en Buenos Aires*. Buenos Aires: Editorial de La Universidad de Buenos Aires.

———. 2006. "Nuevas xenofobias, nuevas políticas étnicas en la Argentina." In Alejandro Grimson and Elizabeth Jelin, eds., *Migraciones regionales hacia la Argentina*. Buenos Aires: Prometeo Libros.

Grimson, Alejandro, and Elizabeth Jelin, eds. 2006. *Migraciones regionales hacia la Argentina*. Buenos Aires: Prometeo Libros.

Grimson, Alejandro, and Gabriel Kessler. 2005. *On Argentina and the Southern Cone: Neoliberalism and National Imaginations*. New York: Routledge.

Gupta, Akhil. 1995. "Blurred Boundaries: The Discourse of Corruption, the Culture of Politics, and the Imagined State." *American Ethnologist* 22: 375–402.

Gupta, Akhil, and Aradhana Sharma. 2006. "Globalization and Postcolonial States." *Current Anthropology* 47(2): 277–307.

Gupta, Akhil, and James Ferguson. 1997a. "Culture, Power, Place: Ethnography at the End of an Era." In Akhil Gupta and James Ferguson, eds., *Culture, Power, Place: Explorations in Critical Anthropology*. Durham, N.C.: Duke University Press.

Gupta, Akhil, and James Ferguson, eds. 1997b. *Culture, Power, Place: Explorations in Critical Anthropology*. Durham, N.C.: Duke University Press.

Guss, David M. 2000. *The Festive State: Race, Ethnicity, and Nationalism as Cultural Performance*. Berkeley: University of California Press.

Hahn, Dwight R. 1992. *The Divided World of the Bolivian Andes: A Structural View of Domination and Resistance*. New York: Taylor & Francis.

Handler, Richard. 1984. "On Sociocultural Discontinuity: Nationalism and Cultural Objectification in Quebec." *Current Anthropology* 25(1): 55–71.

———. 1986 "Authenticity." *Anthropology Today* 2(1): 2–4.

———. 1988. *Nationalism and the Politics of Culture in Quebec.* Madison: University of Wisconsin Press.

Hanks, William F. 1990. *Referential Practice: Language and Lived Space among the Maya.* Chicago: University of Chicago Press.

———. 2000. *Intertexts: Writings on Language, Utterance, and Context.* Lanham, Md.: Rowman & Littlefield.

Harman, Inge Maria. 1987. "Collective Labor and Rituals of Reciprocity in the Southern Bolivian Andes." Ph.D. dissertation, Cornell University.

Harris, Olivia. 1978. "Complementarity and Conflict: An Andean View of Women and Men." In J. S. LaFontaine, ed., *Sex and Age as Principles of Differentiation.* London: Academic Press.

———. 2000. "The Mythological Figure of the Earth Mother." In *To Make the Earth Bear Fruit: Ethnographic Essays on Fertility, Work and Gender in Highland Bolivia.* London: Institute of Latin American Studies.

Hervey, Sandor. 1999. "Context: The Ghost in the Machine." In Roy Dilley, ed., *The Problem of Context.* New York: Berghan Books.

Herzfeld, Michael. 1982. *Ours Once More: Folklore, Ideology and the Making of Modern Greece.* Austin: University of Texas Press.

Hinojosa Gordonava, Alfonso. 2007. "España en el itinerario de Bolivia: Migración transnacional, género y familia en Cochabamba." In Susana Novick, ed., *Las migraciones en América Latina: Políticas, culturas y estrategias.* Buenos Aires: Catálogo.

Hinojosa Gordonava, Alfonso, Liz Pérez Cautín, and Guido Cortéz Franco. 2000. *Idas y venidas. Campesinos tarijeños en el norte Argentino.* La Paz: PIEB.

Howard-Malverde, Rosaleen. 1981. *Dioses y diablos: Tradición oral de Cañar, Ecuador.* Paris: A.E.A.

———. 1997. *Creating Context in Andean Cultures.* New York: Oxford University Press.

Isbell, Billie Jean. 1974. "Parentesco andino y reciprocidad. Kukaq: Los que nos aman." In Giorgio Alberti and Enrique Mayer, eds., *Reciprocidad e intercambio en los Andes Peruanos,* 110–152. Lima: Instituto de Estudios Peruanos.

———. 1985. *To Defend Ourselves: Ecology and Ritual in an Andean Village.* Prospect Heights, Ill.: Waveland.

Izkó, Javier. 1992. *La doble frontera: Ecología, política y ritual en el altiplano central.* La Paz: HISBOL/CERES.

Jagger, Gill. 2007. *Judith Butler: Sexual Politics, Social Change and the Power of the Performative.* New York: Routledge.

Jakobson, Roman. 1960. "Linguistics and Poetics." In T. Sebeok, ed., *Style in Language.* Cambridge, Mass.: MIT Press.

———. 1970. "Subliminal Verbal Patterning in Poetry." In R. Jakobson and S. Kawamoto, eds., *Studies in General and Oriental Linguistics, Presented to Shirô Hattori on the Occasion of His Sixtieth Birthday.* Tokyo: TEC.

Jakobson, Roman, and L. G. Jones. 1970. *Shakespeare's Verbal Art in Th'Expense of Spirit.* The Hague: Mouton.

Jakobson, Roman, and Claude Lévi-Strauss. 1973. "Les chats de Charles Baudelaire." In *Questions de poétique.* Paris: Éditions de Minuit.

Jetté, Christian, and Rafael Rojas. 1999. *Cochabamba, Potosi, Tarija, Chuquisaca: Pobreza, genero y medio ambiente.* La Paz: CEP.

Johnson, Mark. 1987. *The Body in the Mind: The Bodily Basis of Meaning, Imagination, and Reason.* Chicago: University of Chicago Press.

Kapsoli, Wilfredo. 1991. "Los pishtacos: Degolladores degollados." *Bulletin de l'Institut Français des Études Andines* 20(1): 61–67.

Kearney, Michael. 1991. "Borders and Boundaries of State and Self at the End of Empire." *Journal of Historical Sociology* 4(1).
———. 1994. "Desde el indigenismo a los derechos humanos: etnicidad y política más allá de la mixteca." *Nueva Antropología* 14(46): 49–68.
Kurin, Richard. 1991. "Cultural Conservation through Representation: Festival of Indian Folklife Exhibitions at the Smithsonian Institution." In I. Karp and S. Lavine, eds., *Exhibiting Cultures: The Poetics and Politics of Museum Display*. Washington, D.C.: Smithsonian Institution Press.
Lagos, María. 1994. *Autonomy and Power: The Dynamics of Class and Culture in Bolivia*. Philadelphia: University of Pennsylvania Press.
Langer, Erick. 1989. *Economic Change and Rural Resistance in Southern Bolivia, 1880–1930*. Stanford: Stanford University Press.
Larson, Brooke. 1998. *Cochabamba, 1550–1900: Colonialism and Agrarian Tranformation in Bolivia*. Durham, N.C.: Duke University Press.
Laumonier, Isabel, Manuel María Rocca, and Eleonora M. Smolensky. 1983. *Presencia de la tradición Andina en Buenos Aires*. Buenos Aires: Ediciones Belgrano.
Lederer, William J., and Eugene Burdick. 1958. *The Ugly American*. New York: Norton.
Lefebvre, Henri. 1959. *La somme et le reste*. Paris: La Nef de Paris Éditions.
———. 1991. *The Production of Space*. Translated by D. Nicholson-Smith. Oxford: Blackwell.
Low, Setha M., and Denise Lawrence-Zúñiga. 2003a. "Locating Culture." In Setha M. Low and Denise Lawrence-Zúñiga, eds., *The Anthropology of Space and Place: Locating Culture*. Oxford: Blackwell.
Low, Setha M., and Denise Lawrence-Zúñiga, eds. 2003b. *The Anthropology of Space and Place: Locating Culture*. Oxford: Blackwell.
Loxley, James. 2007. *Performativity*. New York: Routledge.
Luna, Félix. 1993. *Breve historia de los Argentinos*. Buenos Aires: Planeta.
Luykx, Aurolyn. 1999. *The Citizen Factory: Schooling and Cultural Production in Bolivia*. Albany: State University of New York Press.
Magliano, M. J. 2007. Migración de mujeres Bolivianas hacia Argentina: Cambios y continuidades en las relaciones de género In *Les Cahiers ALHIM*. N° 14.
Maguid, Alicia. 1997. "Migrantes limítrofes en el mercado de trabajo del área metropolitana de Buenos Aires, 1980–1996." *Estudios migratorios Latinoamericanos* 12(35): 31–62.
Malloy, James. 1970. *Bolivia: The Uncompleted Revolution*. Pittsburgh: University of Pittsburgh Press.
Mannheim, Bruce. 1987. "Couplets and Oblique Context: The Social Organization of a Folksong." *Text* 7(3): 262–288.
Martínez, Gabriel. 1983. Los dioses de los cerros en los Andes. La Paz: HISBOL.
———. 1989. Espacio y pensamiento I: Andes meridionales. La Paz: HISBOL.
Marx, Karl. 1977. *Selected Writings*. Edited by David McLellan. Oxford: Oxford University Press.
Mayer, Enrique. 1974. "Las reglas del juego en la reciprocidad Andina." In Giorgio Alberti and Enrique Mayer, eds., *Reciprocidad e intercambio en los Andes Peruanos*. Lima: Instituto de Estudios Peruanos.
———. 2001. *The Articulated Peasant: Household Economies in the Andes*. Boulder, Colo.: Westview.
Medlin, Mary Ann. 1983. "Awayqa Sumaj Calchapi: Weaving, Social Organization and Identity in Calcha, Bolivia." Ph.D. dissertation, University of North Carolina at Chapel Hill.
Meisch, Lynn. 2002. *Andean Entrepreneurs: Otavalo Merchants and Musicians in the Global Arena*. Austin: University of Texas Press.
Merleau-Ponty, Maurice. 1962. *The Phenomenology of Perception*. Translated by C. Smith. London: Routledge.

Mueggler, Eric. 2001. *The Age of Wild Ghosts: Memory, Violence and Place in Southwestern China.* Berkeley: University of California Press.

Mugarza, Susana. 1989. Presencia y ausencia boliviana en la ciudad de Buenos Aires. *Estudios migratorios Latinoamericanos* 1(1): 98–106.

Munn, Nancy. 1977. "The Spatiotemporal Transformations of Gawa Canoes." *Journal de la Société des Océanistes* 33(54–55): 39–53.

———. 1986. *The Fame of Gawa: A Symbolic Study of Value Transformation in a Massim (Papua New Guinea) Society.* Cambridge: Cambridge University Press.

———. 1996. "Excluded Spaces: The Figure in the Australian Aboriginal Landscape." *Critical Inquiry* 22 (spring): 446–465.

Muñoz Elsner, Diego. 2000. Políticas publicas y agricultura campesina: Encuentros y desencuentros. La Paz: IIED.

Murra, John. 1972. "El control 'vertical' de un Máximo de pisos ecológicos en la economía de las sociedades Andinas." In J. V. Murra ed., *Visita de la Provincia de León de Huánuco en 1562,* Vol. 2. Huánuco: Universidad Nacional Hermilio Valdizán.

———. 1978. "Los limites y limitaciones del 'archipiélago vertical' en los Andes." *Avances* 1: 75–80.

———. 1985. "'El archipiélago vertical' revisited." In S. Masuda, I. Shimada, C. Morris. eds., *Andean Ecology and Civilization: An Interdisciplinary Perspective on Andean Ecological Complementarity.* Tokyo: University of Tokyo Press.

Nader, Laura. 1974. "Up the Anthropologist—Perspectives Gained from Studying Up." In Dell Hymes, ed., *Reinventing Anthropology.* New York: Vintage.

Nagengast, Carole, and Michael Kearney. 1990. "Mixtec Ethnicity: Social Identity, Political Consciousness, and Political Activism." *Latin American Research Review* 25(2): 61–91.

Nobrega, Ricardo. 2008. "Migraciones y modernidad brasileña: Italianos, nordestinos y bolivianos en San Pablo." In Susana Novick, ed., *Las migraciones en América Latina políticas, culturas y estrategias.* Buenos Aires: Catálogos—CLACSO.

Novick, Susana, ed. 2008. *Las migraciones en América Latina políticas, culturas y estrategias.* Buenos Aires: Catálogos—CLACSO.

Ong, Aihwa. 1999. *Flexible Citizenship: The Cultural Logics of Transnationality.* Durham, N.C.: Duke University Press.

Orlove, Benjamin S. 1974. "Reciprocidad, desigualdad y dominación." In G. Alberti and E. Mayer, eds., *Reciprocidad e intercambio en los Andes Peruanos.* Lima: Instituto de Estudios Peruanos.

Orlove, Benjamin S., and Glynn Custred. 1980. "The Alternative Model of Agrarian Society in the Andes: Households, Networks, and Corporate Groups." In B.S. Orlove and G. Custred, eds., *Land and Power in Latin America: Agrarian Economies and Social Processes in the Andes.* New York: Holmes & Meier.

Orta, Andrew. 1996. "Ambivalent Converts: Aymara Catechists and Contemporary Catholic Missionization in the Bolivian Altiplano." Ph.D. dissertation, University of Chicago.

———. 2004. *Catechizing Culture: Missionaries, Aymara, and the "New Evangelization."* New York: Columbia University Press.

Oteiza, Enrique, Susana Novick, and Roberto Aruj. 1997. Migración y discriminación: Politicas y discursos. Buenos Aires: Grupo Editor Universitario.

Oxford Atlas of the World. 2001. 8th ed. Oxford: Oxford University Press.

Paerregaard, Karsten. 2002. "Power Recycled: Persistence and Transformation in Peruvian Transnationalism." In Ton Salman and Anneleis Zoomers, eds., *The Andean Exodus: Transnational Migration from Bolivia, Ecuador and Peru.* Amsterdam: CEDLA.

———. 2008. *Peruvians Dispersed: A Global Ethnography of Migration.* Lanham, Md.: Lexington Books.

Pandya, Vishvajit. 1990. "Movement and Space: Andaman Cartography." *American Ethnologist* 17(4): 775–794.

Paz, R.A. 1978. Geografía y política en los problemas fronterizos pendientes. In P. Randle, ed., *La conciencia cerritorial y su déficit en la Argentina actual*. Buenos Aires: OIKOS.

Platt, Tristan. 1978. "Symétries en miroir: Le concept de yanantin chez les Macha de Bolivie." *Annales E.S.C.* 33(5–6): 1081–1107.

———. 1982. *Estado boliviano y ayllu andino: Tierra y tributo en el norte de Potosí*. Historia Andina 9. Lima: Instituto de Estudios Peruanos.

———. 1987. "The Andean Experience of Bolivian Liberalism: 1825–1900: Roots of Rebellion in 19th Century Chayanta (Potosí)." In S. Stern, ed., *Resistance, Rebellion, and Consciousness in the Andean Peasant World: 18th to 20th Centuries*. Madison: University of Wisconsin Press.

Poole, Deborah. 1984. "Ritual-Economic Calendars in Paruro: The Structure of Representation in Andean Ethnography." Ph.D. dissertation, University of Illinois at Urbana-Champaign.

Presta, Ana Maria. 1990. "Hacienda y comunidad: Un estudio en la provincia de Pilaya y Paspaya, siglos 16–18." *Revista Andes* (Universidad Nacional de Salta) 1: 31–46.

Programa Argentino de Desarrollo Humano. 1997. "Capítulo 2: Trabajo y migraciones." In *Informe Sobre Desarrollo Humano en la Provincia de Buenos Aires*. Buenos Aires: Honorable Senado de la Nación/Banco de la Provincia de Buenos Aires.

Rasnake, Roger Neil. 1988. *Domination and Cultural Resistance: Authority and Power among an Andean People*. Durham, N.C.: Duke University Press.

Ricoeur, Paul. 1974. "Structure, Word, Event." In Don Ihde, ed., *The Conflict of Interpretations: Essays in Hermeneutics*. Evanston, Ill.: Northwestern University Press.

Rivera Cusicanqui, Sylvia. 1983. "Luchas campesinas comtemporáneas en Bolivia: El movimiento 'Katarista,' 1970–1980." In R. Zavaleta, ed., *Bolivia Hoy*. Mexico: Siglo XXI.

———. 1990. "Liberal Democracy and Ayllu Democracy in Bolivia: The Case of Northern Potosí." In J. Fox, ed., *The Challenge of Rural Democratization: Perspectives from Latin America and the Phillipines*. London: F. Cass.

Rockefeller, Stuart Alexander. 1998. "'There Is a Culture Here': Spectacle and the Inculcation of Folklore in Highland Bolivia." *Journal of Latin American Anthropology* 3(2): 188–149.

Rojas Ortuste, Gonzalo. 1996. *Participación popular: Avances y obstáculos*. La Paz: Unidad de Investigación y Análisis/SNPP.

Rojo, Alejandro. 1976. *Las villas de emergencia*. Buenos Aires: Editorial el Coloquio.

Rouse, Roger. 1991. "Mexican Migration and the Space of Postmodernism." *Diaspora* 1(1): 8–23.

———. 1992. "Men in Space: Power and the Appropriation of Urban Form among Mexican Migrants in the United States." Unpublished ms.

———. 1995. "Questions of Identity: Personhood and Collectivity in Transnational Migration to the United States." *Critique of Anthropology* 15(4): 351–380.

Sahlins, Marshal. 1967. "The Segmentary Lineage: An Organization of Predatory Expansion." In R. Cohen and J. Middleton, eds., *Comparative Political Systems: Studies in the Politics of Pre-Industrial Societies*. Garden City, N.Y.: Natural History Press.

Saignes, Thierry. 1995. "Indian Migration and Social Change in Seventeenth-century Charcas." In B. Larson, O. Harris, and E. Tandeter, eds., *Ethnicity, Markets and Migration in the Andes: At the Crossroads of History and Anthropology*. Durham, N.C.: Duke University Press.

Salazar-Soler, Carmen. 1991. El pishtaku entre los campesinos y los mineros de Huancavelica. *Bulletin de l'Institut Français des Études Andines* 20(1): 7–22.

Sallnow, Michael. 1987. *Pilgrims of the Andes*. New York: HarperColllins.

Salman, Ton, and Annelies Zoomers. 2002. *The Andean Exodus: Transnational Migration from Bolivia, Ecuador and Peru*. Amsterdam: CEDLA.

Sargent, Charles S. 1974. *The Spatial Evolution of Greater Buenos Aires, Argentina, 1870–1930.* Tempe, Ariz.: Center for Latin American Studies.

Sassen, Saskia. 1998. *Globalization and Its Discontents.* New York: New Press.

———. 2001. *The Global City: New York, London, Tokyo.* Princeton, N.J.: Princeton University Press.

Sassone, Susana María, and Carolina Mera. 2007. "Barrios de migrantes en Buenos Aires: Identidad, cultura y cohesión socioterritorial." Preactas v Congreso Europeo CEISAL de Latinoamericanistas—Bruselas (Bélgica), Abril 11–14, 2007. Available at http://www.reseau-amerique-latine.fr/ceisal-bruxelles/MS-MIG/MS-MIG-1-Sassone_Mera.pdf (accessed March 21, 2009).

Shields, Rob. 1999. *Lefebvre, Love and Struggle: Spatial Dialectics.* London: Routledge.

Shorter Oxford English Dictionary. 1979. *The Shorter Oxford English Dictionary.* London: Clarendon.

Silverblatt, Irene. 1987. *Moon, Sun and Witches: Gender Ideologies and Class in Inca and Colonial Peru.* Princeton, N.J.: Princeton University Press.

Silverstein, Michael, and Greg Urban. 1996. *Natural Histories of Discourse.* Chicago: University of Chicago Press.

Skar, Sarah Lund. 1994. *Lives Together, Worlds Apart: Quechua Colonization in Jungle and City.* Oslo: Scandinavian University Press.

Stearman, Allyn MacLean. 1985. *Camba and Kolla: Migration and Development in Santa Cruz, Bolivia.* Orlando: University of Central Florida Press.

Stephenson, Marcia. 1999. *Gender and Modernity in Andean Bolivia.* Austin: University of Texas Press.

Stoller, Paul. 2002. *Money Has No Smell: The Africanization of New York.* Chicago: University of Chicago Press.

Tolen, Rebecca Jane. 1995. "Wool and Synthetics, Countryside and City: Dress, Race and History in Chimborazo, Highland Ecuador." Ph.D. dissertation, University of Chicago.

Toranza, Carlos. 1992. *Lo pluri multi, o el reino de la diversidad.* La Paz: ILDIS.

Torres, Horacio. 2001. "Cambios socioterritoriales en Buenos Aires durante la década de 1990." *Eure* (Santiago) 27(80).

Tsing, Anna. 2002. "Conclusion: The Global Situation." In Jonathan Xavier Inda and Renato Rosaldo, eds., *The Anthropology of Globalization: A Reader.* Malden, Mass.: Blackwell.

———. 2005. *Friction: An Ethnography of Global Connection.* Princeton, N.J.: Princeton University Press.

Tuan, Yi-Fu. 1977. *Space and Place: The Perspective of Experience.* Minneapolis: University of Minnesota Press.

———. 1996. *Cosmos and Hearth: A Cosmopolite's Viewpoint.* Minneapolis: University of Minnesota Press.

Tulchin, Joseph S. 1982. "How to Know the City." In S. R. Ross and T. F. McGann, eds., *Buenos Aires: 400 Years.* Austin: University of Texas Press.

Turino, Thomas. 1993. *Moving away from Silence: Music of the Peruvian Altiplano and the Experience of Urban Migration.* Chicago: University of Chicago Press.

Turner, Terence. 1977. "Narrative Structure and Mythopoesis: A Critique and Reformulation of Structuralist Concepts of Myth, Narrative, and Poetics." *Arethusa* 10(1): 103–163.

———. 1996. "Social Complexity and Recursive Hierarchy in Indigenous South American Societies." In G. Urton, ed., *Structure, Knowledge and Representation in the Andes: Studies Presented to R. T. Zuidema on the Occasion of His Seventieth Birthday. Journal of the Steward Anthropological Society* 24(1–2): 37–60.

————. 2002. "The Beautiful and the Common: Inequalities of Value and Revolving Hierarchy among the Kayapó." *Salsa—Journal of the Society for the Anthropology of Lowland South America* 1(1).

Twain, Mark. 1992. "To the Person Sitting in Darkness." In Louis J. Budd, ed., *Twain: Collected Tales, Sketches, Speeches, and Essays, 1891–1910*. Vol. 2. New York: Library of America.

Ulpana Vicente, Filomón. 1981. *Yachayninchej: El saber agricola de San Lucas*. Sucre, Bolivia.

Verdery, Katherine. 1994. "Beyond the Nation in Eastern Europe." *Social Text* 38 (spring): 1–19.

Walter, Richard J. 1982. "The Socioeconomic Growth of Buenos Aires in the Twentieth Century." In S. R. Ross, and T. F. McGann, eds., *Buenos Aires: 400 Years.* Austin: University of Texas Press.

Weber, Max. 1999. "Social Action and Social Relationships." In Wolf Heydebrand, ed., *Max Weber: Sociological Writings*. New York: Continuum.

Weismantel, Mary. 2001. *Cholas and Pishtacos : Stories of Race and Sex in the Andes*. Chicago: University of Chicago Press.

Whiteford, Scott. 1981. *Workers from the North: Plantations, Bolivian Labor, and the City in Northwest Argentina*. Austin: University of Texas Press.

Whitman, Walt. 2002 [1855]. "Starting from Paumanok." In *Leaves of Grass*. New York: Modern Library.

Williams, Raymond. 1973. *The Country and the City*. New York: Oxford University Press.

Zorn, Elayne. 1997. "Marketing Diversity: Global Transformations in Cloth and Identity in Highland Peru and Bolivia." Ph.D. dissertation, Department of Anthropology, Cornell University.

Zuidema, R. T. 1964. *The Ceque System of Cuzco: The Social Organization of the Capital of the Inca*. Leiden: E. J. Brill.

Zulawski, Ann. 1995. *They Eat by Their Labor: Work and Social Change in Colonial Bolivia*. Pittsburgh: University of Pittsburgh Press.

INDEX

STUART ALEXANDER ROCKEFELLER has done fieldwork over the last two decades in highland Bolivia and in the Bolivian migrant community of Buenos Aires, Argentina. His research interests include folklore festivals, the anthropology of place and scale, immigrant social movements, and rumors and gossip. He has taught at New York University, Rutgers University, Haverford College, and Fordham University. Currently he is a visiting scholar and instructor at the Center for the Study of Ethnicity and Race, Columbia University.

Lightning Source UK Ltd.
Milton Keynes UK
UKHW021856170123
415517UK00012B/1393